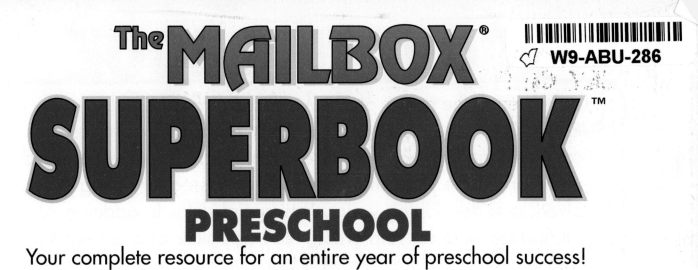

The MAILBOX® SUPERBOOK™
PRESCHOOL

Your complete resource for an entire year of preschool success!

Editor:
Ada H. Goren

Contributing Editors:
Jayne M. Gammons, Marie Iannetti, Lori Kent,
Angie Kutzer, Mackie Rhodes

Contributors:
Barbara Backer, Nancy Barad, Jan Brennan, Deborah Burleson, Rachel Castro, Marie Cecchini, Carleen Coderre,
LeeAnn Collins, Lisa Cowman, Tricia Daughtry, Holly Dunham, Jean Feldman, Ann Flagg, John Funk,
Linda Gordetsky, Lucia Kemp Henry, Lori Kent, Gayla King, Carrie Lacher, Linda Ludlow, Bambina Merriman,
Betty Silkunas, Dayle Timmons, Allison Ward, Virginia Zeletzki

Art Coordinator:
Cathy Spangler Bruce

Artists:
Jennifer Tipton Bennett, Cathy Spangler Bruce,
Clevell Harris, Kimberly Richard, Donna K. Teal

Cover Artist:
Jim Counts

www.themailbox.com

The Education Center, Inc.
Greensboro, North Carolina

ABOUT THIS BOOK

Look through the pages of *The Mailbox® PRESCHOOL SUPERBOOK™*, and discover a wealth of ideas and activities specifically designed for you—the preschool teacher! We've included tips for starting the year, managing your classroom, getting parents involved, and developing youngsters' social skills. In addition, you'll find activities for reinforcing the basic skills and concepts in the preschool curriculum. We've also provided reference materials, literature and music lists, arts-and-crafts projects, holiday and seasonal activities, timesaving reproducibles, and bulletin-board ideas and patterns. *The Mailbox® PRESCHOOL SUPERBOOK™* is your complete resource for an entire year of preschool success!

Library of Congress Cataloging-in-Publication Data

The mailbox superbook , preschool : your complete resource for an
    entire year of preschool success! / editor, Ada H. Goren ;
    contributing editors, Jayne Gammons ... [et al.] ; contributors,
    Barbara Backer ... [et al.] ; art coordinator, Cathy Spangler Bruce
    ; artists, Jennifer Tipton Bennett ... [et al.].
        p.   cm.
    ISBN 1-56234-195-2 (paper)
    1. Education, Preschool—Curricula.   2. Education, Preschool—
Activity programs.   3. Teaching—Aids and devices.   4. Preschool
teaching.   I. Goren, Ada H.   II. Backer, Barbara.   III. Mailbox.
LB1140.4.M375   1998
372.1102—dc21   98-5940
                                                          CIP

Manufactured in the United States
10 9 8 7 6 5 4 3

TABLE OF CONTENTS

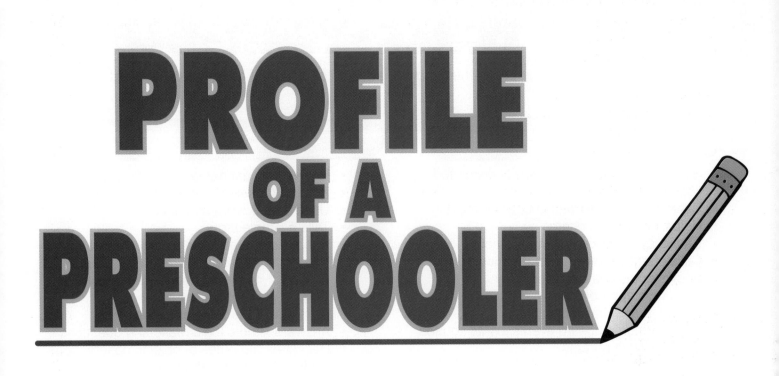

DEVELOPMENTAL PROFILE OF A THREE-YEAR-OLD

Here's a ready reference on the range of abilities of a typical three-year-old child.

SOCIAL-EMOTIONAL

- Has short attention span; easily distracted
- Joins and plays with other children
- Takes turns/shares with encouragement
- Helps with simple chores
- Shows sympathy/concern for others
- Calls attention to own performance
- Shows enthusiasm for work/play
- Uses toys appropriately
- Prefers more challenging tasks
- Finds humor in absurd events/sights/sounds
- Identifies with parents

COMMUNICATION/LANGUAGE

- Knows first/last name, age, and sex
- Recites nursery rhymes; sings songs
- Uses 3- to 5-word sentences
- Tells a simple story
- Recalls elements from story just read
- Names pictures of familiar objects/items
- Follows 2- to 3-step sequenced directions
- Relates personal experiences
- Asks questions for information
- Answers simple logic/reasoning questions
- Describes attributes of objects/observations
- Takes turns in conversation

COGNITIVE

- Orders graduated containers/blocks/rings by size
- Understands simple opposites: big/little, long/short, fast/slow
- Sorts by one attribute (color or size)
- Counts up to five objects
- Matches pictures of like objects
- Recognizes/matches up to six colors
- Understands object function
- Matches simple shapes
- Understands simple time concepts (day/night)
- Groups objects by common attributes
- Understands same/different
- Understands positional concepts (on, in, under)
- Identifies real life/pictured absurdities
- Repeats 3-digit and 3-word sequences

SPEECH MILESTONES

- Has vocabulary of almost 1,000 words
- Has 85% speech intelligibility
- Uses the following grammar forms:
    pronouns (I, she, they)
    auxiliary verbs (am, is, are)
    noun and verb plurals
    -ing endings (walk*ing*)
    prepositions (in, on)
    possessives (mommy*'s* shoe)
    articles (a, the)
- Produces all vowel sounds
- Consistently produces sounds for *m, p, b, h, w*
- May produce sounds in front of mouth that typically are made in back (*t*up for cup)
- May produce simplified consonant blends (pane for *p*lane)
- May substitute more easily produced sound for another (wing for *r*ing)

FINE MOTOR

- Builds a 9- to 12-block tower
- Demonstrates hand preference
- Stabilizes paper with one hand; writes with other
- Draws vertical line, circle, and cross
- Draws recognizable picture
- Cuts continuously along a line
- Strings 1/2-inch beads
- Screws on lids
- Completes 5-piece formboard/puzzle
- Builds 3-block bridge
- Drives nails/pegs into semisoft surface
- Rolls/shapes play-dough forms

GROSS MOTOR

- Walks up/down stairs alternating feet (holds rail)
- Walks several steps on tiptoe
- Walks line on floor
- Balances on one foot several seconds
- Throws ball overhead
- Catches bounced ball
- Kicks ball
- Runs around obstacles
- Climbs easy playground ladders/equipment
- Performs consecutive and forward jumps without falling
- Rides tricycle

SELF-HELP

- Puts on shoes (may be incorrect feet)
- Undresses, manipulating simple fasteners
- Unzips front zipper
- Fastens snaps
- Buttons/unbuttons large buttons
- Brushes hair independently
- Toilets self (with some help to clean/dress)
- Washes and dries hands
- Brushes teeth (with help)
- Eats independently
- Pours liquid from small pitcher into cup
- Spreads soft foods with a blunt knife
- Uses napkin to wipe mouth
- Serves self from container (some spilling)

PLAY

- Begins cooperative play
- Organizes/engages in pretend play
- Sequences play to tell a story
- Assigns roles to props (dolls/puppets)
- Creates imaginary characters
- Uses different voices for different play characters

compiled by Rachel Castro, Bambina Merriman, and Mackie Rhodes

DEVELOPMENTAL PROFILE OF A FOUR-YEAR-OLD

Here's a ready reference on the range of abilities of a typical four-year-old child.

SOCIAL-EMOTIONAL

- Has extended attention span; easily distracted
- Prefers playing with peers rather than alone
- Spontaneously takes turns/shares
- Chooses/identifies special friends
- Accepts responsibility
- Shows awareness of/concern for another's feelings
- Talks about own feelings, emotions, attitudes
- Uses appropriate social responses (says thank you, raises hand)
- Controls/expresses emotions in acceptable ways
- Responds appropriately to small-group instruction
- Shows interest in own body/exploring gender differences

COMMUNICATION/LANGUAGE

- Plays with words (rhymes, repetitions, nonsense words)
- Asks/gives meanings of new words
- Sings songs/rhymes of 30 or more words
- Uses up to 8-word sentences
- Retells stories with essential elements in logical sequence
- Answers content questions about story (facts may be confused)
- Follows three unrelated commands in order
- Asks variety of questions
- Responds appropriately to many question forms (answers may be incorrect)
- Describes past events
- Describes objects by shape, size, color
- Describes own activities
- Uses quantity terms (all, some, most)

COGNITIVE

- Knows own street and city
- Groups by two characteristics (shape, color)
- Classifies objects into categories (food, toys)
- Knows and names up to six colors
- Understands one-to-one correspondence
- Counts/creates sets up to ten
- Imitates simple parquetry patterns
- Completes up to 20-piece puzzles
- Matches/identifies simple shapes
- Sequences three pictures to tell story
- Has expanded knowledge of time concepts (today, tomorrow, yesterday)
- Understands directional concepts (top/bottom)
- Repeats 4-digit and 4-word sequences
- Completes sentences about simple analogies (Fire is hot, but ice is cold.)
- Understands comparatives (big/bigger)
- Predicts outcome of story/event

SPEECH MILESTONES

- Has vocabulary of over 1,500 words
- Has 100% speech intelligibility (not error-free)
- Uses the following grammar forms:
  - possessive pronouns (his, her, their)
  - regular past tense with -ed (walked)
  - irregular past (came instead of comed)
  - no and not appropriately
  - contractions (it's, there's)
  - prepositions (beside, around, between)
  - future-tense verb forms (will)
  - connector words (and, but, because)
- Consistently produces sounds for n, ng, f, k, g, t, d, y (as in you)
- Produces consonant blends with 90% correctness

FINE MOTOR

- Uses mature grasp on pencil
- Copies simple shapes (square, triangle, diamond)
- Draws stick figure
- Draws person with up to six recognizable parts
- Uses irregular/uneven strokes to copy letters/ numbers
- Creases paper
- Puts paper clip on paper
- Cuts out circle and other simple shapes
- Performs simple sewing on lacing card
- Uses key to open small padlock
- Puts small pegs in pegboard

SELF-HELP

- Dresses/undresses with little help
- Knows front and back of clothes
- Buttons small buttons
- Engages separating zipper
- Laces shoes (may not tie laces)
- Hangs up coat
- Blows/wipes nose without help
- Washes face
- Toilets self independently
- Uses fork/spoon skillfully
- Uses blunt knife to cut easy foods
- Gets drink from water fountain
- Puts away personal belongings; cleans up

GROSS MOTOR

- Walks up/down stairs alternating feet (without holding rail)
- Walks on tiptoe for up to ten feet
- Walks balance beam without falling
- Hops on one foot
- Jumps forward up to ten times without falling
- Skips, alternating feet
- Gallops
- Catches a thrown ball
- Kicks rolling ball toward target
- Pumps legs while swinging

PLAY

- Plays cooperatively with peers for extended periods
- Involves others in pretend play
- Represents more realistic situations in pretend play
- Enjoys playing dress-up
- Builds large block/chair structures to center play around
- Begins playing group games with simple rules

compiled by Rachel Castro, Bambina Merriman, and Mackie Rhodes

WHAT DO WE DO IN PRESCHOOL?

- **Circle time** is a group gathering during which we share our ideas, plans, and observations. Circle activities are designed to stimulate youngsters' thinking, enrich their social skills, and expand their attention spans.

- **Gross-motor activities** give children the opportunity to use their muscles—as well as their imaginations—as they engage in fun, healthy exercises, such as running, jumping, and climbing.

- **Fine-motor activities** help improve small-muscle development and eye-hand coordination. Some common items found in the fine-motor/manipulative area include puzzles, beads and laces, pegboards, crayons, and scissors.

- **Art activities** help youngsters creatively express their thoughts and feelings. They help reinforce fine-motor skills and concept development in areas such as colors, shapes, and size relationships.

- **Dramatic-play activities** help children express themselves, practice life skills, improve social skills, increase self-esteem, build vocabulary, and solve problems. And, well, dramatic play is just plain fun!

- **Music activities** promote youngsters' listening skills, creative expression, and social skills. In music, children can explore sound, volume, tempo, and rhythm.

- **Science activities** offer children many hands-on opportunities for observation, exploration, investigation, making predictions, and experimentation.

- **Sand and water activities** allow youngsters to experiment with textures and the properties of different substances. These activities also promote the development of other skills, such as math, science, and language.

- **Block play** gives children experience with many different concepts, such as shape and size discrimination, spatial relationships, number skills, balance, organization, cause and effect, and classification. Cooperative play skills, problem solving, and creativity are also promoted in block play.

- **Storytime** is designed to help youngsters develop an appreciation and enjoyment of literature. Reading activities enhance children's vocabulary and comprehension skills, and also expand their knowledge base.

PARENTS AS PARTNERS

Strengthen ties between home and preschool with these ideas for parent communication and involvement. Let moms and dads know what's happening at school and encourage them to extend their children's learning at home. Parents are your partners in making each child's preschool experience a success!

ideas contributed by Jan Brennan and John Funk

What's Going On?

Keep families informed about the skills and concepts you are covering at school. On a monthly or quarterly basis—whichever works best for you—send home a list or simple chart showing the new skills and concepts you'll be working on with your class. Encourage parents to work on these skills and concepts at home, too.

As a variation, send home a note each time you begin a new theme. List some of the activities you have planned and explain how they fit into various curriculum areas. Give a few suggestions for activities parents can do at home to support your thematic unit.

This Month In Preschool
We are working on...
- zipping and buttoning
- the color orange
- learning our birthdays
- the numbers 4 and 5
- studying about leaves

ROLL 'EM!

If a picture is worth a thousand words, then a video must be worth a million! Prepare a video that documents the highlights of a typical school day: arrival, circle time, snacktime, centers, rest time, a visit to the playground, etc. Then invite youngsters to take turns sharing the video with their families overnight. Working parents who find it difficult to visit the classroom will especially appreciate the chance to see their little ones in action!

"WHAT DID YOU DO AT SCHOOL TODAY?"

Help little ones answer this often-asked question by providing them with a visual reminder. If you've spent the day reading a story about Johnny Appleseed, doing apple artwork, and preparing an apple snack, provide each child with a sheet of paper from an apple-shaped notepad to take home. Or stamp an apple shape on each child's hand as she walks out the door. Make sure you explain the reminders to parents ahead of time so they can be on the lookout for these visual clues and ask appropriate questions.

Once children are accustomed to taking home these clues, they may no longer need a visual reminder. Try telling youngsters a key word, such as "bubbles" or "eggs," that they can remember to help spark discussions about the school day's events.

A LOANING LIBRARY

Preschoolers are usually bursting with pride over special class projects and books they help to create. Share the joy by allowing parents to borrow some of these class treasures for an overnight look-see. Simply package each book or tape (or a video showing large projects) in a large zippered plastic bag. Label the bag with a permanent marker and provide a sign-out sheet with a matching label. Then invite families to check out their little ones' accomplishments from this very special class library!

Our Transportation Songs

Our Transportation Songs

Julie Adams
Ricky Birch ✓
Amanda Stone

Help With Show-And-Tell

Often preschoolers need guidance in selecting items to bring to school for show-and-tell. Make this an easier task—and one in which parents can be involved—by centering sharing time around your current theme. Send home a duplicated note with a simple message, such as "Tomorrow, please bring something [red] for Show-And-Tell." Parent and child can work together to find an appropriate item.

> Tomorrow, please bring something red for Show-And-Tell.

MONTHLY TREASURE HUNTS

This activity will do double duty by encouraging parents and children to spend time together *and* by helping you out with classroom supplies. Each month send home a note asking families to work together to gather specific items for use at school. For example, in September you might ask that families go on a nature walk and collect pinecones or acorns. In December you might ask for scraps of ribbon and wrapping paper. And in May, ask families to collect all kinds of seeds. You'll receive lots of treasures, and parents and children will have some treasured time together.

Home Cookin'

If you've ever seen the look on a youngster's face when she walks into your classroom with a plateful of her mom's home-made cookies, then you know the pride that accompanies providing a snack for the class. Ask each of your students' families to take a turn providing a snack or special treat. Encourage each family to involve their child in preparing an easy recipe, perhaps a family favorite or one that reflects their heritage. If desired, ask parents to write up their recipes; then compile them into a recipe book and duplicate copies for each child to take home once everyone has participated.

It's December

Please work with your child to collect extra wrapping paper, ribbons, or bows. We'll do lots of fun things at school with your donations!

Thank you!

Learning At Home

Preschoolers' parents are often anxious to find out how to help their children extend their learning experiences at home. Consider sending home a newsletter with suggestions for activities and reading material that will tie into your topics of study. You might want to give suggestions every week, every other week, or only once a month, depending on your schedule and curriculum. Simply duplicate the form on page 19; then fill in each box with appropriate ideas and information. Make a copy for each family and send home these nifty notes with your youngsters.

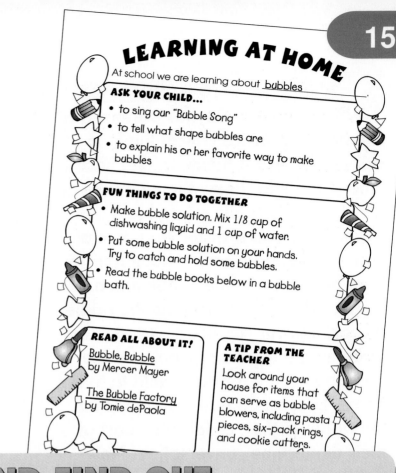

LEARNING AT HOME

At school we are learning about _bubbles_

ASK YOUR CHILD...
- to sing our "Bubble Song"
- to tell what shape bubbles are
- to explain his or her favorite way to make bubbles

FUN THINGS TO DO TOGETHER
- Make bubble solution. Mix 1/8 cup of dishwashing liquid and 1 cup of water.
- Put some bubble solution on your hands. Try to catch and hold some bubbles.
- Read the bubble books below in a bubble bath.

READ ALL ABOUT IT!
Bubble, Bubble
by Mercer Mayer

The Bubble Factory
by Tomie dePaola

A TIP FROM THE TEACHER
Look around your house for items that can serve as bubble blowers, including pasta pieces, six-pack rings, and cookie cutters.

READ AND FIND OUT

Here's a fun and easy way to encourage parents and children to read together. Each month choose a good children's book and write one or two questions about the story on a piece of paper. For example, if you select *The Very Hungry Caterpillar* by Eric Carle (Philomel Books), one question might be "How many things did the hungry caterpillar eat through?" Package the book and questions together in a large zippered plastic bag. Invite each child, in turn, to take the bag home. Ask parents to first read the questions, then the book, to their children. Have them jot down their children's answers to the questions on a sheet of paper and return the bag to school the next day. Then the story can continue on its way until every child has had a turn to read and find out!

THEME RIDDLES

What's a great way for parents and children to practice critical-thinking skills together? A theme riddle! Each time you begin a new theme, make up a very simple riddle related to it. For example, if you are studying animals, your riddle might say, "I have four legs. I am black and white. I look like a horse. What am I?" Include the riddle as part of your regular newsletter, or write it on a separate sheet of paper and duplicate it for each child to take home. Encourage parents to present the riddle to their children as part of their dinnertime conversation. Now that's good thinking!

Hey, Diddle, Diddle—
Can you guess this riddle?

I have four legs.
I am black and white.
I look like a horse.
What am I?

MENORAH

Word Of The Week

Parents can try this weekly activity to help build their youngsters' vocabularies. Each week select a word related to your current theme and draw or cut out a clip-art picture that represents it (nouns will be easiest, of course). Duplicate the picture for each child to take home. Ask each child's parents to post the picture on their refrigerator. They may want to provide the magnetic letters that spell the word or simply write the word on a slip of paper and post it next to the picture. Before you know it, your little ones will be word wizards!

Family Of The Week

What better way to get families involved in your classroom than to get them talking about themselves? Each week send home a copy of the invitation on page 20 with a different child. Set aside time each week for the children to learn about the Family Of The Week. This project will help emphasize the differences and similarities in family structures, as well as help classmates get to know one another better.

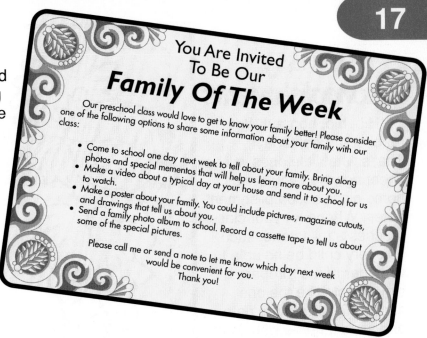

You Are Invited
To Be Our
Family Of The Week

Our preschool class would love to get to know your family better! Please consider one of the following options to share some information about your family with our class:

- Come to school one day next week to tell about your family. Bring along photos and special mementos that will help us learn more about you.
- Make a video about a typical day at your house and send it to school for us to watch.
- Make a poster about your family. You could include pictures, magazine cutouts, and drawings that tell us about you.
- Send a family photo album to school. Record a cassette tape to tell us about some of the special pictures.

Please call me or send a note to let me know which day next week would be convenient for you.
Thank you!

FAMILY BLOCKS

If you don't have time in your schedule for the "Family Of The Week" idea (above), try this simpler way for families to share information about themselves. Create a set of family blocks for the children to share, discuss, and play with. For each child, collect two same-sized juice boxes. Thoroughly clean and dry each box. To make a family block, tape two boxes together, back-to-back. Then cut a sheet of white or light-colored construction paper so that it matches the height of the boxes and wraps completely around the block, slightly overlapping on one edge. Send the cut-to-fit paper home with each child, along with a copy of the note on page 20. After each family returns its decorated paper, wrap the paper around a block and tape it in place. Then invite each little one to describe the pictures on his block and tell about his family. Leave the family blocks in a center where children can use them during their free-choice play.

Classy Accomplishments

"Hip, hip, hooray! We reached a goal today!" That's what little ones will be cheering when you send home class accomplishment notes. Whenever your class reaches a milestone, such as every child being able to write her name, prepare a simple note like the one shown. Duplicate the note and send it home with each child. Parents will enjoy being a part of their children's success!

HIP, HIP, HOORAY! WE REACHED A GOAL TODAY!

We can all write our first names!

KEEPING TRACK

If you like the idea of regularly communicating with parents about their children's personal progress but are wary of keeping track of who you've contacted, try this simple idea. Purchase a set of 5" x 8" index cards. On each card, print the names of three children in your class. Then stack the cards and leave them in a handy location. The names on the top card are the students whose parents you'll contact that day. Send home a quick note with those three children, noting at least one positive aspect about each child's learning or behavior. (If you're really pressed for time, consider using preprinted notes available at your teacher-supply store.) Then move the top index card to the bottom of the stack and you're ready to make the contacts for the next day!

Anita
Thai
Nicholas

LEARNING AT HOME

At school we are learning about _____.

ASK YOUR CHILD...

FUN THINGS TO DO TOGETHER

READ ALL ABOUT IT!

A TIP FROM THE TEACHER

Invitation

Use with "Family Of The Week" on page 17.

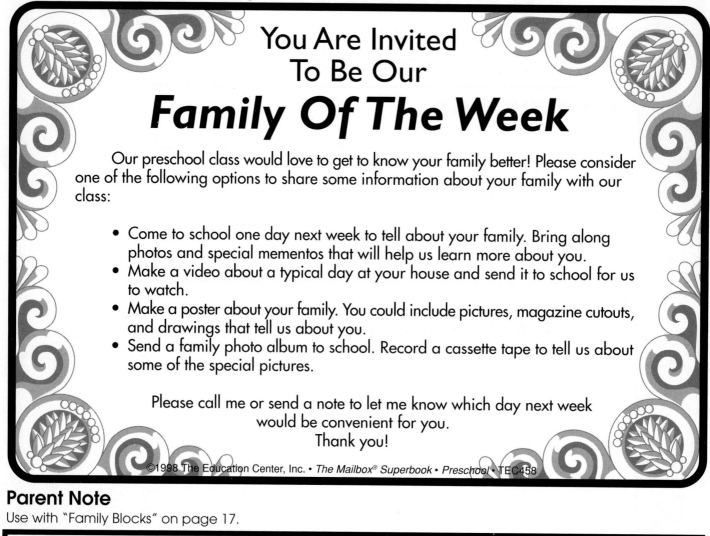

You Are Invited To Be Our

Family Of The Week

Our preschool class would love to get to know your family better! Please consider one of the following options to share some information about your family with our class:

- Come to school one day next week to tell about your family. Bring along photos and special mementos that will help us learn more about you.
- Make a video about a typical day at your house and send it to school for us to watch.
- Make a poster about your family. You could include pictures, magazine cutouts, and drawings that tell us about you.
- Send a family photo album to school. Record a cassette tape to tell us about some of the special pictures.

Please call me or send a note to let me know which day next week would be convenient for you.
Thank you!

Parent Note

Use with "Family Blocks" on page 17.

Dear Family,

Our preschool class would love to get to know your family better! So we are constructing a set of family blocks for the children to share. Please decorate one side of the attached paper with photos, drawings, magazine pictures, and words that tell about your family members. Please return the decorated paper to school by _____. Then stop in to see our finished family blocks!

(date)

Thank you for your cooperation!

Take a look through this unit to find everything you'll need to make this year's parent conferences the best ever. From sign-up sheets to salutations, we've got it covered.

ideas contributed by Lori Kent

Dear Kent Family,
Welcome to a new school year! I would love to meet with you on _____ to discuss the _____ upcoming year. Please answer the following questions so that we can talk about them during this conference time.

— List three topics your child would like to learn about this year.
— List three skills you would like your child to acquire this year.
— What does your child look forward to most about school?
— What does your child look forward to least about school?

I'm looking forward to meeting you.

Sincerely,
Mrs. Goren

BRIGHT BEGINNINGS

Get the new school year off to a bright beginning by scheduling a conference with each family prior to the start of school! Before the first day of class, mail a letter to each family scheduling a specific conference time and requesting that parents write down responses to these suggested questions:
— List three topics your child would like to learn about this year.
— List three skills you would like your child to acquire this year.
— What does your child look forward to most about school?
— What does your child look forward to least about school?

During each conference discuss the responses to the questions. Encourage the child to participate in the conversation by asking him to tell you what he would like to learn about. Then end the conference by showing the family around your classroom, pointing out important areas such as the child's cubby, bathrooms, and play areas. Later use the information gathered from students to help plan thematic units based on their interests.

Draw-A-Man Journal

Parents will clearly see the developmental progress of their children when you share these journals during conference times. Prepare a journal for each child by stapling several sheets of paper—equal to the number of months in your school year—between construction-paper covers. Personalize each journal with a child's name.

During the first week of school, provide each child with crayons and his journal; then have him complete the first page. Instruct him to draw a picture of a man or "Daddy." Do as little prompting as possible, allowing the child as much time as needed to complete his picture. When he has completed his drawing, write the date on the page. Have each child complete one drawing a month (preferably during the same week each month). Then, during parent conferences, share each child's journal with his parents, pointing out the progress made throughout the year. At the end of the school year, send home each student's journal as a meaningful keepsake for parents.

Storyboards

Let pictures tell the story of your classroom activities for parents who are waiting for their scheduled conferences. Use tape to hinge together two sheets of poster board (or cardboard). Attach to the poster board photographs of students participating in classroom activities such as circle time, center time, and recess. Write a caption under each photo that explains what is taking place. Decorate the poster board with cutouts and stickers that correspond to the pictures. Then display the completed storyboard on a tabletop near the entrance to your classroom. Parents will be delighted to get a picture-perfect view of their child at school.

Very Important Preschooler

Parents will know they have a V.I.P. in their family when you use this nifty way to share information during parent conferences. Reproduce a class supply of the V.I.P. report on page 23. Use information gathered from classroom observations and evaluations to fill in the skill boxes on each child's report. Then list the goals you have for that child in the appropriate box. Invite each student to tell you his goals (what he would like to learn during the year) and write those in the corresponding box. Finally, make a copy of each child's V.I.P. report to give to parents.

During parent conferences, share the information on the sheet with each family. Encourage parents to share their goals for their child; then write those goals on your copy of the report. File your copy for reference throughout the school year.

Tea For Two—Or Three

Create a warm and inviting atmosphere for parents during conference time with this cozy idea. The day before scheduled conferences begin, invite your students to prepare a batch of cookies using your favorite recipe. On the day of conferences, make a pot of tea or coffee; then arrange some of the cookies on a decorative plate. (If you have conferences over a period of more than one day, store the remaining cookies in an airtight container.)

Before each conference, spend a few moments getting to know parents over a cup of tea and cookies. Parents will welcome an opportunity to chat with you before you share conference information.

Very Important Preschooler

Name _____

Date _____

Student Goals

Social	Motor	Language

Math	Teacher Goals	Parent Goals

Note To The Teacher: Use with "Very Important Preschooler" on page 22.

Conference Notice

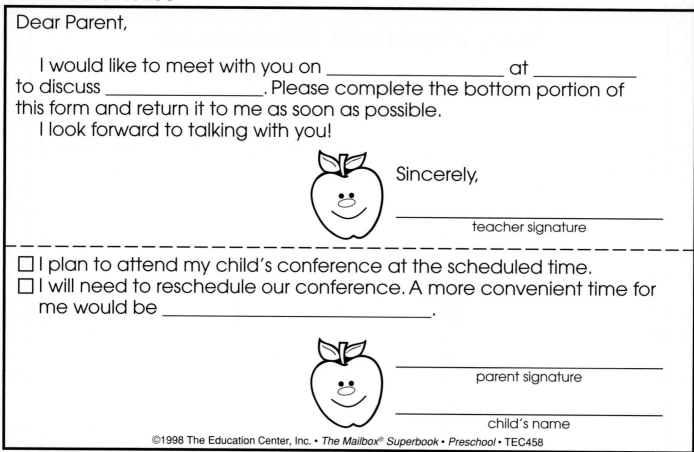

Dear Parent,

I would like to meet with you on _____ at _____ to discuss _____. Please complete the bottom portion of this form and return it to me as soon as possible.

I look forward to talking with you!

Sincerely,

_____
teacher signature

- ☐ I plan to attend my child's conference at the scheduled time.
- ☐ I will need to reschedule our conference. A more convenient time for me would be _____.

_____
parent signature

_____
child's name

Volunteer Form

Dear Parent,

Becoming involved in your child's education helps solidify the home/school connection and provides your child with a sense of continuity. You can help to enhance our preschool program by sharing your time, talents, and expertise with the children. Please glance over the following list of ways you can help in our classroom and check those that interest you. Please return this survey as soon as possible.

Thanks for making a difference!

Name of Parent(s) _____

Telephone Numbers: Work _____ Home _____

_____ Read a story to a group of children.

_____ Assist with or plan a special project or holiday event.

_____ Share a hobby or your occupation and show tools used in your hobby/career.

_____ Prepare classroom learning materials at home (tracing, cutting, coloring, etc.).

_____ Provide materials for special projects.

SETTIN' UP SHOP

Preparing for a new school year is always fun, exciting, and lots of work! Use the ideas in this unit to help you organize your classroom materials, learning centers, and much, much more. Ready to get started? Let's set up shop!

by Lori Kent

WHO'S HERE TODAY?

With this management tip, your little ones will practice name-recognition skills as you take attendance. Prepare an attendance chart by gluing a picture of each student onto a separate library-card pocket. Attach the pockets to a large sheet of tagboard; then laminate it for durability. Use an X-acto® blade to slit the laminating film across the opening of each pocket. Next cut a supply of index cards in half; then personalize a half for each child in your class. Tape each child's name onto a separate wide craft stick. Place the chart and the sticks near the entrance of your classroom.

At the beginning of the year, assist each child in locating his personalized stick, then placing it into his corresponding pocket. Later in the year, request that each child locate his stick and place it into his pocket by himself. With this method you'll be able to see at a glance who is present and who is not.

Who's Here Today?

Tia

Paul

Ashley

CUBBIE BUCKETS

Creating cubbie space is a drop in the bucket with this handy idea! Purchase a class supply of sand buckets with handles. (Check after-season sales for discounted buckets; then stock up!) Invite each child to decorate a bucket using paint pens; then write each child's name on his bucket. Fasten a class supply of large cup hooks along a wall in your classroom; then hang a bucket from each hook. Students will delight in storing small belongings in their buckets. Then, at the end of the school year, invite each child to take his bucket home as a memento of his preschool year.

A PLACE FOR ME

These personalized placemats are just right for designating circle-time seating. Use a permanent marker to personalize a plain vinyl placemat for each child. If desired, tape each child's photo next to his name. Before a group time, arrange the mats on the floor; then invite each child to sit on his mat.

You might also use these handy mats as work areas for individual projects or center activities. They wipe clean in a jiffy!

"PLACE-MAPS"

Your little ones will practice one-to-one correspondence and matching skills when you provide them with a "place-map" to assist them in setting tables for snacks or mealtimes. On each plain vinyl placemat in a class supply, use a permanent marker to outline a plate, a cup, a napkin, and eating utensils. Then when it's time for meals, have each child match the corresponding table items to the appropriate places on her mat. Lunch is served!

IT'S NO SMALL "FEET"!

If standing in line is difficult for your little ones, try this management tip. Draw a pair of feet on several colors of construction paper. Cut out the feet; then arrange the pairs in an area of your classroom that requires children to stand in line—such as by the door or sink. Cover each pair of feet with a piece of clear Con-Tact® covering. When it is time to line up, simply have each child stand on a pair of feet. Your little ones are sure to enjoy stepping from one pair of feet to another as they wait for their turns. Now that's putting our best feet forward!

DIVIDE AND CONQUER

Use this creative idea to conquer the battle over limited storage space *and* define classroom center areas. Collect several lidded boxes similar to those that hold copier paper. Cover each box and its lid separately with Con-Tact® covering. Place storage materials in each box; then label its lid with the contents. Line the boxes up; then stack them one atop the other to create a portable storage wall that helps define and separate classroom centers.

FLOOR GRAPHS

Youngsters will enjoy graphing activities time and time again with this sturdy, reusable floor graph. Unroll a roll-up-type window shade; then use a permanent marker to program the shade with a grid of large squares or rectangles. Now you have a graph that's ready to use at a moment's notice.

GRAPHING POGS®

Graphing is easy when you use these graphing Pogs®. To make one, tape a child's photo to the top of a margarine-tub lid. Use a permanent marker to write the child's name under her picture. Now when you are working on a group graph, each child has her own marker to cast her vote. Easy!

HANG IT UP

If you're hung up over a way to store all of your charts, posters, and large bulletin-board pieces, try this easy management tip. Simply use clothespins to clip the desired item onto a clothes hanger. Hang the hangers from a rod suspended in a storage closet, or place a rolling garment rack in an unused corner of your classroom. Now all of your large materials are stored neatly and are available right at your fingertips.

READY TO ROUND UP THE YEAR

INSTANT DISPLAY

Floor space becomes display space for your book collection when you use this idea in your reading or group area. Purchase a length of plastic rain gutter (available at a home improvement store). Place the gutter along a wall near your reading or group area. Arrange books inside the gutter for an instant display that encourages budding literacy skills.

Henny Penny

Cinderella

The Three Little Pigs

CENTER ROTATION

Your little ones will feel independent as they select and change learning centers with this management system. From tagboard, cut a different-colored seasonal or geometric sign for each of your learning centers. Label each cutout with the center's name. Make smaller, matching shapes for each center, equal to the number of children you want in that center at one time. Hot-glue each small shape onto a separate clothespin. Clip the clothespins to the appropriate signs. When visiting a center, a child removes a clothespin from the sign and clips it onto his clothing. When all the clothespins are removed from the sign, the center is full. When a child is ready to leave the center, he replaces the clothespin on the sign.

SPREAD A CENTER

Make more room for centers in a flash with this quick and easy idea. Purchase a vinyl tablecloth and spread it in an unused corner, a hallway, or an open area of your classroom. Place a center activity, such as small manipulatives, on the tablecloth. The cloth visually defines the center area and cleanup is a breeze. Just gather the manipulatives into the center of the cloth; then pour them back into their proper container.

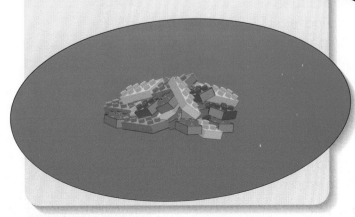

TRAYS FOR STORAGE

Five-drawer office organizers are a great way to save space and store small manipulatives. Label the outside of each drawer with the name of a different manipulative. If desired hot-glue a corresponding manipulative piece next to each name. Each drawer holds a large supply of manipulatives and the traylike design makes it easy for little hands to handle.

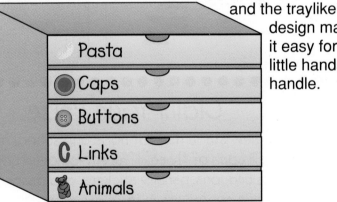

Pasta
Caps
Buttons
Links
Animals

CLEAN AS A WHISTLE

Make short work out of cleaning and sanitizing small plastic manipulatives by letting your washing machine do all the work. Place some manipulatives inside a mesh lingerie bag. Toss the bag into your washer along with some laundry soap and a small amount of bleach. Set your machine on the gentle cycle; then sit back and relax. Your manipulatives will come out sparkling clean and sanitized.

YOU'RE A GUARANTEED WINNER!

Won't your new students be thrilled tio hear they're winners in the Preschool Sweepstakes? Use these ideas to plan a memorable home visit for each lucky child in your new preschool class.

ideas contributed by Linda Ludlow and Angie Kutzer

CONGRATULATIONS!

Announce the good news to each student with a phone call. Introduce yourself and tell her to be on the lookout for the Preschool Prize Patrol that will be visiting her soon. As you speak with the child's parent, schedule a convenient time to drop by for a home visit. A few days before the visit, mail a winning postcard (duplicated from page 32 onto heavy tagboard) to the child. Your new student will be eagerly awaiting your arrival.

CONGRATULATIONS

!

The Preschool Prize Patrol will be visiting your home on

at

.

y Smith

See you then!

Preschool Prize Box

To prepare for your award-winning home visits, assemble a class supply of small, cube-shaped gift boxes. For each child, duplicate the welcome letter found on page 33. Place a prize ticket from "Claim Your Prize" at the bottom of each box; then fill each box with the items listed in the letter. Insert the personalized welcome letter last; then close the box. For extra excitement, gift wrap each box before tying a helium-filled balloon around it. Now you're ready to go on patrol!

You're A Winner!
Redeem this ticket on the first day of school!

Claim Your Prize

Show your new students that home and school are a winning combination. Fill each of three different-colored containers with prizes, such as crayons, pencils, stickers, and assorted party favors. Store these containers in the classroom. Then duplicate a supply of prize tickets from page 33 onto construction paper in the same colors as the prize containers' colors. Put a ticket in the bottom of each new preschooler's prize box (see "Preschool Prize Box"). When the child finds the ticket during the home visit, explain that she is to bring it with her on the first day of school and trade it for a prize. On the first day of preschool, have each child find the prize container that matches her ticket's color, then select a prize. (Be sure to have some extra tickets on hand for children who forget theirs.) Wow, *that's* the ticket!

CRAYONS 8 Large

GLUE

CRAYONS 8 Large

You're A Winner!
Redeem this ticket on the first day of school!

You're A Winner!
Redeem this ticket on the first day of school!

ABOUT THE WINNERS...

Help your students get to know each other by sharing these brag boxes. Once the prize box is emptied during each home visit, ask the child and her parent to prepare the box for a return to school. Instruct them to draw or cut out magazine pictures that tell about the new student and glue them to the outside of the box. Then invite the child to put one of her favorite objects inside the box. Take time during the first day of preschool to have each child share her brag box.

"LOOK, MOM, HERE IT COMES!"

The Prize Patrol! The Prize Patrol! There are sure to be lots of little faces glued to the windows as you arrive for your home visits. Begin each visit by awarding the new preschooler with a prize box as described on page 30. Take time to explain the contents of the box; then spend some time getting to know the new student. The excitement for the first day of preschool just keeps growing!

SMILE!

Make sure you bring a camera along on the visits to capture those winning smiles. Taking photos during home visits will allow you time to have them developed before the first day of school. You will not only be able to put names with faces, but you will also have photos available for a personalized welcome display on that very first day. Say cheese!

Becky

Kevin

The Grand Gala

Before ending each home visit, inform the parent of the grand prize—a chance to meet all of the other young winners and their parents a day or two before school starts! In advance, determine a time and place for everyone to meet, such as a fast-food restaurant's play area, a neighborhood playground, or a nearby park. If desired, provide a large cake with "Congratulations, You're Preschoolers!" written on it. This informal gathering can serve many purposes: parents can begin networking; children can get to know one another; and you can observe parent/child and child/child interactions. Most of all, the stress and tension of the first day of school is lessened for *everyone!*

Postcards

Use with "Congratulations!" on page 30.

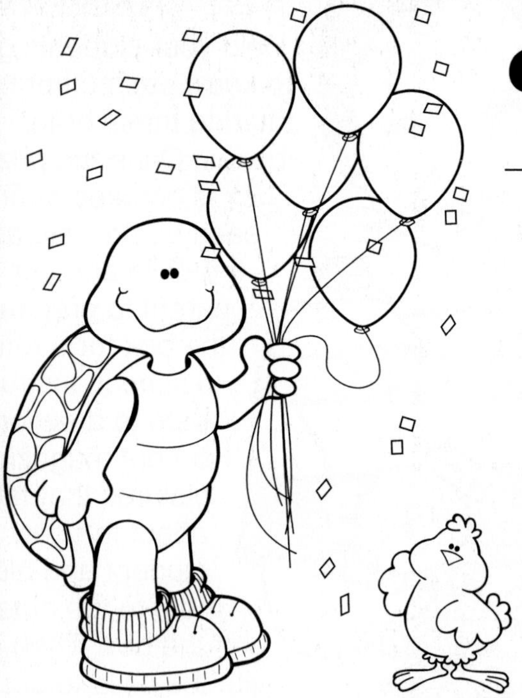

CONGRATULATIONS

_______________________________!

The Preschool Prize Patrol will be visiting your home

on

____

at ______________.

See you then!

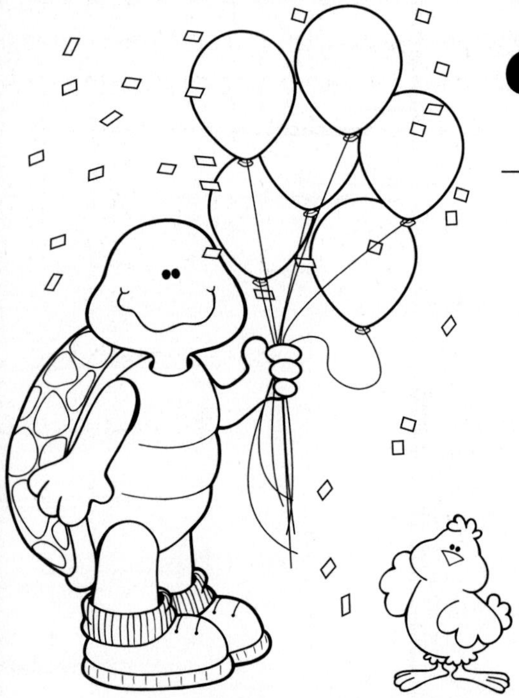

CONGRATULATIONS

_______________________________!

The Preschool Prize Patrol will be visiting your home

on

____

at ______________.

See you then!

©1998 The Education Center, Inc. • *The Mailbox® Superbook* • *Preschool* • TEC458

Welcome To Preschool!

Dear _____,

I am so excited to have you in my class this year! The items in this box will help me tell you about your new classroom and classmates.

- The sticker is to remind you that we will all stick together and help each other.
- The puzzle piece is to remind you that you are needed to make our class complete.
- The cotton ball is to remind you that our class is full of kind words and warm feelings.
- The apple is to remind you that we will learn something new each and every day.
- The eraser is to remind you that we will all make mistakes and that is okay.
- The sunglasses are to remind you that your future is "soooo" bright!

If you'll use these objects as reminders of our visit, we'll *all* be winners!

With Love,

_____

Prize Tickets

Use with "Preschool Prize Box" and "Claim Your Prize" on page 30.

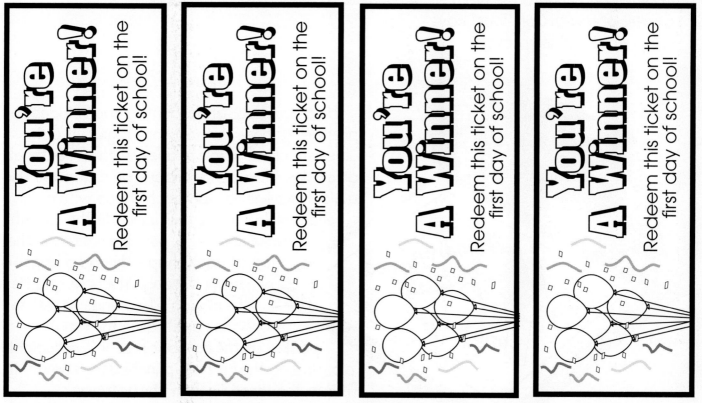

You're A Winner! Redeem this ticket on the first day of school!

You're A Winner! Redeem this ticket on the first day of school!

You're A Winner! Redeem this ticket on the first day of school!

You're A Winner! Redeem this ticket on the first day of school!

SUBSTITUTE SAVVY

When you have to be absent, ensure a successful and less stressful day for everyone by creating this informative substitute notebook. With the turn of just a few pages, most questions about policy, procedure, and your program are answered.

ideas contributed by Jan Brennan

WHO ARE THESE CHILDREN?

Purchase a three-ring notebook that has a transparent panel over the front cover. Take a photo of your class, then have it enlarged to 5" x 7" or 8" x 10". Mount the enlarged photo on a piece of paper cut to fit the front panel of the notebook. Write the children's names under the photo; then slide the paper into the panel. If a paneled notebook can't be found, simply attach the labeled, mounted photo onto the front of a notebook with Con-Tact® covering. What a classy cover!

NAMETAGS ARE NECESSITIES!

Help your substitute identify each student by preparing these durable nametags. Cut out a class supply of simple shapes, such as rectangles or circles, from poster board or tagboard. Use a black marker to label each shape with a different child's name; then laminate the cutouts. To make nametags, punch a hole near the top of each shape, thread a length of ribbon through the hole, and tie the ribbon's two ends together. Store the nametags in the front pocket of the notebook, or in a resealable plastic bag that is hole-punched (as shown) to fit into the three rings of the notebook.

IN CASE OF AN EMERGENCY. . .

Fill the first section of the notebook with information concerning fire drill, inclement weather, and early dismissal procedures. Insert a class roll with a contact person and phone number listed for each child. Also list any medical conditions or allergies beside that particular child's name along with the appropriate steps to follow if an incident occurs.

MATERIALS MAP

Just where are those pattern blocks, that pocket chart, and the hamster food? For the next section of the notebook, prepare a map that shows where to find important items that a substitute teacher will need during the course of the day. Sketch out a simple map of your room; then label the location of each of the needed supplies. Be sure to keep the map current if you rearrange your room frequently!

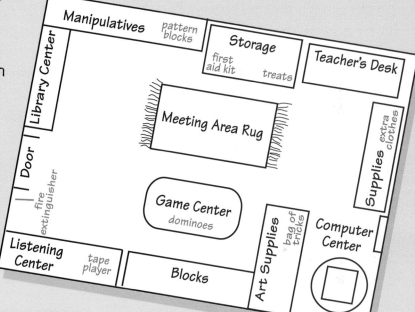

SCHEDULES, SCHEDULES, SCHEDULES

Give substitutes an overview of your class's various schedules in this section. Duplicate the blank schedule on page 37; then fill in your special weekly activities and general daily schedules. Include a copy of your school's or center's monthly schedule of events, a current lunch menu, and a school calendar for the year.

OUR SCHEDULE

Time	Monday	Tuesday	Wednesday	Thursday	Friday
8:30–9:30	Explorations/ Free Choice Centers				
9:30–10:00	Circle Time	Music	Circle Time	Music	Circle Time
10:00–11:00	Work Centers	Circle Time Whole-group activity	Work Centers	Circle Time Whole-group activity	Work Centers
11:00–11:45	Lunch				
11:45–12:15	Recess				
12:15–1:30	Rest/Quiet Time				

WHAT'S THE PLAN?

Into the next section of your substitute notebook, place the specific lesson plans for the day. Use a duplicate of the form on page 42 to provide an outline of the day ahead, or write out the plans in detail—whichever is more comfortable for you. It is also helpful to include a dependable child's name (or several different children) to assist the substitute during each activity. The designated helper will ensure that the others follow the established routine.

BAG OF TRICKS

What does the substitute do when she's at the end of the lesson plans with time to spare? Reach into this bag of tricks, of course! You know it's going to happen, so be prepared with these extra, filler activities. Collect the materials needed to play several quick games, and insert them into a large gift bag. Write simple directions for each game on separate index cards. Punch a hole in the corner of each card, bind them together with a loose-leaf ring, and then put them in the bag, too. Be sure to explain the bag of tricks in your plans and mark its location on the Materials Map from page 35. Those extra minutes will disappear like magic!

NOTEWORTHY NEWS

Fill the last section of the notebook with blank, loose-leaf paper for the substitute to document and relay to you the trials (if any) and celebrations of the day. If desired, include a pocket page at the beginning of the section for any parent notes that were collected for your review. Congratulations—you helped create and guarantee a successful substitute day!

Thanks for letting me come in for you. We had a great day!

Ms. Brown

OUR SCHEDULE

TIME	Monday	Tuesday	Wednesday	Thursday	Friday

Note To The Teacher: Use with "Schedules, Schedules, Schedules" on page 35.

Ready Reference

Stocking Up For Preschool

Scan the master list below; then consider which items you need to order or purchase, and which you want to request from the families of your preschoolers. You may want to request that different families send in different items, so that no one family is overwhelmed. Also keep in mind that there are some items (such as crayons or facial tissues) that you may need to request again later in the year, when your supply runs low.

A few helpful hints:
- Be specific about the number, type, or brand of items you request.
- Give suggestions for stores where parents can find the items on your list.
- Specify a date by which you'd like all supplies turned in.
- Inform parents as to which items will be shared (community property) and which will be marked for each child's individual use.
- Consider snacktime. Is snack provided by your school or center? If not, set up a schedule for parent donations and specify the types of snacks that are appropriate.

Items For Individual Use
resting mat or beach towel
backpack
vinyl placemat
spare clothing/shoes
toothbrush and toothpaste
dishwasher-safe plastic cup and/or bowl
large T-shirt or other art smock
communication notebook

Classroom Supplies
crayons
safety scissors
markers
glue or paste
yarn
facial tissues
baby wipes
play dough
zippered plastic bags
paper plates
paper cups
plastic spoons
napkins/paper towels
paper lunch bags
adhesive bandages
hand lotion
cotton balls/swabs
books for the classroom library
bubbles and blowers
clear Con-Tact® paper
items for texture play:
    rice, grits, pasta, packing foam, etc.

There's more! See page 80 for a reproducible request form for cooking supplies.

Preschool Is Cool!

A B C

WELCOME!

(child's name)

(teacher's name)

©The Education Center, Inc. • *The Mailbox® Superbook* • *Preschool* • TEC458

Preschool Is Cool!

A B C

WELCOME!

(child's name)

(teacher's name)

©The Education Center, Inc. • *The Mailbox® Superbook* • *Preschool* • TEC458

Nametags

Note To The Teacher: Duplicate a class supply of one of these nametags to coordinate with a thematic unit. Or use several of the designs together in order to divide your class into small groups. Color, label, cut out, and then laminate the nametags for durability.

Note To The Teacher: Duplicate a class supply of one of these nametags to coordinate with a thematic unit. Or use several of the designs together in order to divide your class into small groups. Color, label, cut out, and then laminate the nametags for durability.

Preschool Plans

We're Learning About:

Date:

Circle Time Fun

Learning Centers

Language:

Math:

Art:

Discovery:

Manipulatives:

Sand/Water:

Blocks:

Dramatic Play:

Movement

Stories To Read

Special Students

Small Group Activities

Notes

Note To The Teacher: Duplicate and use this form for daily or weekly planning.

Get Set For Centers!

Centers are a big part of most preschool classrooms. Before you set the table in your housekeeping area or stack the wooden blocks on the shelves, check out these ideas to help you organize and manage your centers to get the most out of them.

ideas contributed by Virginia Zeletzki

Consider This...

Before you set up your classroom centers, ask yourself these questions:

How am I going to use centers in my teaching?

Will small groups complete guided lessons at various centers? Or will centers be strictly free play? Will the materials and activities you provide require supervision or can they easily be done independently?

How many centers do I have room for?

Consider the physical space and equipment you're working with. Where is the sink? Where are the electrical outlets? Do you have a portable sand table you could roll outside?

Are there some centers I may want to use only part of the time or seasonally?

If you live in a cold climate, do you want to use the water table only in warmer weather, when you can put it outside? Will the puppet center be open every day?

Will my choices for centers provide for a variety of learning styles?

Do you have both quiet and active centers? Do some centers provide for tactile learning? Are there centers where students can work independently and centers where students can interact with others?

What materials and equipment do I really need? How can I get them?

If you feel it's essential to have a class pet for your science area, can you get a local pet shop to donate one? Can you ask parents to provide materials or build a reading loft?

Once you've made some decisions about the *who, what, when,* and *how* of your classroom centers, turn the page for ideas on furniture arrangement, storage, and management. It's center time!

Use Your Imagination!

Once you've decided which centers to have, you're faced with the task of arranging your furniture to adequately define each area. Keep traffic flow and a clear view of all the centers in mind. The sides of a metal filing cabinet or the front of an air-conditioning unit can make wonderful magnetboards. Low bookshelves or milk crates can be pushed together to make room dividers. Cover the back of an upright piano with flannel to make a storytelling area or with Con-Tact® covering to make a display area for bulletin-board art. Use small area rugs to help define spaces. Place blocks on shelves near your circle-time area so that children can use the open, carpeted space for building during center time. With a little planning and creativity, you'll be set for centers in no time!

Lost & Found

Designate a box or basket as the lost-and-found. If a child finds a loose puzzle piece or any other manipulative and isn't sure where it belongs, have him place it in the lost-and-found. Periodically go through the lost-and-found and return items to their proper places.

Storage Solutions

Now you'll need to store all the wonderful materials you've collected for your centers. If you're not careful, you can end up with a mess of mixed-up pegs, cubes, beads, and buttons! Take a photo, or make a simple drawing, of each material, and glue one picture on each storage container to help little ones get things back into their proper places. Help preschoolers pick up on concepts of color, shape, pattern, and number by utilizing those concepts for storage with any of the following methods:

- Purchase plastic, tinted shoeboxes or storage boxes and designate a different shade for each center. For example, all math materials could go in blue boxes.

- Use coffee cans or sturdy boxes to store materials. Cover the containers with solid-colored Con-Tact® paper; then label each container with a numeral or a shape on one side and a picture of the enclosed material on the other. Label a space on a shelf with the corresponding numeral or shape for each container.

- Cover storage containers with different patterns of Con-Tact® paper before labeling them with pictures of the enclosed materials. Then label a space on a shelf with a corresponding square of Con-Tact® paper, and have children match the patterns as they replace the containers.

Round And Round We Go

If you plan on using your center areas for small-group lessons, you'll need an efficient way to rotate groups from center to center. Try designating a color for each group. Then cut out a balloon shape from each corresponding color of construction paper. Hang the balloon cutouts from clothespins attached to yarn lengths above each center. (Or, if you are not allowed to hang items from your classroom ceiling, simply place a balloon cutout in each center.) Then ask each child to go to the center with the balloon that corresponds to his group's color. When you are ready for each group to rotate, move the balloons and ask children to follow.

How Many?

During free-choice centers, you'll probably want to designate the number of children allowed in each center, in order to avoid crowding and assure that there are enough materials for everyone. Prepare a simple poster to convey the limits to your preschoolers. To begin, prepare a small version of each of your center labels. (If desired, reduce the center labels on pages 61–63.) Glue these to a sheet of poster board or a length of bulletin-board paper, as shown. Next to each center label, glue a library pocket. Label each pocket with a numeral to show how many children may visit that center at any one time. Laminate the finished poster, if desired (don't forget to use an X-acto® knife to slit each library pocket after laminating). Then print each child's name on a separate craft stick.

To use this system, have each child insert the craft stick labeled with her name into one of the library pockets to indicate which center she plans to visit during free-choice time. Once the number of sticks equal to the numeral on the pocket are in place, that center is full.

It's A Theme Thing

If you extend your current theme to each of your classroom centers (see pages 52–57), you'll love this idea for helping keep track of which centers your little ones have visited. For each child, make a necklace using yarn and a theme-related shape. For example, if your class is studying flowers, cut a flower shape for each child from heavy paper. Label each petal with a numeral or shape that corresponds to a label you've placed in a particular center. Over the course of your study, ask each child to wear his necklace as he visits each center. Then hole-punch the corresponding numeral or shape on his neck-lace. Each day at center time—as students don their neck-laces—you can tell at a glance if a student needs to visit a particular center. When you move on to a new theme, send the necklaces home. The cutouts may spark discus-sions between parents and children about the thematic center activities little ones have completed at school.

From Classroom To Classroom

This center idea will make special occasions a real treat—for students and teachers! Rather than trying to set up several unique centers for a holiday or special study in your own class-room, ask each teacher at your level to set up one center in her room. Plan the centers to-gether in advance, so you'll provide a good mix of activities. Then, on the designated day, ro-tate your classes from one room to another, allowing enough time for children to complete each center before moving to a new room. For example, Christmas centers might include a craft in one room, cookie decorating in another, and a story and singing in a third. The children will love it, and there will be less preparation time for each teacher.

Miss Daphne:
—make wrapping paper

Mrs. K:
—Christmas cookies

Miss Terry:
—read and sing "Rudolph The Red-Nosed Reindeer"

The Dramatic-Play Center: Not Just Housekeeping Anymore!

Lights, camera, action! Use the following ideas to transform your dramatic-play area into scenarios that will make even the most reserved preschooler worthy of an Oscar nomination.

ideas contributed by Linda Gordetsky and Angie Kutzer

Let It Snow!

Add a chill to the air when you create this winter wonderland. Sprinkle Styrofoam® packing pieces on the floor to create snow. Make a basic snowman shape by stuffing one large and one small white, plastic trashbag with more Styrofoam® pieces or with newspaper. To make the snowman, insert half of a dowel's length inside the large bag before tying it shut. Then invert the small trashbag over the remaining part of the dowel and tie that bag shut. Provide winter clothing and accessories for children to dress the snowman as well as themselves. Use white athletic socks rolled into balls for soft snowballs. Place arctic animal toys, such as penguins or polar bears, around the area. Complete the scene with plastic mugs, a teapot, an empty can of hot cocoa, and some wintry picture books. What a cool center!

Special Delivery

Set up a post-office scenario to coincide with a community-helper unit or for Valentine's Day. To create this scene, divide the area with a long table to separate the customers from the workers. On this counter, place various office supplies such as pens, stamp pads, and rubber stamps. Include a scale for weighing packages, as well as a cash register and play money. Provide different types of paper, envelopes, pencils, greeting cards, and crayons for customers to make their mail. (Stamps from sweepstakes entries make great stamps for preschool mail.) Hang a class list nearby for children to use when addressing mail. Provide visors for the postal workers to wear. Other props could include an old handbag with a shoulder strap for carrying mail and a large, divided box for sorting mail. This area is sure to be first-class fun!

How Does Your Garden Grow?

Youngsters will dig this opportunity for dramatic play. Bring your sand table or another large container into the dramatic-play area and fill it half-full with potting soil. Stock the center with plastic flowerpots, artificial blooms, trowels, assorted seeds, a watering can, and plastic vegetables. For added fun, hide plastic fishing worms in the soil for youngsters to discover. Provide smocks, a dustpan, and a broom to keep your growing gardeners and your floor neat and tidy. Watch as imaginations start to sprout up and take root!

Down By The Sea

Invite your beach bunnies to use these props to re-create a "sun-sational" day by the shore. Tape a length of white bulletin-board paper to a low section of a wall in the dramatic-play area. Provide a variety of markers and colored chalk and invite children to draw a background scene complete with sun, sand, and surf. (For younger preschoolers, you may want to sketch the outlines of the sun, waves, and sand for them to color.) Move the sand table into the area or fill a plastic swimming pool with sand. Put in plastic shovels, buckets, castle molds, assorted containers for building, and of course, seashells! Spread several beach towels on the floor; then shine a desk lamp into the area for basking in the "sunshine." Flip-flops, sunglasses, a picnic basket, swimming floats, sun hats, and some background beach music will complete this beach-lover's paradise.

Let's Play School!

Give preschoolers an opportunity to walk in your shoes as they role-play the teacher in the dramatic-play area. Setting up this scene is easy; just look around! Include chalk, an eraser, an easel, a big book, a pointer, a puppet, paper and crayons, and plenty of rewarding stickers for the teacher to use. Provide the teacher with a school-themed sweater or T-shirt and eyeglass frames to wear. Encourage students to take turns; then watch as they emulate their favorite educator in action—you! It's sure to be a real learning experience for *everyone*.

A Preschool Powwow

This preschool version of a Native American village is sure to be a hit. Tape a large, tagboard cone to the top of a round table; then cover both items with a sheet to resemble a tepee. Inside the tepee, place beads and laces for stringing necklaces. Provide craft feathers, construction-paper strips, and tape for making headdresses. "Light" a fire by arranging rocks (or crumpled pieces of dark-colored paper) in a circle; then tuck red and orange tissue paper into the center to resemble flames. Be sure to include a drum and some bean shakers for youngsters to use as they chant and dance. If desired, obtain some real animal skins for your tribe to examine. Look, over there. It's Little Running Bear!

Fast-Food Fantasy

May I take your order? Creating this fast-food fantasy is easy with a little help from your local restaurants. Ask them for a supply of napkins, cups, containers, and bags. Arrange your puppet theater to serve as a drive-thru window, a low shelving unit to be the ordering counter, and a table for dining. Place a cash register with play money on the counter. Provide plastic fast-food items, play dough, spatulas, and other cooking utensils for making and filling the customers' orders. Use red fabric paint or permanent marker to stripe white T-shirts and sentence-strip headbands for the workers to wear. Instruct customers not to crush or throw away any of the materials so that they can be used again. You're sure to be amazed at the realistic dialogue that will take place during this fast-food fun. Order's up!

The Greatest Show On Earth

Hurry, hurry, hurry! Fill your dramatic-play area with circus props and let the show begin! Include such things as clown wigs, rubber balls, plastic hoops, tin-can stilts, and a low balance beam (or a length of 2" x 4" lumber). Yarn whips and chairs are perfect for lion tamers. Beanbags and yardsticks make a great balancing act. Complete the scene by putting a red sticky dot on each child's nose—now they're officially circus clowns! Invite other students to munch on a snack of popcorn or peanuts while enjoying the show. Come one, come all!

The Doctors Will See You Now

Is your playful pooch suddenly pooped? The little veterinarians in this classroom clinic will be glad to check him out. To turn your dramatic-play area into a pet clinic, cover the "examining" table with a white sheet. Then set several pet carriers (or cardboard boxes cut to resemble cages) along one wall to resemble a kennel. Provide plenty of stuffed-toy patients and medical supplies, such as bandage strips, gauze, wraps, masks, empty pill bottles, and toy medical tools. Clipboards and notepads are also handy for taking notes and writing prescriptions. Include an oversized, white dress shirt or jacket for each doctor to wear. This setup is a sure cure for reluctant role-players.

Happy Birthday!

Need a reason to party? Pretend it's someone's birthday! Place a variety of decorating items—such as a tablecloth, cups, napkins, plates, horns, and hats—in a box. Provide play dough, candles, and baking tools for the students to create the cake and other munchies. Assist the party goers in playing Pin The Tail On The Donkey, Bingo, Clothespin Drop, or other party games. Encourage each group that visits the area to set up for the party, celebrate, and then clean up to get the area ready for the next group. Happy dramatic play to you!

THEMATIC CENTERS

Want to keep students focused on the current unit of study, even during center time? Use the following helpful hints and ideas for creating thematic centers. This section starts with general ideas regarding the most common centers, then gives specific modifications for three favorite themes.

ideas contributed by Angie Kutzer and dayle timmons

BUILDING AREA

The basic wooden blocks are good, but why stop there? Look for other building supplies, from commercial sets such as DUPLO® to recycled items. Assorted boxes and cardboard tubes can be covered with Con-Tact® covering and used for various building ideas. Include thematic objects in your building area for children to build things for—such as cars that need bridges, and zoo animals that need cages. Mount architectural posters that correspond to your theme around the area for a little inspiration. Finally, be sure to have an instant camera handy to take pictures of the new constructions that are built. Keep these photos in the building area to encourage other kiddie contractors.

MANIPULATIVE AREA

Add theme-related puzzles, colored play dough, cookie cutters, and lacing cards to this area. Challenge students to make certain objects from play dough that correlate with the theme—such as snowmen for a winter theme or flowers for a gardening theme. Think of creative items for children to string, such as Styrofoam® shapes cut from meat trays during a shape unit or colored pasta to match a specific color unit.

WRITING CENTER

Label sentence strips with thematic words; then attach a matching sticker (or draw your own picture) on each strip to make thematic vocabulary cards for children to use in their writing. Stock the center with a variety of papers and writing tools, some of which can be modified to fit your theme—such as heart-shaped notepads for Valentine's Day. Add thematic stencils to the center. These can be store-bought or teacher-made. Write the words to a thematic fingerplay, song, or poem on chart paper, and post it in the center for students to "read" and "copy."

bear

HOUSEKEEPING AREA

Look carefully at the furniture in the center to see how things can be rearranged. For example, position the puppet theater behind the sink to be a picturesque window. Or use the theater as a drive-through window for a restaurant. With a few props, you can turn your housekeeping center into an office, a grocery store, a hospital, or a salon. Just use your imagination, which in turn will encourage your little ones to use theirs! (See pages 48–51 for more ideas on transforming your dramatic-play area.)

DRIVE-THRU

PAINTING CENTER

Choose theme-related colors of paint for this center. Set out various types of paint, from tempera, to watercolor, to fingerpaint. Add flavoring extracts or scented potpourri oils to the paints to scent them. Or add gelatin, sand, or glitter to the paint to create interesting textures. Paint with thematic objects, such as a pine branch when studying trees, or feathers when studying birds. Use sponge shapes relating to your theme for some printing fun. Provide different painting surfaces for children to explore, such as grocery bags, Styrofoam® trays, and aluminum foil.

DISCOVERY CENTER

Place thematic items in this area that will encourage preschoolers to experiment with the scientific-process skills of observing, comparing, relating, analyzing, and communicating. Collections of all types, from seashells to insects, accompanied by magnifying glasses, are great for discovery. When possible include live specimens to observe that correlate with your theme—such as tadpoles during a pond unit, or a hatching egg during spring. Stock the discovery center with blank journals and crayons so that little ones can record their findings with writing or pictures.

GAME CENTER

Place your computer and activities that reinforce cognitive skills in this area. Look for software that enhances your theme. You probably won't be able to change the programs to coordinate with *every* theme you teach, but keep your favorite themes in mind as you select new titles for your classroom each year. Use thematic, die-cut notepads and stickers to make quick patterning, matching, and counting games. Also include any store-bought games you may have that correlate with your chosen theme, such as Candyland® during Halloween or a color unit.

ART CENTER

To your regular stock of construction paper, add lots of miscellaneous collage materials that will add texture, sparkle, and pattern to young-sters' creations. Keep an eye on the bargain tables at your local sewing and crafts stores for items such as fabric scraps, yarn, rickrack, buttons, sequins, and ribbon. Check out post-seasonal and holiday sales, and stock up for the next school year. To modify the center for specific themes, select items of a specific color, texture, or shape. For example, when studying weather, include cotton balls (clouds), foil (rain or lightning), yellow cupcake liners (the sun), and small bits of doilies or lace (snow) for children to use to create scenes showing the elements.

SAND/WATER TABLE

Anything that can be used to dig or pour can be added to this area. Cups, bowls, measuring tools, shovels, funnels, scoops, and buckets are only a few of the possibilities. Think about other things that can be added to the table to enhance your current theme—such as sailboats when studying air, or construction vehicles during a building unit. For a fun twist, try filling the table with potting soil during a gardening unit, or with O-shaped cereal for a unit on circles. Whatever the theme, this area is sure to be "sand-sational!"

THANKSGIVING

Mmmm, is that turkey and sweet potato pie? Stuff your centers with these Thanksgiving ideas to keep your little ones gobbling!

Building Area: Provide a set of interlocking building logs, craft sticks, clay, and broom straw for building the Pilgrims' homes. (Be sure to have books showing pictures of the Pilgrims' clapboard houses for children to use as references.)

Manipulative Area: Add fruit, vegetable, and turkey puzzles. Put out red, yellow, and orange play dough along with leaf- and fruit-shaped cookie cutters. Include a tub of colored macaroni pieces and yarn lengths for making Native American necklaces.

Writing Center: Add stencils of fruits, vegetables, and a cornucopia. Look for fruit-scented markers for writing, tracing, and coloring. Put up a chart of Native American symbols for children to copy. Include theme-related vocabulary cards, such as *pumpkin, turkey, feather,* and *family.*

Housekeeping Area: Cover the table with a tablecloth that has a Thanksgiving motif. Place a cornucopia full of plastic fruits and vegetables in the center of the table. Provide plenty of plates, cups, and napkins, and encourage children to set the table for a specific number of guests. Stock the kitchen shelves with real, unopened cans of food. Provide aprons for the cooks of this great feast.

Painting Center: Set out paint in fall colors. Add lemon extract to the yellow paint, cinnamon spice to the brown, and pumpkin spice to the orange. Encourage students to use vegetable and fruit halves to make prints. Paint with feathers instead of brushes.

Discovery Center: Peel, core, and cut two apples into 1/8-inch slices. String the slices from one apple. Soak the other apple slices in lemon juice before stringing. Let students observe the apples for several days to see which slices turn browner. Eat the dried apples at snacktime one day. Do they taste different than regular apple slices?

Game Center: Look for a turkey-shaped notepad. On each of five sheets, draw a different set of dots from one to five. Label each of five more sheets with a different numeral from one to five. Encourage students to match the numeral turkeys to the correct dotted turkeys.

Art Center: Add feathers, pinecones, and wiggle eyes for making turkeys. Bring in a collection of real, colorful leaves to glue on paper-plate rings for beautiful fall wreaths. Have strips of construction paper and tape available for students to use in making their own Native American headbands.

Sand/Water Table: Fill the table with a large bag of popped popcorn or with leaves. Encourage students to experiment with a bowl of mixed nuts and water to see which nuts float and which nuts sink. Add plastic fruits, vegetables, bowls, salad tongs, pots, and wooden spoons so children can make vegetable soup or fruit salad.

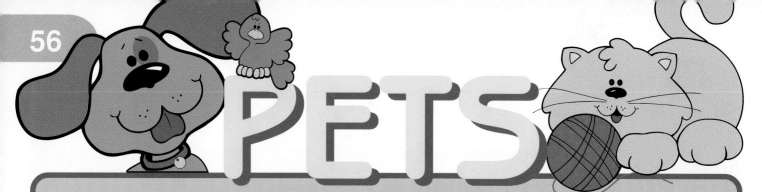

PETS

Invite your youngsters to crawl, hop, swim, pounce, and romp on over to these learning centers enhanced with a pet theme. What "purr-ific" ideas!

Building Area: Add lots of animal figures that need pens and cages built for them. Then let the building begin!

Manipulative Area: Make pet lacing cards. Laminate die-cut notepad sheets; then punch holes around each sheet's perimeter. Provide play dough and pet-shaped cookie cutters, and have students create their own unique pets.

Writing Center: Provide pet stencils and pet-shaped notepads. Make pet vocabulary cards—each showing a magazine picture of a pet labeled with its name. Add several coloring books containing pet pictures for copying, tracing, and coloring.

Housekeeping Area: Turn the area into a veterinary clinic by adding pet figures and medical tools—such as gauze, wraps, and toy stethoscopes. Or try a grooming salon equipped with stuffed animals, empty shampoo bottles, brushes, combs, and bows.

Painting Center: Post a picture of a distinctly patterned pet, such as a dalmatian, in the center. Set out the appropriate paint colors; then encourage little ones to paint a duplicate of the picture on their paper.

Discovery Center: Adopt a class pet or two during your unit for students to observe, take care of, and write about in journals. Goldfish, rabbits, frogs, worms, or hamsters are just a few of the possibilities.

Game Center: Set out a bowl of dog-bone treats and a die. Have a small group of children take turns rolling the die and taking the corresponding number of bones from the bowl. After each child has rolled the die three times, assist him in counting his total number of bones. Who has the most? Return the bones and play another round.

Art Center: This is a perfect time to add craft feathers, fur, felt, sequins (scales), or leather scraps to this center. Encourage children to create a pet-store window full of different textured pets.

Sand/Water Table: Fill the water table with an assortment of toy fish and nets for scooping. Or hide bones in your sand table for your young pups to find.

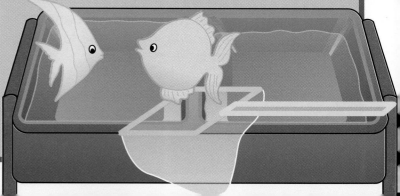

Though the weather outside is frightful, these winter centers are just delightful. Invite your children to warm up to learning!

Building Area: Encourage children to make homes for winter animal toys, such as penguins, polar bears, and seals that you put into the area. Provide white Styrofoam® shapes to use as icy building blocks. Styrofoam® packing pieces can serve as snow for toy construction vehicles to load, push, plow, and dump.

Manipulative Area: Knead iridescent glitter into white play dough for a glistening, snowy effect. Provide a snowman cookie cutter or a round cutter that children can use to create their own snowman forms. Set out a variety of decorative items, such as colored aquarium rocks and twigs, for embellishing the snow figures. Add winter puzzles to the area, along with an assortment of white beads and white laces for stringing.

Writing Center: Encourage children to draw snowmen using assorted circle stencils. Provide a supply of dark paper and white crayons (or chalk) for drawing snowy scenes. Make vocabulary cards for winter thematic words, such as *mitten, snow, sled,* and *ice.* Make a pointer by gluing a wooden Christmas ornament to the tip of a wooden dowel for students to use as they read a favorite winter rhyme or fingerplay you've written on a chart.

Housekeeping Area: Add plenty of winter dress-up clothes and accessories. If your area is large enough, consider dividing it in half. On one side create an outdoor scene by covering the floor with a white sheet. Add a sled; a small, artificial tree; and some sock snowballs. On the other side, arrange the furniture cozily around an imitation fireplace made by covering the back of a bookshelf with brick-patterned background paper. Stock the kitchen with warm foods and the cookware needed to prepare them—such as plastic mugs, spoons, a container of hot cocoa, a kettle, soup cans, bowls, pots, and a Thermos.®

Painting Center: Invite children to fingerpaint on cookie sheets using whipped cream or shaving cream. Add snowflake sponges for printing on a supply of dark-colored construction paper. Stir sparkly glitter into white paint for shimmering, snowy designs.

Discovery Center: Bring in a snowball from outside or an ice cube from the freezer. Set it in a pie plate and invite students to observe and describe what happens.

Game Center: Label each of five snowman cutouts with a different numeral from one to five. Direct a student to place the correct number of cotton balls on each cutout.

Art Center: Add lots of white materials, such as doilies, cotton balls, coffee liners, dried beans, felt, yarn, Styrofoam®, and tissue paper for interesting texture collages.

Sand/Water Table: Fill the table with crushed ice, white confetti, or mounds of shaving cream. Let little ones explore using shovels and buckets.

Making The Most Of Every Center

Adding new and different items to your various centers can make them more enjoyable and stimulating for your students. Check out these suggestions; then scout around your house for the various items, ask parents for donations, or shop local yard sales. You may come across some great finds of your own!

Art Center

Besides the usual:
paper
crayons
markers
safety scissors
glue or paste
paint
paintbrushes
play dough

Try adding:
foam paintbrushes
mini paint rollers
sponges
glitter or textured paint
cookie cutters
child-size rolling pins
plastic knives
tissue paper
crepe paper
sheets of craft foam
gift wrap
index cards
wallpaper scraps
doilies
colored masking tape
stencils

glue sticks or rollers
shaped paper punches
colored chalk
decorative-edge safety scissors
hole punchers
rubber stamps
ink pads
crinkled gift-wrap stuffing
pipe cleaners
craft feathers
fabric scraps
paper plates
paper lunch bags
colored sand
yarn
Magna Doodle®

Sand and Water Table

Besides the usual:
sand
water
rice
plastic containers
scoops

Try filling the table with:
foam packing pieces
bubble solution
grits
shaving cream
crinkled gift-wrap stuffing

Try adding to water:
ice cubes
vinyl sea animals
measuring cups and spoons
waterwheel
water pump

toy boats
eyedroppers
funnels
mild dish detergent
wire whisks or eggbeaters

Try adding to sand:
measuring cups
measuring spoons
funnels
plastic confetti shapes

plastic sand molds
toy construction vehicles
berry baskets
metal washers and magnets

Reading and Listening Center

Besides the usual:
books
tape player
cassette tapes

Try adding:
big books
class books
child-size rocking chair
child-size beanbag chair
floor pillows
stuffed animals
flannelboard
flannelboard stories

Ready Reference

Block Center

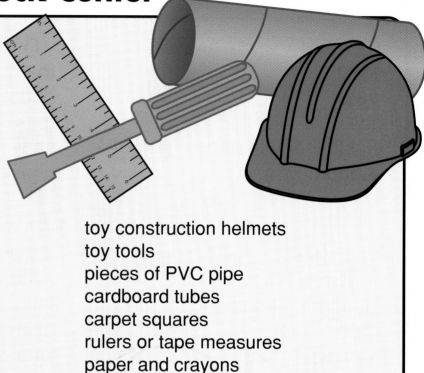

Besides the usual:
wooden blocks
DUPLO® building sets
cardboard brick blocks
foam blocks
toy vehicles

Try adding:
toy traffic signs
wooden or vinyl people figures
wooden or vinyl animal figures
dollhouse
wooden or plastic train set
vinyl or carpet road map
pulleys

toy construction helmets
toy tools
pieces of PVC pipe
cardboard tubes
carpet squares
rulers or tape measures
paper and crayons

Dramatic-Play Center

Besides the usual:
dress-up clothes
dishes and utensils
plastic foods
dolls
broom, mop, and dustpan

Try adding:
more clothing items, such as
   jewelry
   purses and wallets
   bandanas, ties, and scarves
   elbow-length gloves
telephone (toy or real)
telephone directory

empty food containers (boxes or
   plastic)
toy cash register
play money
toy tools
placemats
silk flowers in a vase
kitchen towels
toy shopping cart or basket
baskets and trays
stuffed animals
puppets

(Also see pages 48–51 for ideas on transforming your dramatic-play center.)

Block Center

A Language Area

Note To The Teacher: Enlarge each label, color it, and cut on the bold lines. Glue it to a sheet of construction paper slightly larger than the label. Laminate if desired. Mount it near the appropriate activity area.

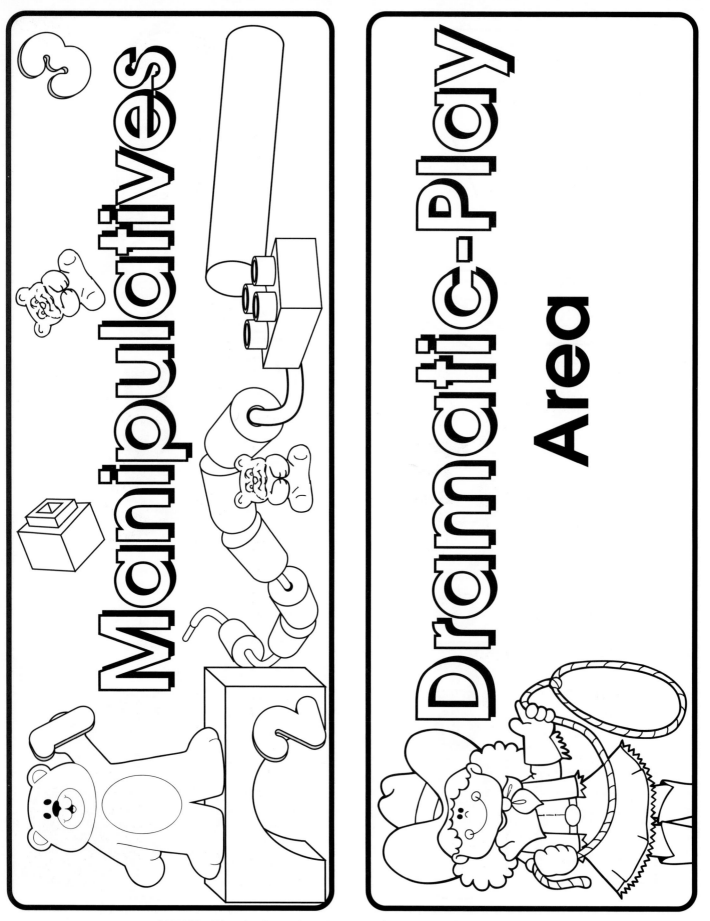

Manipulatives

Dramatic-Play Area

Note To The Teacher: Enlarge each label, color it, and cut on the bold lines. Glue it to a sheet of construction paper slightly larger than the label. Laminate if desired. Mount it near the appropriate activity area.

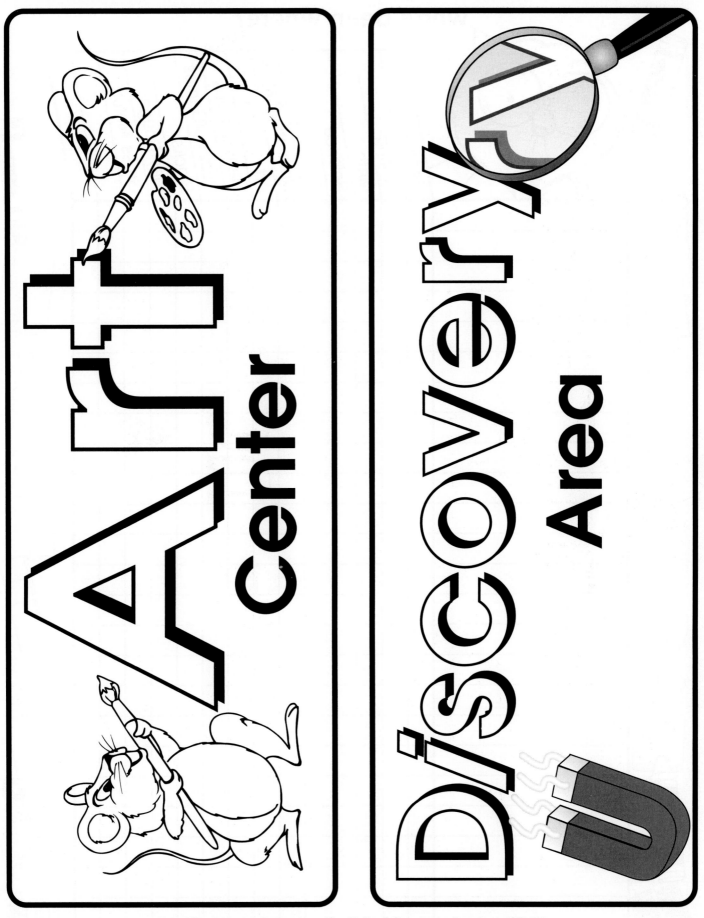

Art Center

Discovery Area

Note To The Teacher: Enlarge each label, color it, and cut on the bold lines. Glue it to a sheet of construction paper slightly larger than the label. Laminate if desired. Mount it near the appropriate activity area.

Who's Been Where?

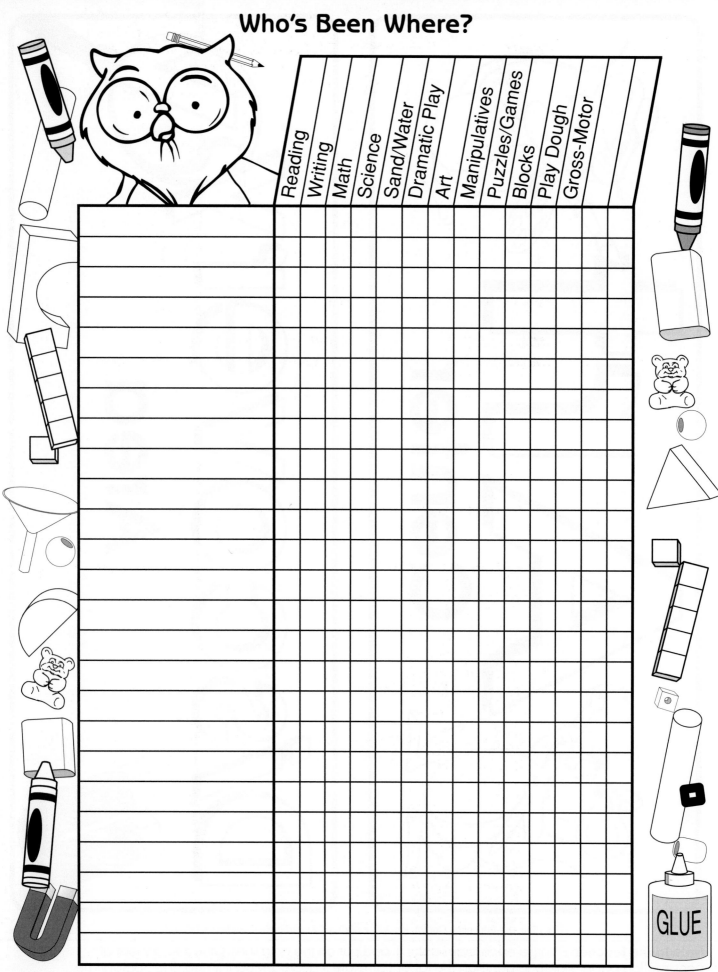

	Reading	Writing	Math	Science	Sand/Water	Dramatic Play	Art	Manipulatives	Puzzles/Games	Blocks	Play Dough	Gross-Motor

MANAGEMENT TIPS

Use the management tips provided here to help
keep your classroom running smoothly throughout the year.
ideas contributed by Linda Gordetsky and Jean Feldman

The Gang's All Here!

Here's an easy way to have youngsters account for their attendance as well as for you to make a quick visual check of your absentees. To prepare, cut a clean half-gallon milk or juice carton into thirds. Fit the bottom section of the carton into the top section; then discard the middle section. Cover the shortened carton with construction paper or solid Con-Tact® covering; then decorate it to resemble a house. Similarly, cover and decorate an inverted rectangular tissue box to resemble a school building. Cut enough half-inch long slits in the top of both the house and the school to equal the number of students in your class.

Then take a picture of each child on her first day at preschool. Trim the photo; then mount it onto a tagboard circle labeled with the child's name. Attach the circle to a craft stick, and insert the puppet into a slit in the house. As each child arrives daily, have her move her puppet from the house to the school. With a quick glance, it'll be easy to see whether or not the gang's all here!

Playtime Pals

Encourage a variety of playtime friendships among youngsters with this idea for grouping students. In advance obtain a supply of clear clip-on nametags. Cut out a supply of tagboard cards sized to fit in the nametags. Decide the number of youngsters that will be allowed in each play area, such as blocks or housekeeping; then decorate and label that number of cards in an identical fashion. Slip each card into a separate nametag and put the tags in a box. Before playtime invite each child to select a tag from the box. Help the child put on his tag; then have him join the other children wearing matching tags in his chosen play area. Wow! Instant fun! Instant friends!

Blocks

Seasonal Incentives

Motivate youngsters to behave appropriately year-round with this idea. At the beginning of each season, create a bulletin board that corresponds with that season. For each child, add to the display a seasonal construction-paper cutout labeled with her name. For example, you might display cutouts of leaves for fall, snowmen for winter, flowers for spring, and suns for summer. Throughout the year, as you randomly catch a student behaving appropriately, invite her to attach a sticky dot to her cutout. When a child's cutout is filled with dots, have her exchange it for a special treat, such as a party ring, an artificial flower, a small bottle of bubbles, or any other small token. Then give her a new cutout so she can work toward another prize. At year's end, you'll proudly tell little ones, "You've had a good year!"

Swimming Right Along

Youngsters will be swimming right along in the pool of good behavior with this self-checking system. To prepare, create an ocean scene on a bulletin board. Layer several different shades of blue and green paper strips to represent the ocean water. Place a pushpin in the bottom water layer for each child; then randomly place pins along the other layers. Cut out and label a construction-paper fish for each child. Punch a hole in each fish cutout; then hang each on a pin in the bottom layer of water. To use, have a child move his fish up a layer each time he is caught in appropriate behavior. When his fish reaches the top, invite him to choose a gummy fish, a fish cracker, or another treat; then have him return his fish to the bottom to swim his way to the surface once again. Observers are sure to think there's something fishy going on here—this class behaves swimmingly!

Chores Chat

Youngsters will swell with pride and a sense of responsibility when they tell about how they keep their belongings organized and in place! After students arrive each day, call them together for a brief group time. During this time remind them of their routine arrival chores—such as putting away bookbags, hanging up coats, or putting lunchboxes in an assigned place—and ask each child to tell the group which chores he remembered to do. Give those children who may have left out a chore the opportunity to do it at this time; then invite the class to sing this song to the tune of "Row, Row, Row Your Boat." After singing, praise the students for helping to keep the class running smoothly. This daily chores chat will go a long way toward creating proud, responsible citizens.

We've done all our chores.
We've done all our chores.
Listen, and we'll tell you now,
We've done all our chores!

Special Delivery

Make sure important notes and student work make it home with these special-delivery tubes. To make a tube, cover a clean potato-chip canister with construction paper or Con-Tact® covering. Use a permanent marker to label the canister with "Special Delivery." To use, roll up papers to be sent home with a child and slip them into the canister; then place the lid on the canister. Explain to the child that he will be taking home a special delivery to his parents. Encourage him to return the empty canister the following day so that it can be used for his next special delivery. Ding! Ding! Special delivery for Mom and Dad!

Sign In, Please

Use this daily attendance recording system to promote—and even assess— youngsters' name-writing skills. To prepare a sign-in board, laminate a sheet of poster board to display on your classroom door or on a wall near the door. Attach one end of a length of yarn to an erasable marker; then attach the other end of the yarn to the poster. To use, have each child sign her name (or her mark) on the poster each day as she arrives at school. Then use the sign-in board to note which children are present for the day. Before erasing the names at the end of the day, record anecdotal notes about each child's name-writing skills. A sign-in sheet that pulls double-duty—cool!

Please Sign In

John
shela
T
Ben
St
Pm
Ann
rck
hana

Erasable Marker
navy blue

Circle-Time Strategy

Invite youngsters to create a strategy for making their own unique circle-time mats; then use these mats to create your own strategic plan for circle-time organization and socialization. To make a mat, have each child examine a file folder; then decide how she plans to decorate and personalize the folder to make it uniquely her own. Ask each child to describe her plan to you; then invite her to decorate her folder accordingly. Laminate the folders. Then, prior to circle time, strategically arrange the mats on the floor so that favorable social and behavioral interactions between students might be achieved. Throughout circle-time activities, be sure to reinforce your strategic efforts by encouraging positive interactions between neighboring students. Circle-time strategy equals circle-time success.

Cheryl

MUSICAL MANAGEMENT

Help little ones tune in to each segment of your day with one of these lively songs. Music will get your youngsters' attention, and will help them learn and enjoy daily routines.

songs contributed by Marie Cecchini, Jean Feldman, and Betty Silkunas

Hello, Hello, Hello

Greet youngsters at the start of your day with this upbeat tune.

(sung to the tune of "If You're Happy And You Know It")

Hello, hello, hello,
Hi to you!
Hello, hello, hello,
Hi to you!
I'm so glad you came today;
We will learn and work and
  play!
Oh, hello, hello, hello,
Hi to you!

If desired personalize this song by substituting a different child's name for the word "you" in each of the second, fourth, and last lines. Repeat the song as many times as necessary to mention each child in your class.

I See You

Use this song to help little ones get settled and ready to listen before a group activity.

(sung to the tune of "Frère Jacques")

I see brown eyes;
I see green eyes;
Blue eyes, too!
I see you!
Quiet all the talk now.
Show me that you know
  how.
Gosh-oh-wow! Gosh-oh-
  wow!

Songs For Lining Up

Make this daily routine fun for your preschoolers by singing either of these catchy songs.

(sung to the tune of "Good Night, Ladies")

Line up, children.
Line up, children.
Line up, children.
It's time to line up now.

(sung to the tune of "Jingle Bells")

Let's line up,
Let's line up,
Quick as one, two, three.
Come and form a nice
    straight line
Right here in front of me.

Snacktime Song

Prepare your students for snacktime with this tasty tune.

*(sung to the tune of
"Row, Row, Row Your Boat")*

Snack, snack, snacktime's here.
Won't you have a seat?
Fold your hands right in your
    lap,
Let's get set to eat!

Dream Sweet Dreams

Lead youngsters in a quiet rendition of this tune as they prepare their cots or mats for rest time.

(sung to the tune of "Frère Jacques")

Time for resting,
Time for resting,
Preschool friends,
Preschool friends.

Close your tired eyes now.
Close your tired eyes now.
Dream sweet dreams.
Dream sweet dreams.

It's Time To Wiggle

Try this tune when your students have an overabundance of energy.

(sung to the tune of "Ten Little Indians")

Wiggle, wiggle, shake and jiggle!
Shake your arms and giggle, giggle.
Shake your legs; it's time to wiggle.
Now let's all sit down!

Cleanup Time

When your room's a mess—don't be stressed! Just give little ones a musical reminder to help you straighten up! Repeat the verse until your room is squeaky clean.

(sung to the tune of "Heigh-Ho" [The Dwarfs' Marching Song])

Heigh-ho, heigh-ho,
A-cleaning-up we'll go.
So everyone
Join in the fun!
Heigh-ho, heigh-ho.

Good-Bye Song

End your school day on a happy note with this lively tune and the accompanying motions.

(sung to the tune of "She'll Be Comin' Round The Mountain")

Oh, it's time to say good-bye
to all my friends.
(Wave good-bye.)
Oh, it's time to say good-bye
to all my friends.
(Wave good-bye.)
Oh, it's time to say good-bye.
Give a smile and wink your
eye.
(Smile and wink.)
Oh, it's time to say good-bye
to all my friends.
Good-bye, friends!
(Wave good-bye.)

Transitions And Time Fillers

Fill transition times and spare moments with these fun activities designed just for preschoolers!

ideas contributed by Jean Feldman

Come-And-Play Trays

As your little ones arrive, capture their attention while reducing their separation anxiety with these instant tray activities. To prepare, obtain a tray or box lid for each child. Arrange materials for a different activity—such as cookie cutters and play dough for sensory play, laces and short lengths of straw for stringing, or crayons and paper for drawing—on each tray. As each child arrives, invite her to use a tray of materials. You can almost hear the tray say, "Come and play! Come and play!"

Eye Spy

When you have some extra time to fill—or if you just want to engage students in a quiet activity—challenge youngsters with these bottles that help promote visual discrimination and memory skills. To prepare, fill a clear, plastic soda bottle two-thirds full with sand or salt; then put five different small items—such as a crayon, a paper clip, a rubber band, a plastic flower, and a toy animal—into the bottle. Glue the lid onto the bottle; then shake the contents. To use, challenge a child to shake, tilt, and rotate the bottle to find and identify the five things inside. What do your eyes spy?

Treasured Trash

Convert the humdrum task of cleaning up into an adventurous treasure hunt with this neat idea. Before beginning your cleanup activities, glance around the area and silently target several items to represent treasured trash. Explain to the class that several pieces of treasure are hidden among the scattered trash and items in the room. If a child happens to pick up and put away one of these special items during cleanup time, he will be rewarded with a special treasure. Then invite students to engage in cleanup until the job is complete, rewarding each child who finds a treasured item with a special sticker or small prize. These trash-turned-to-treasure tokens are great cleanup-time motivators!

Sing A Song Of Silence

Cue youngsters to settle down quickly and quietly with a song of silence. Simply mouth a voiceless version of a familiar song or fingerplay (while performing hand gestures) during a transition. Before long, youngsters will sing along, ending the song on a note of silence—and order—so that you can begin your next activity.

Flower Power

Employ the power of flowers to help line up youngsters or to move them to new activities. To prepare the flowers, cut a construction-paper flower from each of the eight basic colors. Attach each cutout to the end of a straw; then put the flowers in a vase or decorated can. To use, pick a flower from the vase and call out its color. Have each child wearing clothing of that color line up or move to an assigned center or activity area.

What To Do

Chase away your students' there's-nothing-to-do blues with this boxful of ideas. To prepare, cover an empty tissue box with a solid piece of Con-Tact® covering. If desired decorate the box with stickers and glitter-paint pens. Look in school supply catalogs to find—then cut out—pictures of materials, toys, and games representing those in your classroom. Glue each picture onto a separate notecard; then place the cards in the decorated box. Whenever a child has time to fill, invite her to pull a card out of the box, then obtain the pictured item(s) to use. No more blues; there's plenty to do!

Picture Me

Making transitions from one activity to another will be a snap with this idea. To prepare, mount a photo or self-portrait of each child on a separate tagboard card; then attach the hook side of a piece of Velcro® to the back of each card. At the end of a group activity or at line-up time, place each child's picture—one at a time—on the flannelboard. Have each child move to his assigned area or stand in line when his picture is placed on the board. Picture this: picture-perfect transitions!

Animal Crackers

It's a zoo in here! Or so it will seem when you use this activity as a time filler. In advance fill an emptied animal-cracker box with small plastic zoo animals or animal pictures. Then pass the box of animals around the group. On her turn have each child remove an animal from the box, then perform actions and noises made by that animal. For a variation, use a box of real animal crackers; then invite each child to eat her cracker at the end of the activity.

Making Tracks

Put down these prehistoric footprints and convert your line-up time into a learning opportunity. Simply cut out a class supply of dinosaur footprints from various colors of construction paper. If desired, label each footprint set with a different numeral. Then sequence and attach the line of footprints to the floor with clear Con-Tact® covering or clear packing tape. When it's time to line up, explain to the class that they will play a listening game. To play, call a child; then have that child stand on the set of prints that you name by color or numeral. Or have youngsters count off, then move to the footprints corresponding to their assigned numbers. Or invite each child to stand on a pair of footprints corresponding in color to an article of clothing he is wearing. Any way you line 'em up, youngsters will be making tracks with this idea!

Give The Signal

Here's an efficient way to direct outbound traffic from your classroom. To make a simple traffic signal, label an eight-inch red construction-paper circle with "Stop" and a same-sized green construction-paper circle with "Go." Glue the cutouts together back-to-back; then string a length of yarn through a hole punched near the rim of the circle. Tie the yarn ends together. Hang the traffic signal—with "Stop" facing out—beside your classroom door. After lining youngsters up to go to a different school location, explain that you will switch the signal to "Go" when the class is quiet and ready to leave. Quiet. Ready. Let's go!

Go

Stop

Cell Phone

A very special phone call may provide the perfect incentive for youngsters to make a transition from one activity to another. To receive such a call, keep a toy, battery-operated cellular phone handy on a high shelf in the classroom. Just before a transition time—such as cleanup or snacktime— ring the phone; then answer it, pretending to talk to a storybook character, the president, or even your school's director/principal. During your phone conversation, be sure to mention that it's time for a specific transition; then conveniently repeat your caller's reminders about expected behaviors for that transition. For example, you might say, "Yes, Gingerbread Man, I'll remind the children to pick up *all* the toys and put them away. Thanks for your call. And watch out for that fox! Bye-bye." Then return the phone to the shelf to await your next special caller.

I'm Ready

Prepare youngsters for the next activity with this quick chant. Invite students to repeat each line and gesture after you perform it. Then conclude with a "thank-you" to students for showing their readiness by making eye contact with you.

Big ears to hear.	*Cup hands behind ears.*
Big eyes to see.	*Loop fingers like pretend glasses in front of eyes.*
Now I'm ready.	*Point to self.*
One, two, three.	*Clap hands three times; then put hands in lap.*

LET'S GET COOKIN'

Mix together equal portions of planning and organization, health and safety practices, and preliminary preparations. Add a cup of nutritious ingredients, a tablespoon of hands-on learning opportunities, and a pinch of creativity. Then get ready to cook up some fun! Let's get cookin'!

ideas contributed by Carleen Coderre

Essential Ingredients

- measuring cups and spoons
- nonbreakable mixing bowls
- kid-friendly kitchen gadgets (such as spatulas, eggbeaters, and potato mashers)
- a few sharp knives (securely placed out of little hands' reach!)
- cookie sheets, pots and pans, muffin tins
- electric frying pan, toaster oven, blender
- oven mitts and dish towels
- disposable plates, bowls, cups, and utensils
- aluminum foil, waxed paper, plastic wrap, zippered plastic bags
- parent request forms for recipe items and supplies (see page 80)

First Things First: Safety And Health

- Prepare foods with good nutritional value.
- Be aware of students' food allergies. Adjust recipes if necessary.
- Have youngsters wash their hands before cooking.
- Clean and disinfect all food preparation surfaces.
- Closely supervise children during all cooking activities, particularly when you are using electrical appliances.
- Use nonbreakable dishes and utensils.
- Know what to do if a child chokes on his/her food.
- Allow hot items to cool before giving them to youngsters.
- Don't let children sample mixtures with raw eggs or meat.

Before Starting

- Illustrate recipes on step-by-step picture cards or charts.

- Gather the necessary supplies and ingredients.

- Have a supply of paper towels on hand.

During The Activity

- Invite youngsters to actively participate in every step of the recipe preparation.
- Encourage students to use their five senses while preparing the recipe.
- Introduce cooking vocabulary and terms.
- Refer to pictured recipe cards and measuring utensils when appropriate.
- Invite youngsters to observe transformations that take place as a recipe is prepared.
- Use lots of descriptive language, as well as open-ended questioning techniques.
- Turn spills, mistakes, and cooking disasters into learning opportunities by discussing how these could have been avoided.

And Finally...

- Involve youngsters in preparing the table and in cleaning up afterwards.

- Invite student comments about the texture, flavor, feel, smell, and sound of their food as they handle and eat it. If desired record comments on a sheet of chart paper.

- Promote the use of good manners, healthy habits, and turn-taking at the table.

LOOK WHAT'S COOKING!

Dear Family,

We're preparing to mix up a big batch of learning and we need your help.

What's cooking? _____
(name of recipe)

In order to get cookin', we need the following supplies:

_____

_____

_____

_____

Please supply the item(s) listed above by: _____ .
(date)

Let me know if you'll be unable to send in something we've requested.

Thanks for helping us get cookin'!

Sincerely,

_____
(teacher)

YEARLONG DISPLAYS

ideas contributed by Deborah Burleson

Happy Birthday

February

3	Sean Johnson
7	Anna Parker
19	Danny Craigman
23	Kristin Smith

March

4	Mandy Dixon
10	Scott Lyons
16	Liza Jones
30	Allen Brady

April

2	Debbie Walker
5	Donna Teal
5	Hannah Lloyd
21	Billy Apple

May

6	Jackson Crane
12	Jesse Horton
15	Susan Hill
26	Cathy Bruce

How about a "beary" special birthday display? Make 12 enlarged copies of the bear pattern on page 87 on brown construction paper. For each bear, cut a party hat from different-colored construction paper and a gift box from birthday wrap. Label and assemble a bear for each month as shown; then laminate the bears. Add personalized strips with children's birthdates to the gift boxes. Mount the display on a classroom wall and add gift-bow hat toppers; then add an uninflated Mylar® balloon above the current month's bear.

BE INFORMED!

PARENTS...
Please remember to send all library books back to school by Wednesday of each week.

LOST & FOUND:
1 Batman lunchbox

1 red sweater

Have you signed up for conferences?
Monday
David Causey
Brenda Oakes

Tuesday
Tia Leonard
Matt Nelson

Wednesday
Sally Hughes
Jay Jackson
Ricky Stanford

Thursday
Dawn Lewis
Nick Green
Joe Carter

Friday
Linda Stacy
Seth Wilson

Coming Next Week:
Field trip to the fire station!

Cut a length of white bulletin-board paper to resemble the top of a fence; then staple it to a blue background. Instruct each child to use crayons, markers, yarn, and paper scraps to decorate a paper plate to resemble himself. Attach the faces so that they peek over the top of the fence, and add hand shapes as shown. Use the fence as a background for mounting photos, newsletters, and other important information that parents need to see.

Enlarge the chilly character on page 88 to fit the corner of your bulletin board. Duplicate the ice-pop pattern, also on page 88, onto each of the nine basic colors of construction paper. Cut out the ice pops; then label each one with the correct color word. Use clear-drying glue and iridescent glitter to give each pop an icy look. Tape two tongue depressors to the back of each ice pop. Hot-glue more tongue depressors together to form the letters in the title.

Put color and texture within children's reach with this display. Cut a flowerpot from bulletin-board paper. Print the title on the pot; then mount the pot near the bottom of a wall. Cut a large tagboard flower from each of the nine basic colors. To each flower, add a white center labeled with the color word. Cover the petals of each flower with a different-textured material, such as felt, cotton, foil gift wrap, satin, corduroy, or denim. Attach the flowers, along with crepe-paper stems, to the wall above the flowerpot.

Draw and cut out a supply of brown hexagons; then glue them to a length of white bulletin-board paper to resemble a honeycomb. Then mount the paper on a wall. Duplicate the bee patterns on page 89 so that there are 55 bees total. Laminate the bees if desired. Label the honeycomb with numerals one through ten; then attach the correct number of bees around each numeral. Buzz, buzz!

Mmm...mouthwatering math! Cut ten pizza slices from yellow felt. Color the edge of each slice and label each one with a different numeral from one to ten. Cut 55 circles from red felt, and back each one with the hook side of a piece of self-adhesive Velcro®. Mount the slices on a bulletin board, along with the title. Store the felt circles (pepperoni) in a pizza box nearby. Invite youngsters to stick the corresponding number of pepperoni pieces to each pizza slice.

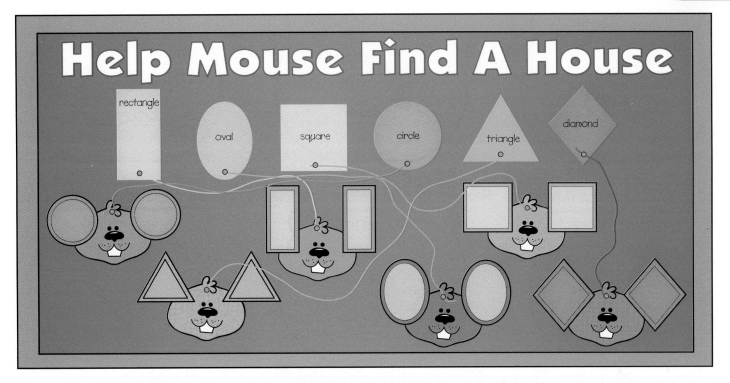

Help Mouse Find A House

These mice will help little ones with matching shapes. Enlarge the six mice on page 90. Color and laminate the mice; then attach them to the bottom of a bulletin board as shown. Add a pushpin at the top of each mouse's head. Cut out a large construction-paper shape to match each mouse's ears. Label and laminate the shapes. Mount them above the mice; then add the title. Pin a long length of yarn to the bottom of each shape. Instruct students to wrap the loose end of each yarn length around the pushpin on the mouse with the matching shaped ears.

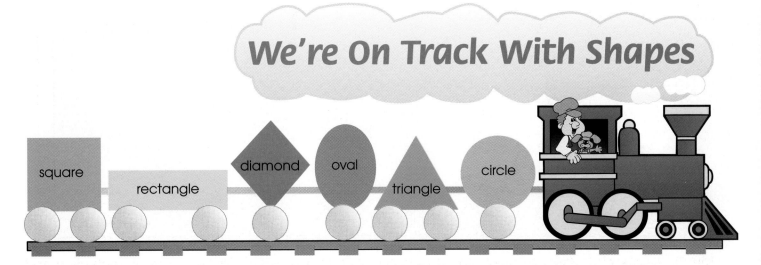

We're On Track With Shapes

Let shapes chug around your classroom with this display. Enlarge and color your favorite train-engine pattern; then cut each of the basic geometric shapes from a different color of construction paper. Label each shape with its name. Laminate all of the pieces; then attach them to a wall. Connect the train pieces by adding aluminum-foil rails and wheels.

Need A Helper? Go Fish!

Make several enlarged fishbowls from the pattern on page 91. Label each bowl with a classroom chore; then have children use diluted blue paint to fingerpaint water inside the fishbowls. Using different colors of construction paper, duplicate a fish from the pattern on page 89 for each child. Personalize each fish; then laminate the fish and the fishbowls. Attach the fishbowls and the title to a door or wall. Assign helpers by attaching fish to each bowl.

Stir up some good help with this tasty display. Use a checked tablecloth as a bulletin-board background. Enlarge and color the chef on page 91. Tear off several lengths of aluminum foil to resemble baking sheets. Use a permanent marker to label each one with a class job. For each child, duplicate the cookie pattern on page 89 onto manila paper. Personalize the cookies; then laminate them. Assemble the board as shown, changing the helpers often. Yummy!

Penguin Pattern
Use with "Cool Colors" on page 83.

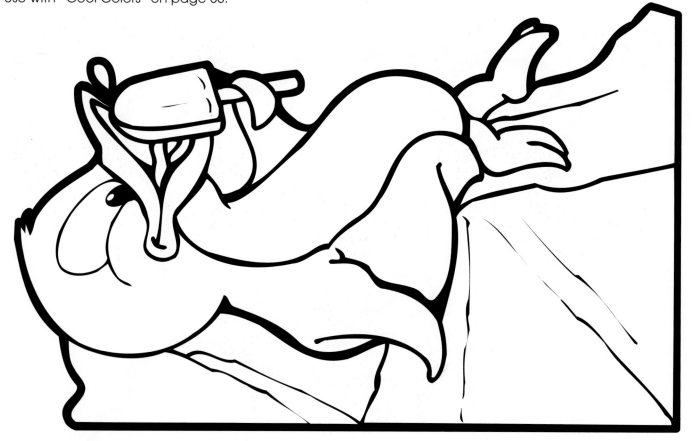

Ice-Pop Pattern
Use with "Cool Colors" on page 83.

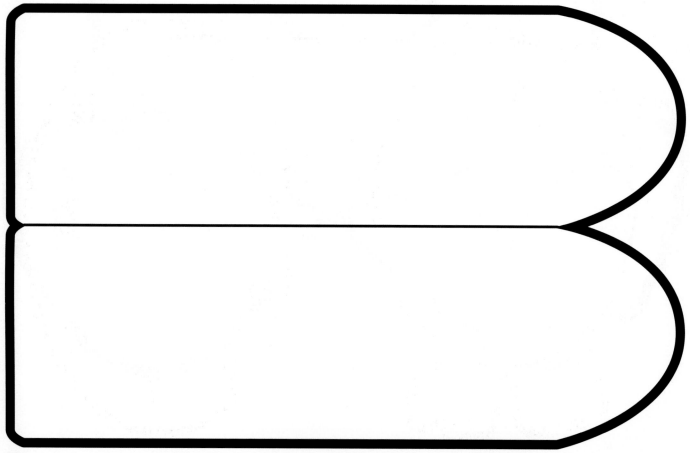

Fish Pattern
Use with "Need A Helper? Go Fish!" on page 86.

Cookie Pattern
Use with "A Batch Of Good Help" on page 86.

Mice Patterns
Use with "Help Mouse Find A House" on page 85.

Fishbowl Pattern

Use with "Need A Helper? Go Fish!" on page 86.

Chef Pattern

Use with "A Batch Of Good Help" on page 86.

ideas contributed by Carrie Lacher

A COLORFUL COLLECTION OF IDEAS

You'll be tickled pink with these activities to help you teach colors to your preschoolers! After introducing colors one at a time by using some of the suggestions on pages 92–95, try some activities that will involve little ones in discriminating among colors and mixing up color combinations (see pages 96–98). With these cool color ideas, you've got it made in the shade!

DAZZLING DECOR

Set the mood as you introduce each new color by decorating your classroom in the color you plan to study. Try some of the following suggestions, or come up with your own colorful ideas.

Using materials in the color you want to introduce:

- Hang crepe-paper streamers from the ceiling.

- Cover some windows and mirrors with cellophane.

- Create a bulletin board using background paper and a border in two shades of the color. Cut—or have youngsters help you cut—magazine pictures of objects in the same color. Post the pictures on the board.

- Drape yards of inexpensive nylon chiffon fabric across windows, over tables, or along the tops of bookshelves. Or suspend swags of fabric from the ceiling with lengths of yarn or fishing line.

- Post a construction-paper sign on your classroom door with a catchy phrase that will inform parents and students which color is currently your focus:
    - Our Room Is Blue—Just For You!
    - Ready For Red?
    - Say Hello To Yellow!
    - Have You Seen? We're All In Green!
    - Orange Is Everywhere!
    - Take A Peek At Purple!

Even you and your students can be part of the decor. Designate a special day when everyone will wear one or more articles of clothing in the current color. Now, *that's* color coordinated!

COLOR IN THE CLASSROOM

Each time you introduce a new color, use this activity to encourage your little ones to search for it in your classroom. Using construction paper in the current color of study, cut out a class supply of letters corresponding to the color word's beginning letter. For example, if you are focusing on red, cut a class supply of Rs from red construction paper. Place a roll of clear tape and the cut-out letters in a basket in your circle-time area. Then ask each child, in turn, to take a letter cutout and a small piece of tape. Have her find something red in your classroom and tape the letter cutout to the object or picture. Continue until every child has had a turn, giving assistance as necessary.

If you don't have access to a die-cutting machine to make the letters quickly, simply write the color word on small slips of paper, using a marker of that color. Either way, this activity will have your youngsters saying, "What a colorful classroom we have!"

I see a

COLOR IN THE COMMUNITY

After hunting for colors inside, lead your little ones outside for a game of I Spy with a colorful twist. In advance, help youngsters make special spyglasses. Provide each child with a cardboard toilet-tissue tube, a paintbrush, and tempera paint in the color currently being studied. Have each child paint the outside of his tube; then set all the tubes aside to dry thoroughly.

When the tubes have dried, have each child pick up a special color-seeking spyglass and follow you outdoors for a walk around the neighborhood. Instruct your students to be on the lookout for items in that special color. If desired, carry a clipboard with paper and pencil and make a list of all the items your students identify. When you return to the classroom, review the list and praise your preschool color spies!

A MOUTHFUL OF COLOR

If you're looking for a sensory experience to really capture the concept of a color, then tasting is tops! Each time you focus on a new color, provide a snack and/or drink in that color for your little ones to enjoy. Check out the list below or scour your grocery store's shelves for other yummy tinted treats! (Be sure to check for food allergies before serving any new food or drink.)

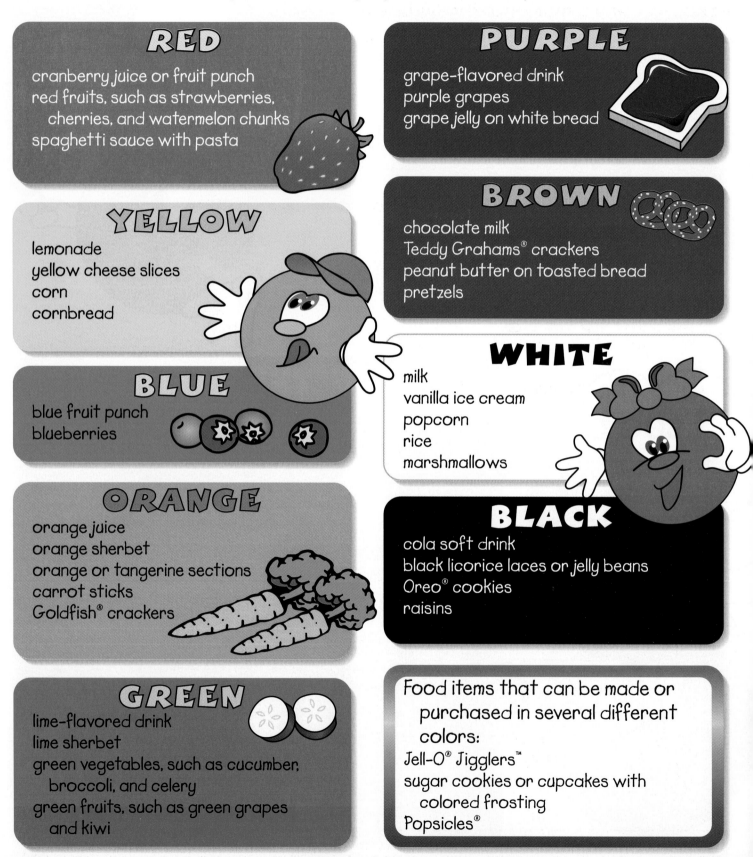

RED
cranberry juice or fruit punch
red fruits, such as strawberries,
    cherries, and watermelon chunks
spaghetti sauce with pasta

YELLOW
lemonade
yellow cheese slices
corn
cornbread

BLUE
blue fruit punch
blueberries

ORANGE
orange juice
orange sherbet
orange or tangerine sections
carrot sticks
Goldfish® crackers

GREEN
lime-flavored drink
lime sherbet
green vegetables, such as cucumber,
    broccoli, and celery
green fruits, such as green grapes
    and kiwi

PURPLE
grape-flavored drink
purple grapes
grape jelly on white bread

BROWN
chocolate milk
Teddy Grahams® crackers
peanut butter on toasted bread
pretzels

WHITE
milk
vanilla ice cream
popcorn
rice
marshmallows

BLACK
cola soft drink
black licorice laces or jelly beans
Oreo® cookies
raisins

Food items that can be made or
    purchased in several different
    colors:
Jell-O® Jigglers™
sugar cookies or cupcakes with
    colored frosting
Popsicles®

SENSORY SUGGESTIONS

Youngsters will really dig a sensory table filled with color! As you introduce each new color, fill your sensory table with a different material from the list below (mix and match the colors and appropriate materials, according to what you have available). Then add scoopers, grabbers, and containers. Hide some small manipulatives (such as teddy-bear counters or LEGO® blocks) in matching colors for little ones to discover. Your students will soon be sinking deep into color-identification skills!

NOTE: Small objects can be a choking hazard for little ones. Be sure to provide adequate supervision.

Red: shredded Mylar ®

Blue: pom-poms

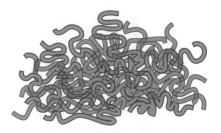

Yellow: popcorn kernels

Green: dried split peas

Orange: craft feathers

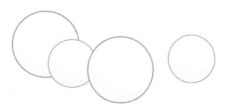

Purple: plastic Easter grass

Brown or black: craft fur cut into geometric pieces

White: Styrofoam® balls in assorted sizes

Any color: colored rice

SHADY SHAVING CREAM

A few drops of food coloring or a bit of powdered tempera paint added to a mound of shaving cream will provide yet another "sense-ational" color experience for your youngsters. Just squirt, stir, and scribble!

CRAYON CLUES

After your preschoolers have spent time focusing on each basic color, they'll be ready for some activities that involve more than one color. Look to that old standby—a box of crayons—to help you get started. Ask each child in a small group to select a crayon. Have her identify the crayon's color; then write the color word and the child's name at the top of a sheet of plain paper. Tape the crayon to the paper. Then instruct each child to find items in your classroom that match her crayon's color. As a student discovers an item, write that item's name on her page. After each child in the group has found several items, collect the papers and continue with other groups.

To extend this activity, send each child's paper home with her, with the crayon still attached. Attach a duplicated note encouraging families to help their child continue the color search at home. Happy hunting!

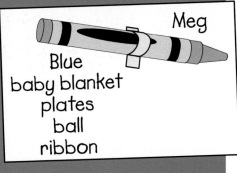

Meg

Blue
baby blanket
plates
ball
ribbon

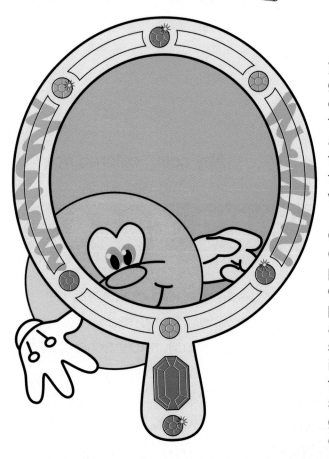

A LOOKING GLASS OF COLOR

The world will look mysterious and magical when youngsters peer at it through rose-colored—or blue- or green- or yellow-colored—glasses! To make these special looking glasses, duplicate a class supply of the frame pattern on page 99 on heavy tagboard. Have your assistant or a parent volunteer help you cut out each frame, including the center section. Then ready your art table with the cutout frames, several colors of plastic wrap or cellophane, glue, and crayons.

Working with one small group at a time, ask each child to begin coloring a frame. Have him choose a color of plastic wrap or cellophane. Assist the child in cutting a piece of the see-through material to fit over the opening of a frame; then help the child glue the wrap or cellophane in place. If desired, provide decorative materials—such as sequins, glitter, or plastic gems—so that students can further embellish the frames of their looking glasses. When the glue has dried, invite youngsters to peer through their special looking glasses and describe what they see. Encourage each child to trade glasses with a friend for another colorful view of your classroom.

COLORFUL PHOTOS

Smile! In a flash, your pre-schoolers will be practicing color identification and matching skills with this activity! Ask each child to name her favorite color; then request that she find as many classroom items as she can in that color. Have her gather all the items onto a tabletop. Then snap her picture with the objects. Select a half-sheet of construction paper in the same color and mount the developed photo in the center. Group all the photos showing the same color together and add a sized-to-match top sheet (again in the same color) labeled with the color word. Stack each color grouping together, and bind the book with a cover that bears the title "Our Classroom Color Book." Share the book with your students, helping them correctly identify each color and the various items shown in each photo.

A RAINBOW OF READING

Something shady's going on in your reading area! At least, it will be when you stock up on these books about colors.

Of Colors And Things
Written by Tana Hoban
Published by Greenwillow Books

Lunch
Written by Denise Fleming
Published by Henry Holt And Company, Inc.

Brown Bear, Brown Bear, What Do You See?
Written by Bill Martin, Jr.
Published by Henry Holt And Company, Inc.

I Went Walking
Written by Sue Williams
Published by Harcourt Brace & Company

Brown Cow, Green Grass, Yellow Mellow Sun
Written by Ellen Jackson
Published by Hyperion Books For Children

Freight Train
Written by Donald Crews
Published by Greenwillow Books

Color Dance
Written by Ann Jonas
Published by Greenwillow Books

Who Said Red?
Written by Mary Serfozo
Published by Simon & Schuster's Children's

My Crayons Talk
Written by Patricia Hubbard
Published by Henry Holt And Company, Inc.

COLOR COMBINATIONS

Try the activities on this page to give little ones experience with mixing colors and discovering how secondary colors are formed.

"MARBLE-OUS" PLAY DOUGH

For more color-mixing creativity, involve small groups of youngsters in some play-dough predictions. In advance, prepare a batch of uncolored play dough, following the recipe below. Then give each child in the group a portion of dough. Squeeze a few drops of red, blue, or yellow food coloring or liquid watercolor onto each child's ball of dough; then encourage him to knead the color into the dough, creating a marbleized effect. Ask the child to choose a second color and to predict what will happen if he kneads in this color. As he works the second color into the dough, direct his attention to areas where the two colors mix. Was his prediction accurate? If desired, place each child's ball of dough into a zippered plastic bag. Encourage youngsters to take their dough home and share their color-mixing knowledge with their families.

ICY COLORS

Put the freeze on boredom with this color-mixing activity. In advance, fill three clear, plastic containers with water. Squeeze a few drops of food coloring into each container to make one container each of red, blue, and yellow water. Freeze the containers thoroughly. Then fill three large bins with warm water and place these on a low table. Use food coloring to create a different primary color in each bin. Place scoopers and pourers—such as measuring cups, ladles, turkey basters, and small pitchers—into the water. Place the containers of colored ice near the bins of warm water.

When all is ready, invite youngsters to don protective aprons and gather around. Show students the molded ice and help them correctly identify each color. Then ask little ones to predict what will happen when you place the ice into the water. Carefully unmold the colored ice and place an ice chunk into each bin of water. (Combine the ice and water to create the secondary colors.) Encourage the children to scoop and pour water over the ice. Direct their attention to the changing colors of water and the diminishing size of the ice. Water play has never been so cool!

UNCOLORED PLAY DOUGH
(makes enough for six children)

3 cups white flour
3/4 cup table salt
3 cups warm water
3 tablespoons cream of tartar
3 tablespoons vegetable oil

Whisk together all ingredients in a large pot until free of lumps. Place on medium heat and stir constantly until mixture pulls away from the sides of the pot and forms a large ball. Turn out onto a floured board and knead while still very warm. Knead in additional flour until the dough achieves a silky texture.

GETTING INTO SHAPES

Use the activities in this unit to give youngsters lots of experience with looking at, touching, singing about, and even *eating* the basic shapes! Start with one shape at a time; then gradually combine shapes in your activities to build youngsters' discrimination skills. Once your little ones have gotten into shapes, use the reproducible booklet on pages 105–107 for a ship-shape review!

ideas contributed by dayle timmons

ONE AT A TIME

Begin your study of shapes with only three concepts: circles, triangles, and squares. Introduce each of these one at a time, and spend a few days focusing on each one before presenting them to youngsters in combination. After little ones have mastered these three easily distinguishable shapes, move on to introduce hearts, stars, or diamonds—again, one at a time. Save ovals and rectangles for last; they will be the most difficult for preschoolers to identify. As you introduce each new shape, designate it as the Shape Of The Day.

SHAPES EVERYWHERE

Give little ones opportunities to hunt for the Shape Of The Day both at home and at school. Prepare a note to parents similar to the one shown, and make a copy for each child. When youngsters bring in their items, hold a shapely sharing session so they can tell about the objects they found.

Then extend the shape hunt to your classroom with a shape-specific spy game. Provide a large magnifying glass. Hand the glass to one child at a time and ask him to look around your classroom until he spies an item that matches the Shape Of The Day. Have him point to the shape or use his finger to outline the shape. If desired, write the shape name on a sticky note and invite the finder to label the item he found.

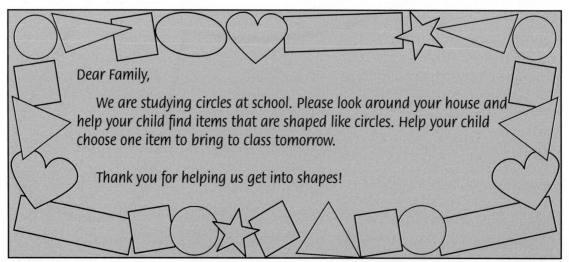

Dear Family,

We are studying circles at school. Please look around your house and help your child find items that are shaped like circles. Help your child choose one item to bring to class tomorrow.

Thank you for helping us get into shapes!

CUT IT OUT!

Combine practice with shapes and scissor skills. Make several tagboard stencils of your Shape Of The Day, and add them to your fine-motor center. Encourage little ones to use the stencils to trace, and then cut, the Shape Of The Day from construction paper several times. Collect each child's cutouts and assist her in gluing them to a sentence strip to create a shape crown she'll be proud to wear!

SHAPES IN THE SAND (OR WATER)

Add some Shape-Of-The-Day items to your sand or water table. For example, when focusing on squares you might add square nesting cups, square plastic containers and lids, plastic berry baskets, and plastic blocks or linking cubes.

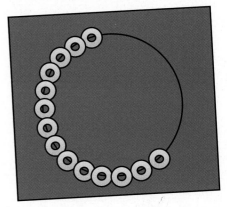

THE REAL THING

Gather several real objects that match your Shape Of The Day. For example, when focusing on circles, you might collect empty toilet-paper tubes, empty thread spools, empty curling-ribbon spools, paper cups, pencil erasers, container lids, and film canisters. Set out shallow trays of tempera paint and construction paper that's been cut into your Shape Of The Day. Then invite little ones to make shape prints on paper using the objects.

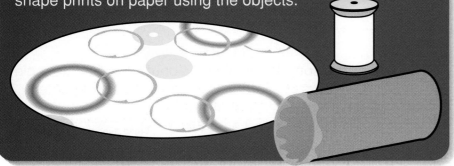

OUTLINES

For each child, pencil the outline of your Shape Of The Day onto a sheet of drawing paper. Then provide small items in the corresponding shape, such as Cheerios® cereal for circles, self-stick stars for stars, or candy corn for triangles. Invite each child to stick or glue the items over your outline to complete the shape.

SHAPELY SNACKS

Each time you focus on a new Shape Of The Day, bring in (or ask a parent to bring in) a snack in that shape. Check the list of shapely foods below for some suggestions. For more difficult shapes—such as hearts or stars—try rolled cookies, sandwiches, or Jell-O® Jigglers™ cut with cookie cutters.

Circles	Squares	Triangles
pancakes	cheese slices	turnovers
banana slices	saltine crackers	slices of cake or pie
rice cakes	Wheat Thins®	Doritos®
bagels	Chex® cereal	sandwich halves

LOTS OF SHAPES

After you've introduced a few basic shapes individually, try some of these activities involving combinations of shapes to build little ones' discrimination skills.

GET MOVIN'

Incorporate some movement into your shape study. Use masking tape to outline one or more basic shapes on the floor of your classroom (or draw the shapes with chalk on a sidewalk or blacktop area). Invite youngsters to perform various movements on each shape outline, such as "Jump around the square," or "Tiptoe around the triangle."

SINGIN' ABOUT SHAPES

Prior to teaching little ones this song, cut several shapes from different colors of construction paper. Laminate the shapes, if desired. Then, during circle time, hold up one shape at a time as youngsters join you in singing this song to the tune of "Skip To My Lou." Hold up a new shape each time you reach the last line of the song.

[Red, red circle], I see you.
[Red, red circle], I see you.
[Red, red circle], I see you.
[Green square], I see you, too!

SHAPELY COLLAGES

Cut large versions of circles, triangles, and squares from black construction paper. Then pre-cut various smaller sizes of the corresponding shapes from colorful construction paper. (A die-cutter will be helpful for this task, or ask parent volunteers for their assistance.) Mix up all the precut shapes and place them in the middle of a table. Invite each child to choose a black shape, then select matching colored shapes to glue onto his larger version. Display these attractive collages on a bulletin board with the title "Getting Into Shapes."

A SONG BOOK

Make the song from "Singin' About Shapes" into a big book for your class library. Use small sheets of poster board for the pages. Write the first three lines of a verse on the bottom of a page, then write the last line at the top of the following page. Continue with the number of verses you desire. Have the students illustrate the book by cutting the shapes from the appropriate colors of construction paper and gluing them onto the correct pages. Add a cover with the title "Shaping Up!" and more student-cut shapes. Children will be excited to read or sing this book all by themselves!

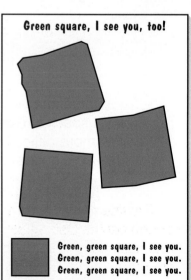

Green square, I see you, too!

Green, green square, I see you.
Green, green square, I see you.
Green, green square, I see you.

FLOATING FOAM SHAPES

Purchase several sheets of colorful craft foam from your local craft store. Cut various shapes from the foam and float these shapes in your water table. Alternately, cut the shapes from Styrofoam® trays. Also provide containers in various shapes, such as square berry baskets or round nesting cups. Ask youngsters to sort the foam shapes into the corresponding shaped containers.

SHAPE SOCK

Make a "feely" sock by inserting a paper or plastic cup into the toe end of a tube sock. Inside the cup, place an attribute block, a building block, or a cookie cutter. Have a child place his hand inside the sock and feel the shape, attempting to identify it. As a variation, place two or three shapes into the "feely" sock and ask a volunteer to remove the shape you name.

SHAPE RUBBINGS

To prepare for this activity, cut sheets of sandpaper into basic shapes, peel the paper off a supply of crayons, and gather a few clipboards. Working with two or three children at a time, have each child choose a sandpaper shape. Use a piece of rolled masking tape to secure each child's shape to a clipboard. Then clip a sheet of white copy paper over the shape. Demonstrate how to rub the length of a crayon across the paper to make the shape "magically" appear. Continue with different crayon colors and shapes on the same or different sheets of paper.

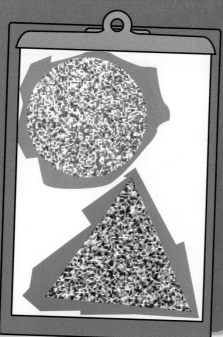

SHAVING-CREAM SHAPES

Spray some shaving cream onto a tabletop or cookie sheet for each child. Encourage youngsters to use their index fingers to draw shapes as you call them out. Walk around to check each child's work, and provide guidance when necessary. As a variation, use pudding in place of shaving cream. Mmm…shapes are yummy!

PLAY-DOUGH PRACTICE

Provide more tactile experiences with shapes in your play-dough center. Set out play dough, cookie cutters, rolling pins, and cutting tools, such as plastic knives or craft sticks. Encourage your students to cut the dough into shapes, either using the cookie cutters or freehand with the cutting tools.

SPONGE-AROUND SHAPES

Invite little ones to make unique shape pictures with this painting method. To prepare, cut a variety of shapes from tagboard, set out several shallow trays of tempera paint, and attach a supply of one-inch-square sponges to clothespins. Working with two or three children at a time, have each child choose two or three shapes and arrange them on a 12" x 18" sheet of white construction paper. Use rolled pieces of masking tape to secure the shapes. Then have the child dip a sponge into the paint color of his choice and sponge all around the edges of one shape. Have him repeat the procedure with other paint colors on the other shapes. Then remove the tagboard shapes. Display the finished artwork on a bulletin board.

SHAPE CHANT

Cut a class supply of shapes from different colors of construction paper. Distribute a shape to each child; then seat the children in a circle. Teach youngsters the chant below, explaining that on each child's turn she should fill in a classmate's name in the last line. It will probably take several repetitions of the chant with your cues before little ones chime in.

I have a [blue square], yes I do.
[Courtney, Courtney], how about you?

I SEE SHAPES!

Review all the shapes your little ones have studied with the reproducible booklet on pages 105–107. You may choose to use only some of the pages, and they can be placed in any order, with the exceptions of the cover, the first page, and the last page. To prepare, duplicate the desired booklet pages for each child; then cut them apart and staple the booklets together. For each child duplicate two copies of the shapes on page 107 on various colors of construction paper. Ask a parent volunteer to help you cut out the shapes you will need.

When you are ready for students to complete their booklets, set out glue and a supply of shapes on each table. Give each child a booklet. Read through the booklet together, asking each child to choose the correct shape to glue to each page. Invite each child to glue extra shapes to both her booklet cover and her last page. Encourage your youngsters to take these booklets home and share their shape knowledge with their families.

I see a square looking at me.

Square, Square,
What do you...

I see a heart looking at me.

Heart, Heart,
What do you see?

I See Shapes!

by _____

Circle, Circle,
What do you see?

I see a square looking at me.

I see a rectangle looking at me.

Square, Square,
What do you see?

Rectangle, Rectangle,
What do you see?

I see a triangle looking at me.

Triangle, Triangle,
What do you see?

I see a heart looking at me.

Heart, Heart,
What do you see?

I see a star looking at me.

Star, Star,
What do you see?

I see a diamond looking at me.

Diamond, Diamond,
What do you see?

I see an oval looking at me.

I see lots of shapes looking at me!

Oval, Oval,
What do you see?

BODY PARTS

Use this collection of ideas with youngsters to teach—and to reinforce—the different parts of the body.

ideas contributed by Barbara Backer and Mackie Rhodes

PUZZLED PARTS

Make this life-size floor puzzle to help youngsters recognize the parts of the body. To begin, place a length of white bulletin-board paper on the floor. Have a student volunteer lie down on the paper, with his arms resting away from his body and his legs slightly spread. Trace around the child with a permanent marker. Invite small groups of students, in turn, to color the resulting outline. Puzzle-cut the arms, legs, and head of the outline from the body. (If desired, you might also cut away other body parts, such as hands and feet.) Glue each puzzle piece onto poster board; then cut the poster board to maintain the body-part shape. Laminate the pieces for durability. To use, have a child or small group put the body puzzle together, naming the different parts as they work. Extend the use of the puzzle by arranging the arms and legs in different positions; then invite youngsters to position themselves to resemble the puzzle.

This Is Me!

Youngsters will demonstrate their self-awareness through some creative expression with these pictures. Invite each child to create a picture of herself using a variety of craft items, such as yarn, wiggle eyes, craft sticks, and buttons. Label her dictated names for the different body parts represented in her picture; then draw a line between each label and the corresponding part. Have the child write her name on her picture. During group time ask each child to tell the class about her picture. As she names each labeled part of her picture, have her point out that body part on herself. Then display the pictures with the title "This Is Me!"

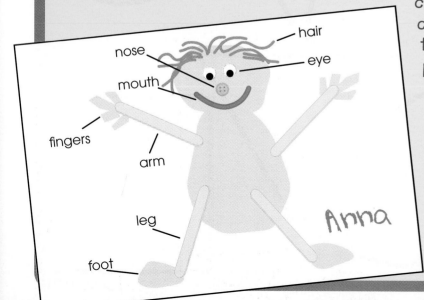

WHERE DOES IT GO?

Challenge students to think about their body parts with this game of associations. In advance, collect a variety of clothing accessories and wearable sports equipment: items such as bracelets, necklaces, rings, gloves, socks, caps, sunglasses, shoulder pads, knee pads, and elbow pads. Display all the items during group time; then ask a student to find an item that is worn on his hand, his knee, his head, or any other body part to which an item corresponds. After the child locates an appropriate item, invite him to model it for the class; then return the item to the collection. Continue in the same manner, giving each child an opportunity to select and model an item. Head, shoulder, knees, elbows—show us where each item goes!

On A Warm, Warm Day

Try this cool body-parts activity outdoors on a warm day. In advance, ask each family to send a swimsuit and towel to school with their child. Also inform them that the students will most likely get paint on many different parts of their bodies, and probably on their swimsuits. Then, on a warm day, take your class outdoors. Invite each child to dip different parts of his body into a tray of washable paint, and to paint with those body parts on a length of bulletin-board paper. Encourage youngsters to experiment painting with their fingers, toes, heels, and elbows, as well as their knees, wrists, chins, and fists. Afterward, invite youngsters to wash the paint off themselves by running through a water sprinkler. Then have children towel-dry before returning to the classroom. If desired, display the dried paintings with the title "Lots Of Art With Body Parts."

My Body Can

Use this rhyme about body parts and their movements to help youngsters make the transition into group or story time.

My little toes can tap, tap, tap.
My little hands can clap, clap, clap.
My little knees can knock, knock, knock.
My little feet can walk, walk, walk.

My head can nod.
My eyes can blink.
My lips can kiss—
And whistle, I think.

My arms can flap.
My fingers snap.
Now I can sit
And make a lap.

GIVE IT A SHAKE, SHAKE, SHAKE

Use the song "Looby Loo" to reinforce body parts with this idea. Tape a large outline of a body on the floor. Have youngsters stand around the outside of the outline. Sing the song, using body-part names corresponding to those which your class has been learning about. Encourage students to put the named body part within the taped outline or take it out as the song directs. Periodically, name a lesser-known body part, such as an ankle, to challenge youngsters' listening skills and body knowledge. Here we go Looby Loo!

Looby Loo

Here we go Looby Loo,
Here we go Looby Light,
Here we go Looby Loo,
All on a Saturday night.

You put your [right hand] in,
You put your [right hand] out,
You give your [right hand] a
    shake, shake, shake,
And turn yourself about. Oh…

BODY BAND

Entice youngsters to use their own body parts as instruments with this idea. To begin, clap a simple rhythm with your hands; then invite students to join in as you repeat the rhythm. After a few rounds, begin another body-part rhythm such as foot-tapping or thigh-slapping. Continue in this manner to model a variety of body parts and rhythms. Then invite each child, in turn, to lead the class in a body-rhythm pattern. Afterward, play some lively music, encouraging students to join in the band by playing any body instrument they choose. What beautiful music!

It's In The Cards

Try one or all of these activities to reinforce body parts with your youngsters. To prepare, duplicate two sets of the body-parts cards (page 113) on tagboard. Laminate the tagboard copies; then cut the cards apart. Use the cards in each activity as suggested.

- Shuffle the two card sets together. Have each child in a student pair draw a card from the stack, then identify the pictured body part on her card. Then have the pair create a silly pose by joining the body parts on themselves that correspond to the body parts shown on their cards.

- Use one set of body-parts cards for this activity. Invite each child, in turn, to draw a card. Ask him to name the body part, locate it on a display poster of a person, and point to the body part on himself.

- Spread out the cards from both sets facedown. Have each child in a pair turn over one card, attempting to find a match. When a match is found, invite the partners to give each other a gentle "high five" with the corresponding body parts.

elbow

Turn something that sounds like red.

Move something that sounds like boulder.

Movin' Right Along

Get youngsters on the move with this listening activity. During a group time ask youngsters to remove their shoes and socks; then explain that you are going to say a real or made-up word that rhymes with a body part. When each child thinks of a body part that sounds like the word, he will move that part until you signal him to stop. For instance, you might ask youngsters to move a body part that sounds like *sand* or *boulder*. After several rounds, invite volunteers to take turns leading the game. Then, to expand the game and the challenge, pair a specific action with each rhyming word—such as, "Turn something that sounds like *red*," or "Open something that sounds like *south*." Little ones will move right along with this activity.

COUNT IT OUT

This idea provides valuable counting practice, as well as an opportunity to follow directions. During a small group time, ask each child, in turn, to perform a specific action with a named body part. For example, you might instruct a child to stomp her foot, blink her eyes, or bump her elbows together. After several practice rounds, challenge each youngster to perform the named action for a specific number of times based on her counting ability. Ask the child to count each of her movements aloud. To extend this activity, whisper the directions to a child; then have her perform the action. Ask the group to imitate her performance. Afterward, repeat the directions to the entire group; then invite them to once again perform the action while chorally counting their movements. Act it out, and count it out.

1, 2, 3, 4, ...

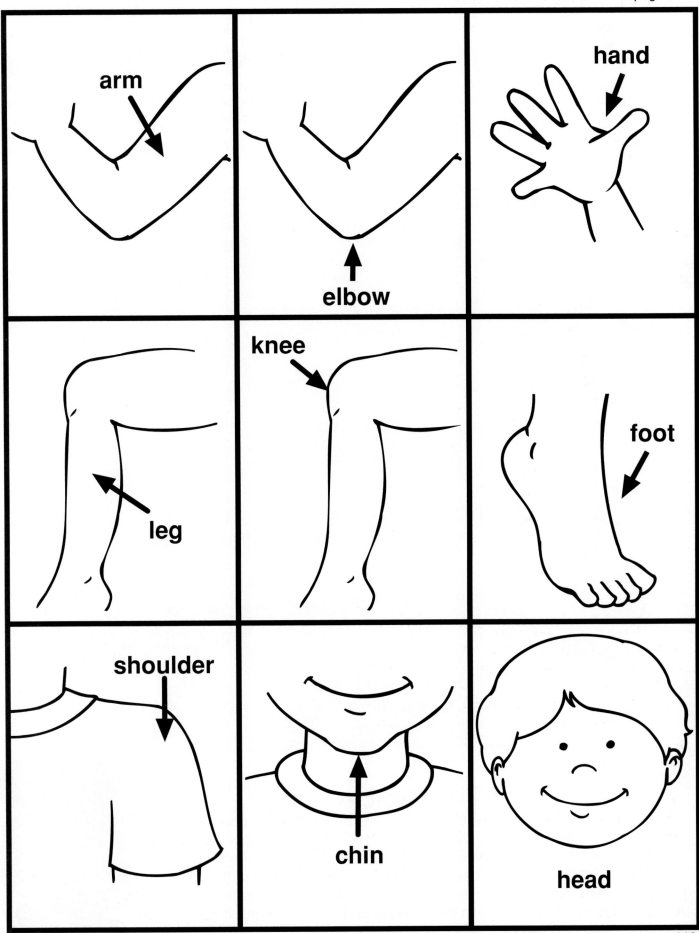

COUNTING
Around The Classroom

2 5 1 6 3 8

Use every area of your preschool classroom—from circle to centers—to reinforce the basic skill of counting. To prepare for these activities, make several sets of the number cards found on pages 117–119. Simply duplicate the patterns onto colored construction paper, cut out the cards, then attach the correct number of stickers to each card. It's as easy as one, two, three!

ideas contributed by Lucia Kemp Henry and Angie Kutzer

Circle Time Counts!

Liven up circle time with this fingerplay and game that will have your youngsters wiggling, giggling, and counting, of course!

The Fantastic Five

One, one, this is one.
Come on, one, let's have some fun.

Two, two, this is two.
Hopping, hopping, me and you.

Three, three, this is three.
Wave your branches like a tree.

Four, four, this is four.
Can you make us sweep the floor?

Five, five, this is five.
Squeeze us tight; then take a dive.

GUESS THE NUMERAL

Use a set of the number cards (pages 117–119) to play this counting game with your little ones. During circle time have a volunteer pick a card from your hand and instruct him not to show it to the rest of the children. Direct him to select a set of students to stand in front of the group to match the numeral on his card, and assist him if necessary. Ask a seated volunteer to guess the numeral on the child's card. If he is correct, give the guesser the next turn to pick a card.

Housekeeping Counts

Pair items found in your housekeeping corner with the number cards (pages 117–119) to provide lots of opportunities for little ones to match, sort, group, and count.

- Stock the shelves with empty food boxes. Label each of ten paper grocery bags with a different numeral from one to ten. Instruct a student to pick a bag and fill it with the correct number of boxes.

- Fill a box with five of each of the following: paper plates, napkins, plastic forks, plastic spoons, and paper cups. Have a child choose a number card from one to five, lay it in the center of the table, and then set the table for the correct number of guests.

- Hang a clothesline in your housekeeping center. Place baby or doll clothes, clothespins, and the number cards inside a basket. Invite a youngster to hang a number card along with the matching number of clothing items on the line to "dry."

WARNING: Counting Under Construction

Blocks are for building *and* counting when youngsters complete these constructive activities!

- Invite a student to choose a number card, then build a road with the corresponding number of blocks. Have him continue building until he has used the whole set of cards.
- Encourage a pair of youngsters to work together to build a block tower. When the tower falls, have the students count to find out how many blocks they used. Then challenge them to build a larger tower, using more blocks than before.
- Designate a specific numeral from one to five (or ten with more advanced students). Instruct each member of a small group to build a structure that uses only the designated number of blocks. Share and compare the finished projects.

BOOKS TO COUNT ON

Include these counting books in your reading area or storytime.

Mouse Count
Written by Ellen Stoll Walsh
Published by Harcourt Brace Jovanovich, Publishers

Gray Rabbit's 1, 2, 3
Written by Alan Baker
Published by Kingfisher

I Can Count
Written by Denise Lewis Patrick
Published by Golden Books Publishing Company, Inc.

One, Two, Three
Written by William Wegman
Published by Hyperion Books
  For Children

Ten, Nine, Eight
Written by Molly Bang
Published by William Morrow And Company, Inc.

Cock-A-Doodle-Doo: A Farmyard Counting Book
Written by Steve Lavis
Published by Lodestar Books

The Art Of Counting

Try this palette of activities to keep little ones counting in your art center.

- Spread out a set of the number cards (pages 117–119). Have a pair of children work together to place the correct number of crayons on each card.

- Place several fat, thin, long, and short paintbrushes together in a container. Instruct a student to sort the brushes into groups, then count the members in each group.

- Encourage little ones to create pictures using a certain number of items—such as four buttons, seven star stickers, or ten toothpicks. If desired use the story *Ten Black Dots* by Donald Crews (Greenwillow Books) as a springboard for this activity.

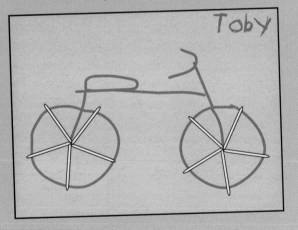

1, 2, 3...Dig!

Watch as youngsters get down to the nitty-gritty with these counting activities for the sand table.

- Invite a child to explore with 1/4-cup, 1/3-cup, 1/2-cup, and 1-cup measuring scoops. Ask her to count measurements, such as how many 1/4-cup scoops it takes to fill the 1-cup scoop.

- Label each of five small plastic flowerpots with a different numeral from one to five. Set them in the sand table with an assortment of 15 artificial blooms. Direct little ones to "plant" the correct number of flowers in each pot.

- Bury a set of ten plastic or wooden numerals in the sand. Have a small group of children find the numerals, sequence them (assist as necessary), and then count aloud as they point to each one.

KEEP ON COUNTING

Encourage parents to continue counting at home with their children. For each child, duplicate onto construction paper the parent note on page 117 along with a set of the number cards from pages 117–119. If possible include the 55 stickers needed to complete the cards. Send the materials home in resealable plastic bags for durable storage. Soon your little ones will be counting everything in sight!

Dear Parent, # 1...2...3...4...5

Here are some ideas to help your child learn to count at home:

- Count socks as you fold laundry.
- Count utensils as you set the table.
- Count flowers or trees outside.
- Count blocks as you build a tower.
- Clap and count as you listen to music.

To use the enclosed counting cards, put stickers on the cards to represent each number. Cut out the cards. Help your child count the stickers and say the numbers.

Number Cards
Use with "Guess The Numeral" on page 114, "Housekeeping Counts" and "Warning: Counting Under Construction" on page 115, and "The Art Of Counting" and "Keep On Counting" on page 116.

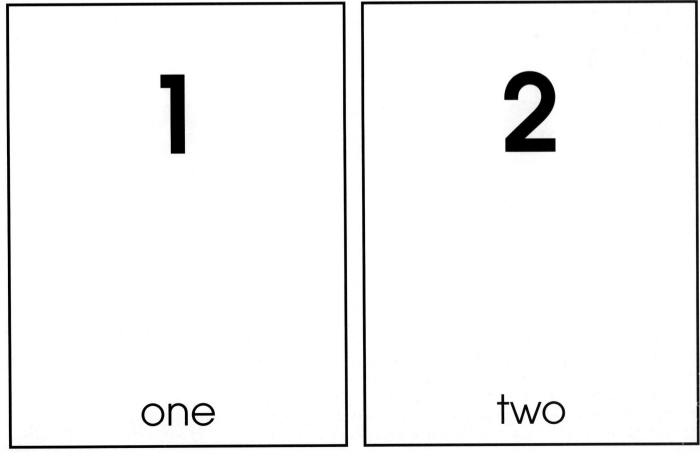

1	**2**
one	two

Number Cards

Use with "Guess The Numeral" on page 114, "Housekeeping Counts" and "Warning: Counting Under Construction" on page 115, and "The Art Of Counting" and "Keep On Counting" on page 116.

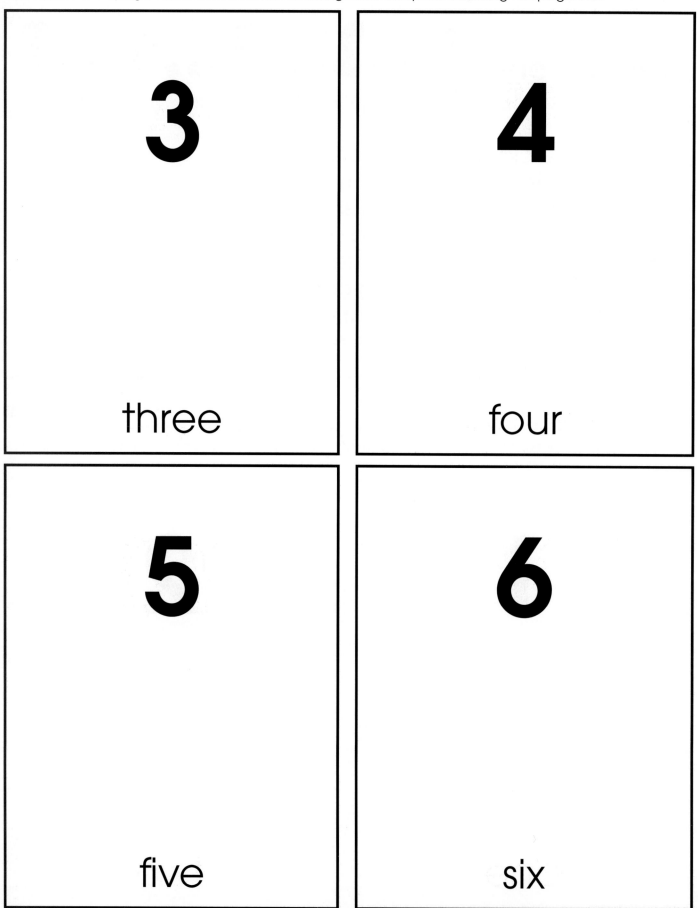

3

three

4

four

5

five

6

six

Use with "Guess The Numeral" on page 114, "Housekeeping Counts" and "Warning: Counting Under Construction" on page 115, and "The Art Of Counting" and "Keep On Counting" on page 116.

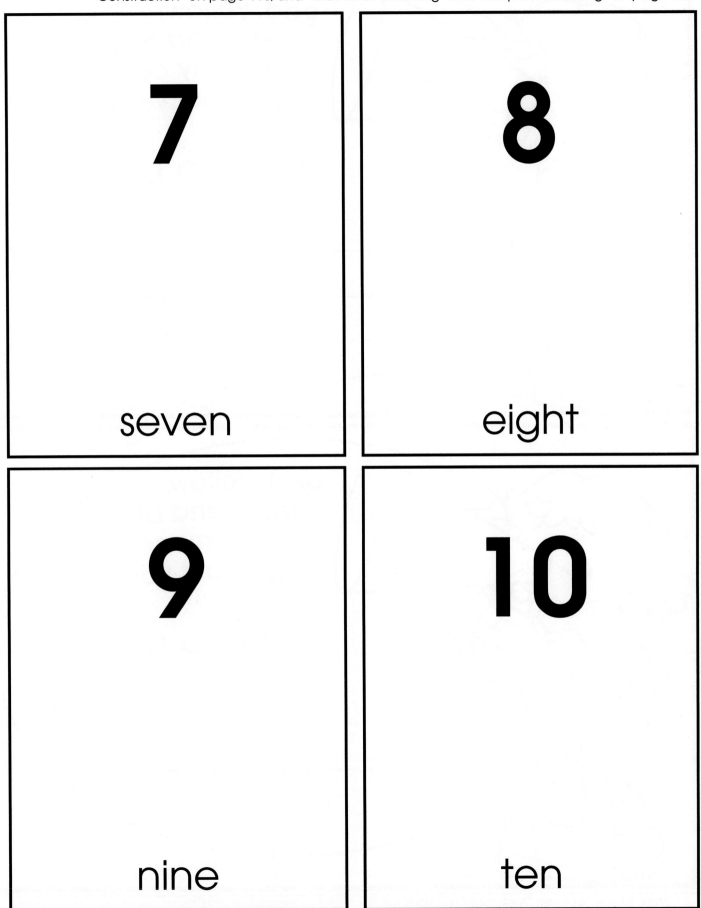

7

seven

8

eight

9

nine

10

ten

Red, yellow,
green, and blue.
I know my colors.
How 'bout you?

Way to go,

_____!

_____
date

©1998 The Education Center, Inc. • *The Mailbox® Superbook* • *Preschool* • TEC458

Red, yellow,
green, and blue.
I know my colors.
How 'bout you?

Way to go,

_____!

_____
date

©1998 The Education Center, Inc. • *The Mailbox® Superbook* • *Preschool* • TEC458

Note To The Teacher: Duplicate an award for each child. Personalize and distribute when appropriate to reward each child's progress.

CELEBRATE!

_____

knows the shapes!

_____
date

CELEBRATE!

_____

knows the shapes!

_____
date

Note To The Teacher: Duplicate an award for each child. Personalize and distribute when appropriate to reward each child's progress.

Just flew in to say,

_____

can count from
1 to 10!
Hooray!

_____
date

Just flew in to say,

_____

can count from
1 to 10!
Hooray!

_____
date

Note To The Teacher: Duplicate an award for each child. Personalize and distribute when appropriate to reward each child's counting progress.

A Birthday BLOWOUT!

Your wish came true! Here's a collection of ideas that will make celebrating birthdays in your classroom a piece of cake!

ideas contributed by Lucia Kemp Henry and Carrie Lacher

A Bag Full Of Fun!

Save time by preparing birthday gift bags for the whole year in just one day! Decorate a class supply of small paper bags. For each child, fill a bag with inexpensive items, such as crayons, coloring sheets, decorative pencils, paperback books, stickers, small toys, and candy. Store the bags in a closet or cabinet. Before a birthday child arrives at school on his special day, personalize a bag and place it at his seat or in his cubby. What a way to start the day!

Happy Birthday Kevin

It's My Birthday!

Create this party vest for each child to wear on his birthday. Use fabric pens and dimensional paints to embellish a small denim or felt vest with birthday-themed designs. If you have sewing talents, consider making a vest from material with a festive print or using appliqués. Your birthday child will enjoy the smiles and greetings that he receives when he wears this festive vest.

A Party Plate With Pizzazz

Celebrate in style with these unique party plates. Search yard sales and thrift shops for an assortment of small, elegant (but inexpensive) china plates. Or make your own by painting the backs of clear glass or plastic plates. (Consult your local craft store for specific directions.) Serve the birthday child a treat on the plate of her choice. It's guaranteed to taste even better!

Birthday Books

Keep the party atmosphere alive during storytime with a Birthday Book Box. Cover a box and its lid separately with festive gift wrap. Fill the box with birthday-themed books (see the list below for suggestions). Invite the birthday child to choose a selection from the box for storytime. Then put the box away until the next special birthday!

The Barn Party
Written by Nancy Tafuri
Published by Greenwillow Books

A Birthday Cake For Little Bear
Written by Max Velthuijs
Published by North-South Books

Can You Guess?
Written by Laurence and Catherine Anholt
Published by Puffin Books

Hilda Hen's Happy Birthday
Written by Mary Wormell
Published by Harcourt Brace & Company

Birthday Buddies
Written by Laura Damon
Published by Troll Associates

Bunny Cakes
Written by Rosemary Wells
Published by Dial Books For Young Readers

Happy Birthday, Dear Duck
Written by Eve Bunting
Published by Clarion Books

It's My Birthday
Written by Helen Oxenbury
Published by Candlewick Press

Finding The Favors

X marks the spot for fun in this hunt for a happy birthday. Cut two squares from each of four different colors of construction paper. Tape one square of each color to a different location in the room, such as a closet, cabinet, or file drawer. At each location, place different items needed for a birthday party. For example, put party hats at the first location, noisemakers at the second location, festive paper goods at the third location, and birthday cupcakes at the last location. Glue the other four squares to a large sheet of paper in the order that you want the objects to be found; then number the squares as shown. Hold this treasure map in front of the group. Encourage your little party pirates to read the map and help direct the birthday child to the birthday loot.

Celebrate With Song

Replace the traditional "Happy Birthday" melody with this special song and watch that birthday boy or girl glow!

Your Special Day
(sung to the tune of "Clementine")

Happy birthday, happy birthday!
You're the birthday [boy] today.
Happy birthday, happy birthday!
It's your very special day!

Happy birthday, happy birthday!
You're an older [boy] today.
Happy birthday, happy birthday!
It's your very special day!

Happy birthday, happy birthday!
You are [five] years old today.
Happy birthday, happy birthday!
It's your very special day!

Cooperative Cake

Add teamwork, fine-motor skills, and creativity together and what do you get? This giant-sized birthday display frosted with fun! Collect several boxes (cake layers) in graduated sizes and a class supply of toilet-paper tubes. Tape the boxes closed; then have a small group decorate each box with colorful construction paper, crepe paper, glitter, glue, and various other art supplies. Once the glue is dry, have students help order and stack the layers; then tape or glue the cake together.

Top your cardboard confection with these personalized candles. Give a toilet-paper tube to each student. Direct her to paint it a color of her choice. After the paint dries, have her "light" her candle by stuffing yellow tissue paper in one end. Label the child's candle with her name and birthdate; then tape all of the candles to the cake. Thenzx invite everyone to make a wish and pretend to blow out the candles. Happy birthday, *everyone!*

How Old Are You?

The verse adults dread is the same verse that children love. Invite each child to show off his new age on this cake-and-candle keepsake. In advance of a student's birthday, send home a copy of the patterns on page 128 and the parent note on page 129 along with a large sheet of construction paper. Ask the child to bring his finished cake to school on the day of his birthday celebration. Begin the day's activities by encouraging the birthday child to show his cake to the rest of the group. Have your students count the candles to discover the child's new age. Write "[Child's name] is [five] today!" across the top of his paper; then have each student sign her name somewhere on the paper. If possible, take an instant photo of the birthday child with his classmates sometime during the day and glue it to the cake. This class greeting is sure to be a treasured keepsake for years to come!

A Handy, Dandy Birthday!

Let your hands do the talking as you teach your little ones how to say "Happy birthday!" in sign language. Explain why people sometimes talk with their hands; then use the steps and illustrations shown here. After some practice, encourage your youngsters to sing the traditional birthday song and sign the words *happy birthday* each time they are sung. Happy birthday to you…

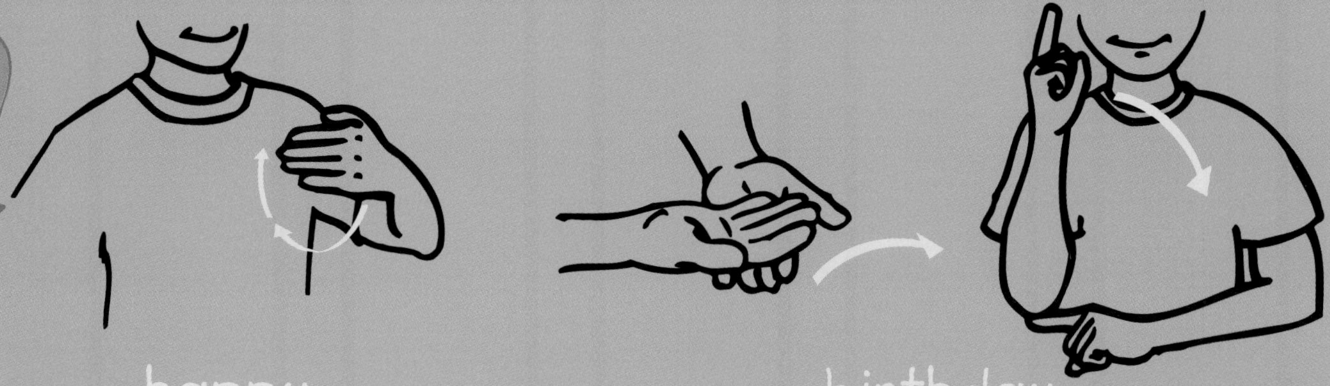

happy   birthday

Birthday Months

Play this circle-time game with your youngsters to help them learn their birthday months. To prepare, stuff a small gift box with paper; then wrap it like a birthday present. Make a list of class birthdays for reference. Seat your students in a circle. Instruct them to pass the gift around the circle while chanting the following rhyme. At the end of the rhyme, have the child holding the gift tell the group her birthday month (and date if she knows it). Then start the chant again and continue until each child has had a turn. Hip, hip, hooray—we know our birthdays!

My birthday is May 4th.

Cake and candles, oh, what fun!
Food and games for everyone!
April, June, November, May…
When will it be your birthday?

Cake And Candle Patterns
Use with "How Old Are You?" on page 126.

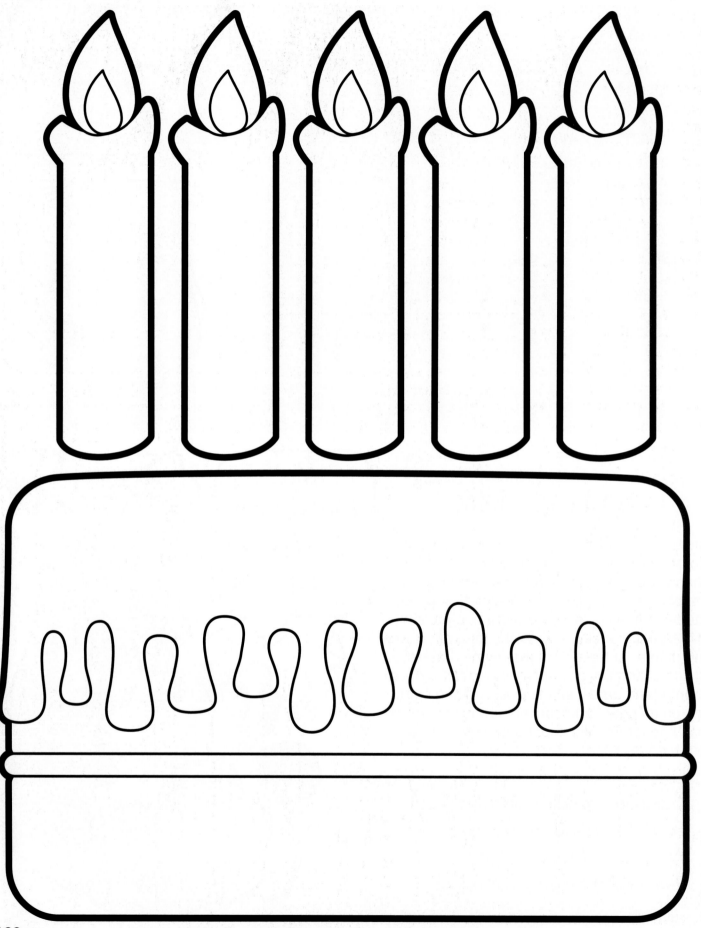

What Would A Birthday Be...

...without a cake? As part of your child's upcoming birthday celebration, ask him or her to prepare this birthday-cake project. Have your child color the appropriate number of candles; then help cut them out, along with the cake pattern. Help your child glue the cake and candles in the center of the construction paper. If you'd like, decorate the cake further with glitter, stickers, or other craft materials you have on hand. Please return the finished cake to school on or before your child's birthday.

Thanks for your help!

_____
(teacher signature)

Birthday Cards

Have A "Hoppy" Birthday!

From

_____
(teacher)

_____
(date)

Wishing You A "Beary" Happy Birthday!

From

_____   _____
(teacher)   (date)

GET READY, GET SET, LET'S GO, GO, GO!

Do you suffer from F.T.F.—Field Trip Frenzy? If so use the ideas in this unit to take the frenzy out of your trips. We'll show you how to *get ready*— with practical tips for planning meaningful trips; *get set*— with handy ideas for organizing your adventure; *then go, go, go* with some fabulous field-trip possibilities and fun follow-up activities. So jump on the bus and get ready to ride!

ideas contributed by Barbara F. Backer

GET READY: Planning Your Trip

Learning will be all the more sweet when you plan field trips based on your students' interests. Observe your little ones during play and center activities, and take note of their interests. For example, if children are using pegs and pegboards to make birthday cakes, plan a trip to a bakery to see how cakes are made. This way you'll cook up a meaningful field trip that is a sweet success!

Although any trip outside the classroom can be a learning experience for young children, think about why you are planning to go to a particular site. What is there to see? Is it too far away? How will the trip enhance the learning experiences of your youngsters? With some advance planning and a little forethought, you'll plan a trip that is jam-packed with learning fun.

Consider learning opportunities that are within walking distance of your classroom. A short walk to observe flowers in bloom provides youngsters with practice walking in a group and listening to directions, and provides countless opportunities to put observation and investigation skills to work. Now, that's a step in the right direction!

Get a handle on any transportation kinks that may put a damper on your fun by driving to your destination prior to your trip. Take note of the route you take and any road conditions that may cause delay. Time your trip so that you can plan departure and arrival times more accurately. While you are at the site, scout out points of interest and collect any available written materials to help prepare your little ones for their excursion. A little roadwork beforehand will surely help pave the way to a hassle-free trip.

GET SET:
Preparing For Your Trip

If you are transporting students in private vehicles, make a detailed map of your route for each parent driver. Write the school's phone number and the phone number of your destination on each map. Just before leaving, verbally review the map with each parent; then double-check to make sure that each child is properly fastened in a seat belt.

Keep your caravan of cars together by tying matching flags or scarves to the antenna of each vehicle. Other drivers will be able to tell that you are traveling together, and your caravan is less likely to become separated.

You'll have field-trip supplies ready to go at a moment's notice when you stock a backpack with bandages, a cold pack, antiseptic wipes, a pair of disposable latex gloves, moist towelettes, emergency first-aid information, spare change, your school's phone number, a memo pad, and a pen. The pack is easy to tote on your back and keeps your hands free. When you return to school, replenish the supplies as necessary.

Help parent volunteers identify the children in their groups by fastening a nametag (see pages 40–41) to the front *and* back of each child in your class. Be sure to include your school's name and phone number on the back of each tag just in case a child becomes separated from his group.

One, two, three, four...count your students; then count some more. Avoid a field-trip fiasco by counting your children before you leave your school and immediately upon arriving at your destination. Encourage parent volunteers to count their groups several times during the outing. Then be sure to count your students as you prepare to leave your destination and when you arrive back at school.

Help parent chaperones keep the children in their groups together with a walking rope. To make one, tie several knots, at regular intervals, in a long length of clothesline cord. The chaperone holds one end of the rope; then each student in the group holds on to a separate knot. With this method little ones feel independent, but are still together in a group.

LET'S GO, GO, GO:
Places To Go And Things To See

Throughout the school year, take nature walks to visit a nearby tree. Observe and record the seasonal changes in the foliage. Then step up literacy skills by compiling the pages into a class book.

The doctor will see your pet now! Arrange for your little ones to tour a veterinarian's office. Have each child bring along a stuffed animal pet. After a tour of the facility, arrange for the veterinary assistant to give each pet a checkup. Students may then take home their pet's checkup records.

Enhance a health unit by taking your students to the produce section of a market. Identify some of the different types of fruits and vegetables; then take instant pictures of them. If possible purchase a sampling of the produce you photographed. When you return to school, have students sort the photos by color, shape, or another characteristic. Then taste the produce purchased. Compare the smell, taste, and texture of each. Take a class poll to determine the favorites. Finally, label the pictures and compile them into a class book.

We saw apples.

We saw grapes.

Your little ones' imaginations will soar to new heights when you visit an airport. Before your trip place a variety of travel-related props in your dramatic-play center. Set up chairs to resemble the inside of an airplane. Provide small trays and cups so your little flight attendants can serve refreshments.

Make advance arrangements with the airport to visit during a time when it is less crowded. Plan to visit a ticket counter and boarding gate, walk through the metal detectors, and watch the luggage circle around the baggage-claim area. If possible make arrangements with a particular airline for youngsters to tour the inside of an airplane. Up, up and away!

Ask local artists for tours of their workshops and demonstrations of their crafts, such as painting, pottery making, sculpting, and weaving. Then ask them to assist your youngsters in creating their own art. When you return to your classroom, set up an atelier (workshop). Provide the materials necessary for youngsters to practice their art skills. Display their pieces around your classroom; then invite parents and friends to the grand opening of your museum.

HOME AGAIN, HOME AGAIN:
Field Trip Follow-Ups

Capture your little ones' field-trip enthusiasm by taking photos of them during your excursion. Select the photos that best depict your outing; then create a memory book by mounting the photos on copies of the album page on page 135. Write students' dictated captions on each page; then bind the pages between construction-paper covers. Invite a different child each day to take the album home to share with his family.

Catch them on tape! Throughout the year bring a video camera along on your field trips. During each trip ask a parent volunteer to take lots of footage of your youngsters. Record each trip on the same videotape. Then, at Open House, set up a mini theater so that parents can view the tape. Serve popcorn and drinks to complete the theater-like atmosphere. Lights, camera, action!

Grin and share it! Write a group-experience story to add meaning to your field trip. Write each child's memorable experiences on a sheet of chart paper; then have each child draw a picture illustrating his favorite part of the trip. Display the chart and pictures in the hallway, or on the door of your classroom for parents and others to enjoy.

Your field-trip hosts will surely feel like "thumb-bodies" after receiving this thank-you note. Write a brief note on a sheet of paper, expressing your appreciation for your host's hospitality. Personalize the note by having each child press his thumb onto an ink pad and then onto the paper. Assist each child in signing his name under his thumbprint.

Field Trip Ahead

On October 3rd, we went to City Park.

Donnie climbed on the monkey bars.

We had fun.

Dear Mr. Kramer,
Thanks for showing us around your doughnut shop! We liked watching the machines make doughnuts. And the samples were yummy!

Your friends,
Miss Taylor's Class

Zach
Tia   Tim
                    Susie
Justina
Ben   Alfie
      Keri
                    Ashley
         Thomas
Gina   Owen

On The Road Again...

Destination: _____

Date: _____

Meeting Place: _____

Time: _____

Your child will need: _____

☐ sack lunch   ☐ money

☐ other   _____

_____

_____

Please sign and return the lower portion of this note no later than _____.
(date)

Preschool Express

_____ has my permission to
(child's name)

go to _____ on _____.
(where)   (when)

_____   _____
(date)   **(parent or guardian's signature)**

☐ I would like to accompany the group as a chaperone.

_____
(parent or guardian's signature)

Field Trip Ahead

Note To The Teacher: Use with "Home Again, Home Again" on page 133.

THE STARS ARE OUT TONIGHT!
Star-Studded Ideas For Family Night

Help parents see that children are the center of your classroom galaxy with these family-night ideas.

ideas contributed by Barbara Backer

Preparing To Launch

Prepare to launch a spectacular family night by preparing the invitation on page 140. Duplicate a class supply of the invitation onto yellow construction paper. Cut out the invitations; then personalize them. Invite each child to drizzle glue around the edges of his caregiver's invitation, then sprinkle on gold glitter. Send the invitations home. Wishing on a star for good attendance won't be necessary with these intriguing invitations!

All Stars

Take pictures of your family night and use them on this schoolwide display. When your guests arrive, take a close-up picture of each caregiver or caregiver with his child. When the pictures have been developed, cut them into star shapes. Display each photo along with a larger personalized construction-paper star on a board titled, "Our Families Are All Stars!" Encourage other teachers involved with family night to add their pictures to the display.

Okoya Family

NAME THAT STAR

Prior to your family night, duplicate onto yellow construction paper a number of nametags, using the pattern on page 141. Cut out the nametags. On the night of your event, arrange the nametags, markers, and safety pins on a table near the entrance to your room. Encourage each caregiver to complete a tag by writing his name as well as his child's name. Twinkle, twinkle, parent stars, now we know just who you are!

The Stars Are Out Tonight!

Mr. Okoya
My name

Kashi
My little star's name

STARGAZING

This idea will identify each child's cubby or table space as well as add pizzazz to your room. For each child, cut a large star from yellow poster board. Label each point of the star with a different sentence starter listed below. Write on each child's star as she dictates her responses. Then ask her to draw a picture of herself in the center of the star. Put each child's star on the appropriate table or cubby. Or hang the stars from the ceiling to promote stargazing.

My favorite center is…
My favorite story is…
My favorite song is…
I like my school because…
My name is…

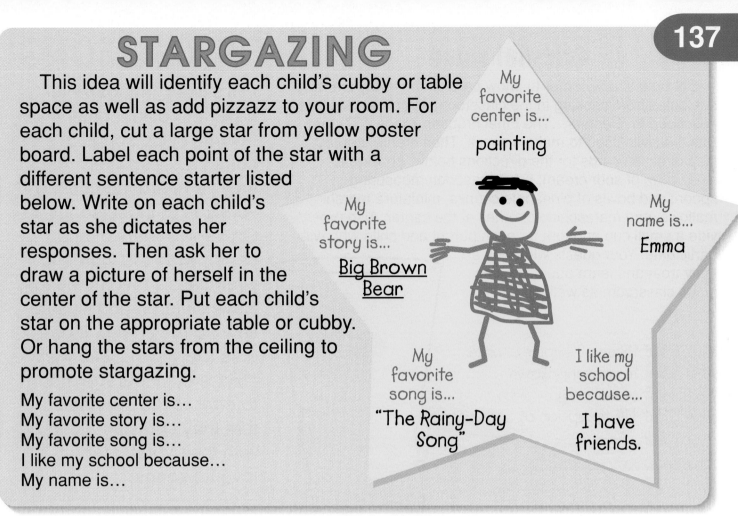

My favorite center is…
painting

My favorite story is…
Big Brown Bear

My name is…
Emma

My favorite song is…
"The Rainy-Day Song"

I like my school because…
I have friends.

In The Movies

Prior to your family night, make a video showing children engaged in typical classroom activities. Be sure to capture each child on the video as well as the activities that take place in each of your centers. During your family night, turn off your TV's volume and play the video continuously. As parents enjoy the show, use this opportunity to point out the process and play-based learning taking place.

COOKING CENTER

• counting   • following directions

• measuring

• understanding picture clues

Centers…The Final Frontier

With this idea parents will appreciate the value of your learning centers in the twinkling of an eye. For each of your centers, cut a star from yellow poster board. Label each star with a different center's title and the concepts that can be reinforced at that center. (Refer to the information on page 10.) Post the stars in the appropriate centers. As parents tour your room, encourage them to take time to read the signs and "play" in the centers as well.

Celestial Salad

Set up a snack center to show parents the many learning outcomes from cooking in the classroom. Prepare a sign as described in "Centers…The Final Frontier" (page 137) that lists the skills used to make a snack. Then create step-by-step direction cards for the directions below. Arrange a small bowl of sour cream; a 1/4-teaspoon measuring spoon; and bowls of pineapple chunks, miniature marshmallows, and maraschino cherries at the center. Also provide a small cup and fork for each parent and child who will participate. Your guests will enjoy a tasty treat and learn about cooking in the classroom as well.

Step 1: Put three pineapple chunks.
Step 2: Put ten marshmallows.
Step 3: Put one cherry.
Step 4: Put 1/4 teaspoon of sour cream.
Step 5: Stir.

Put 3 pineapple chunks

Put 10 marshmallows

Reading And Listening Center

Display class-made books in your reading center. On a cassette tape, record information about your literacy efforts, such as why reading aloud is important, why you make class books, and more. Put the tape in your center along with a tape player and headphones. Display a sign encouraging parents to take a moment to read the books and listen to the tape.

OH, THAT SONG!

It's likely that parents have heard youngsters' favorite class songs at home. It's also likely that they've heard incomplete versions of those songs! On large sheets of chart paper, write the words to your class's favorite songs. Have children add illustrations to the charts. If parents are visiting with their children, encourage them to refer to the charts so that they can sing along with their youngsters' favorite songs.

Twinkle, Twinkle, Little Star

Twinkle, twinkle, little star,

How I wonder what you are!

Up above the world so high,

Like a diamond in the sky.

Twinkle, twinkle, little star,

How I wonder what you are!

EVERYONE LOVES A STORY

Remind parents of the enjoyment of listening to a good story by gathering them together for a brief storytime. Share with parents the benefits of reading aloud daily, such as developing listening skills and imagination. You may wish to describe how other daily activities develop reading skills. For example, pushing a truck on the floor helps develop the visual tracking needed to follow rows of print. Read aloud one of your class's favorite titles. Or share with parents one of the following children's books about preschool.

When Daddy Came To School
Written & Illustrated by Julie Brillhart
Published by Albert Whitman & Company

Busy At Day Care: Head To Toe
Written by Patricia Brennan Demuth
Published by Dutton Children's Books

From Parent To Child

If parents will be attending your event without your students, have them leave notes for the children to discover the next day. Duplicate a class supply of the note on page 141 onto yellow construction paper; then cut them out. Put the notes in the children's cubbies or on their tables. Sprinkle gold star dust (star-shaped confetti or gold glitter) around the notes. Ask each parent to complete a note to her child before leaving your event. Read each parent's note with her child when it is discovered the following day.

To: Cassie

Star light, star bright,
I saw your flower painting last night.
From: Mommy

Invitation
Use with "Preparing To Launch" on page 136.

You're
invited
to an
out-of-this-world
family night
starring the caregivers of

_____.
(child's name)

Date: _____

Time: _____

Place: _____

We've been wishing on this star,
We're hoping to see you,
yes we are!

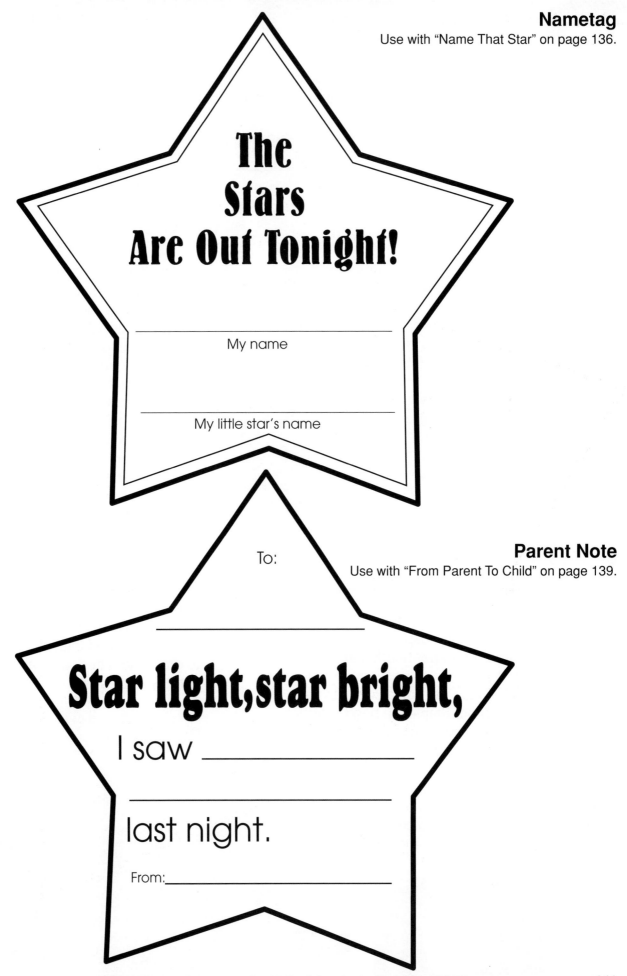

The Stars Are Out Tonight!

_____
My name

_____
My little star's name

Parent Note
Use with "From Parent To Child" on page 139.

To:

_____

Star light, star bright,

I saw _____

_____

last night.

From:_____

PARTY TIME!

What do you get when you combine a pinch of creative decorations, a smidgen of seasonal style, and a dollop of fun and games? A big batch of seasonal celebrations that really sizzle! It's party time!

ideas contributed by Linda Ludlow and Lori Kent

APPLE EXTRAVAGANZA

DECOR

"A-PEEL-ING" CENTERPIECES

Add a little polish to your party table with this "a-peel-ing" apple arrangement. To make an apple for each child, stuff a paper lunch bag half-full of crumpled newspaper. Gather the top of the bag together; then twist to form a stem. Wind the stem with masking tape. Paint the bag red, yellow, or green; then paint the stem brown. Program a leaf shape as shown; then glue a child's photo to the leaf. Tape the leaf to the stem. Arrange the apples in a large basket; then set the basket on your party table.

DRESS

Johnny Appleseed Hats

For each headband, you will need:
- one 9" x 3" construction-paper rectangle
- 1 black construction-paper headband
- 1 apple cutout

Have each child glue the apple cutout to the center of his headband. Staple the band to fit the child's head. Have him round one end of the construction-paper rectangle to resemble a pot handle. Have him use an apple-shaped hole puncher to punch a hole in the rounded end of the handle. Fold down one inch of the opposite end of the handle to create a gluing tab. Help the child glue the handle to the headband.

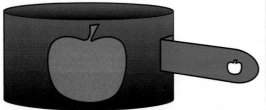

ACTIVITY

Johnny Goes-A-Planting

This guessing game similar to Who's Got The Button? is sure to produce a bumper crop of smiles. Seat children in a circle. Invite a volunteer to be Johnny Appleseed and wear a pot on her head. Have this child stand away from the group with her back toward the circle. Give a child seated in the circle an apple seed (brown pom-pom) to hide in his hands. Have the remaining children pretend to hide seeds in their hands. Have Johnny return to the group and pretend to pour water on the hands of the child she thinks has the seed. If that child has the seed, he stands up and pretends to grow into a tree. He then becomes Johnny. If he doesn't have the seed, he opens his hands to reveal no seed. Johnny then has two more guesses to try and find the seed. If none of her guesses are correct, Johnny says, "Grow, apple tree, grow." The child holding the seed then stands up, pretends to grow into a tree, and takes his turn as Johnny Appleseed.

Squirmy-Wormy Apples

Ingredients (per child):
- 1 small, cored apple
- 2 Tbsp. peanut butter
- 1 Tbsp. granola
- 1 Gummy Worm®

Mix the peanut butter and granola together; then stuff the apple with the mixture. Place one end of the Gummy Worm® in the peanut-butter mixture. Delicious!

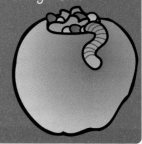

A SUPER SPIDER CELEBRATION

DECOR — SPIDER SETTINGS

Set your party table for some shivery fun with these placemats and spider napkin rings. Invite each child to make a placemat by marble-painting a 12" x 18" sheet of black construction paper with white paint. While the placemats are drying, cut a supply of toilet-tissue tubes into thirds to create rings. Provide each child with a ring, four black pipe cleaners, one large black pom-pom, and two wiggle eyes.

To make a napkin ring, twist the four pipe cleaners together in the center; then bend them to resemble spider legs. Tape the legs to the ring. Squeeze a large puddle of glue onto the intersection of the legs; then place the pom-pom on top. Glue wiggle eyes to the pom-pom to complete the spider. Insert a paper napkin into each napkin ring; then arrange the placemats and napkins on your party table. "Spider-rific!"

DRESS — Spider Headbands

For each headband, you will need:
- 1 black construction-paper headband
- eight 1" x 12" strips of black construction paper (accordion-folded)
- 1 black construction-paper circle
- 2 large wiggle eyes

Have each child glue his wiggle eyes onto the circle, then glue the circle onto his headband. Have him glue four accordion-folded strips to opposite sides of his headband to resemble spider legs. This spider's legs will jump and jiggle just like a real spider's!

ACTIVITY — Web Walkers

Draw a web shape on a large piece of tagboard; then draw a fly shape somewhere on the web. Draw, color, and cut a spider from tagboard. Laminate the web and the spider. Slide a large paper clip onto the spider. Suspend the tagboard web between two tables and tape it in place. Place the spider on the web. Invite a child to help the spider catch the fly by moving it around the web using a magnet underneath the tagboard. That's some fancy web walking!

Spider Bites

Ingredients (per child):
- 1 small chocolate donut
- 8 pretzel sticks
- frosting in a tube
- 2 mini chocolate chips

Push four pretzel sticks into opposite sides of the donut. Squeeze two dots of frosting onto the top of the donut. Press the chocolate-chip eyes onto the frosting. What a tasty spider treat!

DECOR — TURKEY FAVORS

These tiny turkey favors will have your little ones strutting to the party table! To make one, cut a nine-inch square from each of three different colors of tissue paper. Stack the squares; then place several small candies in the center. Gather the tissue paper around the candies. Hold a wooden ice-cream spoon (the turkey's head and neck) along the gathers; then twist a red pipe cleaner around the spoon and tissue paper. Shape the pipe cleaner to resemble a wattle. Fan out the tissue paper to resemble a turkey's plumage. Use a fine-tip marker to draw a turkey face on the ice-cream spoon. Arrange the favors around your party table. Gobble, gobble, gorgeous!

ACTIVITY — Bowling For Turkeys

Your little turkeys are sure to flock to this bowling game that strengthens hand-eye coordination skills. Decorate 6 two-liter soda bottles to resemble turkeys. In an open area of your classroom, line up the turkeys as you would pins for bowling. To play, a child rolls a small rubber ball toward the turkeys. He then counts the turkeys he knocked down and realigns them for the next player.

DRESS

Turkey Pins

For each pin, you will need:
- 1 wooden ice-cream spoon
- 5 small, colorful feathers
- 2 wiggle eyes
- 1 bar pin

Use craft glue to attach the wiggle eyes to the small end of the spoon. Use markers to add a beak and wattle to complete the turkey face. Glue the feathers to the back of the spoon to resemble a turkey's plumage. Glue the bar pin to the back of the turkey.

Turkey Treats

Ingredients (per child):
- 2 round crackers
- 1 tsp. peanut butter
- 2 small pretzels
- 1 piece of candy corn
- 2 mini chocolate chips

Spread peanut butter on one cracker; then place the other cracker on top to make a sandwich. Push the pretzels into the peanut butter to resemble feathers. Place a small dot of peanut butter on the bottom of each chocolate chip and on one side of the candy corn; then press the chocolate-chip eyes and candy-corn beak onto the front of the cracker. Gobble up this treat!

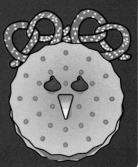

DECOR

FANTASTIC FLAKES

These snowflakes will have your room looking like a winter wonderland in a flurry! Provide each child with a paper doily and a variety of craft supplies (pom-poms, sequins, buttons, and beads) in cool colors, such as white, silver, and blue. Invite her to glue her choice of materials onto the doily to make a snowflake. When the glue is dry, spray a thin coat of adhesive on the doily; then sprinkle the entire surface with iridescent glitter. Tie a length of fishing line to each snowflake; then suspend all the shimmering flakes from your classroom ceiling.

DRESS

Snowman Pins

For each pin, you will need:
- 1/2 of a craft stick
- 2 cotton balls
- 2 wiggle eyes
- 1 construction-paper hat cutout
- 1 orange pipe cleaner
- 1 bar pin

Have a child spread glue on the craft-stick half, then press on the cotton balls. Have her glue the hat and wiggle eyes on the snowman. Clip off one end of the pipe cleaner; then help her glue this below the eyes to create a carrot nose. Help her wrap the remaining pipe cleaner around the stick (between the cotton balls) to create a scarf. Glue the bar pin to the back of the snowman.

ACTIVITY

Snowball Shoot

Students are sure to enjoy slam-dunking snowballs in this game that focuses on hand-eye coordination skills. Make several beanbag snowballs by using a funnel to partially fill white balloons with rice. Knot the end of each balloon. Set three different colors of laundry baskets or large tubs in a row on the floor. Invite a child to stand a specified distance away. Have him name a color, then throw a snowball into the corresponding basket.

❄ ❄ ❄ ❄ ❄

Snowflake Fruit Snacks

Ingredients (per child):
- 1 large marshmallow
- a variety of fruits cut into small pieces
- flaked coconut
- minimarshmallows
- 3 coffee-stirring sticks, cut in half

Make kabobs by skewering minimarshmallows and pieces of fruit onto each of six sticks. Push one end of each stick into the large marshmallow to create a snowflake shape. Sprinkle the entire snowflake with flaked coconut. This snack is "snow" yummy!

DECOR
BLOOMIN' HEART CENTERPIECES

Love will be in bloom when you place these pretty heart-shaped flowers on your party table. To make a flower, have each child drizzle glue onto a construction-paper heart, then shake on red, gold, and silver glitter. When the glue is dry, shake off the excess glitter and tape each heart to the end of a separate straw.

Make a few baskets by painting toilet-tissue tubes with white paint. When the paint is dry, decorate the tubes with heart-shaped stickers. For each basket, cut a 1" x 9" construction-paper handle. Decorate the handles if desired; then glue them to the tubes. To complete the baskets, dip the bottom of each tube into glue; then press it onto a heart-shaped doily. Arrange a few of the flowers in each basket, and set the baskets around your party table. Beautiful!

DRESS
Crown Of Hearts

For each crown, you will need:
- 1 white headband
- pink and red construction-paper heart-shaped cutouts
- faux jewels

Have each youngster glue heart cutouts and faux jewels to his headband.

ACTIVITY
Sweetheart Messages

To prepare for this game, program a class supply of construction-paper hearts with various messages, similar to those found on candy conversation hearts. To play, seat youngsters in a circle. Choose one child to be Cupid. Have Cupid stand a distance away from the group with her back toward the circle. Give a programmed heart to a child in the group, and have him conceal it. Invite Cupid to return to the group by chanting, "Cupid, Cupid, what do you say? Do you know who has a message today?" Allow Cupid to guess who has the heart by asking children, "Do you have a heart today?" Once Cupid guesses correctly, the teacher then reads the message aloud and safety-pins the heart to Cupid's clothing. Cupid then rejoins the group and the guessed child becomes Cupid. Continue play until each child is wearing a heart.

Sweetheart Envelopes

Ingredients (per child):
- 1 unfrosted Pop-Tart®
- 1 Tbsp. white frosting
- Alpha-Bits® cereal
- 1 candy conversation heart

To make an envelope, spread frosting on the Pop-Tart®. Find the cereal letters in your name; then arrange them on the frosting. Place a conversation heart in the upper right-hand corner to represent a stamp. Your tummy will love this special delivery!

BUNNY BLAST

DECOR — BUNNY BUCKETS

These cute bunny buckets are sure to have your little ones hopping to your party table. Give each child a small, white foam cup. Have her glue wiggle eyes and ears, a nose, and whiskers cut from construction paper on the cup. Have her add a cotton-ball tail. To make a handle, push one end of a pipe cleaner through the rim of the cup and twist to secure it. Bend the pipe cleaner; then push the other end through the opposite rim and twist. Stuff the bucket with cellophane grass and a few party treats.

DRESS — Bunny Necklaces

For each necklace, you will need:
- 1 eight-inch square of pastel gingham fabric
- 1 coin
- 2 jumbo cotton balls
- 1 large, round wooden bead
- one 30-inch length of narrow green ribbon

Place the coin in the center of the fabric square. Put the cotton balls on top of the coin; then fold the square as shown. Gather the two points over the folds. Knot the ribbon around the gathered fabric to secure it. Use a permanent marker to draw a rabbit face on the bead. Thread the ribbon and then the cloth through the bead. Separate the fabric so that it forms two ears. Adjust the ribbon so that it is in back of the ears; then tie the ribbon ends together to make a necklace.

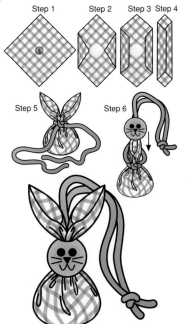

Step 1   Step 2   Step 3   Step 4
Step 5   Step 6

ACTIVITY — Five Little Bunnies

Five little bunnies
(Hold up five fingers.)

Hopping in the sun.
(Hold up two fingers and make them hop.)

Eating all the farmer's carrots, one by one.
(Hold fingers up to mouth and pretend to nibble.)

Here comes Mr. Farmer;
(Make a scared face with a hand on each cheek.)

Oooooh, you'd better run!
(Shake one finger.)

5, 4, 3, 2, 1.
(Count down on fingers.)

Peter Rabbit Pinwheels

Ingredients (per child):
- 1 slice of wheat bread with the crusts removed
- 1 Tbsp. spreadable cream cheese
- 1 tsp. blackberry jam

Use a rolling pin to flatten the bread slightly. Spread the cream cheese and jam onto the bread. Roll the bread into a small jelly roll. Slice the roll into four pinwheels. Nibble away!

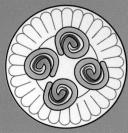

Calendar Of SPECIAL

AUGUST

- Children's Vision And Learning Month

- Friendship Day—First Sunday in August

- National Smile Week—First full week in August

- Book Lovers Day—August 9

- National I Love Cowboys and Cowgirls Day—August 15

- National Aviation Week—Week of August 19

SEPTEMBER

- Children's Good Manners Month
- Library Card Sign-Up Month
- National Better Breakfast Month
- National Honey Month
- Labor Day—First Monday in September
- National Grandparents Day—First Sunday after Labor Day
- National Farm Animals Awareness Week—Third full week in September
- Johnny Appleseed's Birthday (John Chapman)—September 26

OCTOBER

- National Dental Hygiene Month

- National Pasta Month

- National Pizza Month

- National Popcorn Poppin' Month

- Fire Prevention Week—First or second week of October

- Columbus Day—Second Monday in October

- National School Bus Safety Week—Third full week of October

- Halloween—October 31

NOVEMBER

- Peanut Butter Lovers' Month
- International Drum Month
- National Author's Day—November 1
- Sandwich Day (birthday of John Montague, sandwich inventor)—November 3
- National Children's Book Week—Week prior to Thanksgiving week
- American Education Week—Week prior to Thanksgiving week
- Thanksgiving Day—Fourth Thursday in November
- National Game And Puzzle Week—Last week in November

EVENTS

DECEMBER

- International Calendar Awareness Month

- National Poinsettia Day—December 12

- Christmas—December 25

- Hanukkah—Date based on Jewish calendar (usually in December)

- Kwanzaa—December 26–January 1

JANUARY

- National Soup Month

- Oatmeal Month

- Eye Care Month

- New Year's Day—January 1

- International Thank-You Day—January 11

- Pooh Day (A. A. Milne's Birthday)—January 18

- National Hugging Day™—January 21

- Martin Luther King, Jr. Federal Holiday—Third Monday in January

- National School Nurse Day—Fourth Wednesday in January

FEBRUARY

- American Heart Month

- Black History Month

- National Children's Dental Health Month

- Groundhog Day—February 2

- Random Acts Of Kindness Week—Week including February 14

- Read To Your Child Day—February 14

- Valentine's Day—February 14

- Presidents' Day—Third Monday in February

- International Friendship Week—Last full week of February

MARCH

- National Nutrition Month®

- National Peanut Month

- Music In Our Schools Month

- Youth Art Month

- Share A Smile Day—March 1

- Newspapers In Education Week—First full week of March

- St. Patrick's Day—March 17

APRIL

- Keep America Beautiful Month

- National Library Month

- Month Of The Young Child

- Easter—Date based on lunar calendar (between March 22 and April 25)

- April Fools' Day—April 1

- International Children's Book Day—April 2

- Earth Day—April 22

- National Arbor Day—Last Friday in April

MAY

- National Physical Fitness And Sports Month
- National Strawberry Month
- National Family Week—First full week in May
- May Day—May 1
- Mother Goose Day—May 1
- National Weather Observer's Day—May 4
- Mother's Day—Second Sunday in May
- National Transportation Week—Week including third Friday in May
- Memorial Day—Last Monday in May

JUNE

- Dairy Month

- National Fresh Fruit And Vegetable Month

- Pet Appreciation Week—June 6–12

- National Hug Holiday Week—Second week in June

- Flag Day—June 14

- Father's Day—Third Sunday in June

- Celebration Of The Senses Day—June 24

JULY

- National Hot Dog Month

- National Ice Cream Month

- National Picnic Month

- Independence Day—July 4

- Space Week—Week including July 20

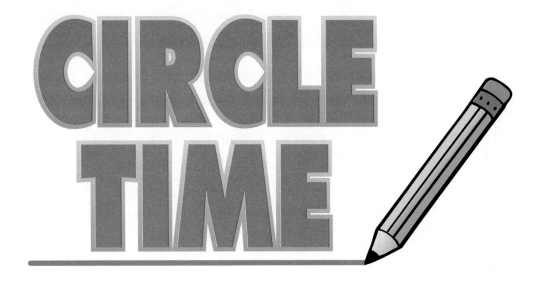

CIRCLE-TIME SAVVY

Add to your circle-time savvy with these cross-curricular activities. The fun and frills brought to this special part of the day will have youngsters claiming circle time as their favorite time!

ideas contributed by Jean Feldman

GREETINGS GALORE

Hello! Hello! Youngsters will gladly sing their greetings to each other with this circle-time tune. Ask students to greet a different child each time you repeat the song.

(sung to the tune of "Skip To My Lou")

Hello, and how are you?	*Wave to friend.*
Hello, and how are you?	
Hello, and how are you?	
How are you this morning?	
I'm fine. Hope you are, too.	*Point to self; then to friend.*
I'm fine. Hope you are, too.	
I'm fine. Hope you are, too.	
Hope you are fine this morning.	

Happy New Shoes

Here's a song to reinforce that special feeling a youngster brings to school when he wears shoes or another article of clothing new to him. While singing to the child, simply replace the underlined words with the name of his special item. As you sing, invite the child to stand up and model his special "wears."

(sung to the tune of "Happy Birthday To You")

Happy [new shoes] to you.
Happy [new shoes] to you.
Happy [new shoes] to you.
[They/It] look(s) good on you!

WHERE, OH WHERE?

Grab youngsters' attention with this contagious tune. Use a different child's name in each line of the song. In no time you'll find youngsters alert and ready for circle-time activities.

(sung to the tune of "Paw Paw Patch")

Where, oh where, is my friend [child's name]?
Where, oh where, is my friend [child's name]?
Where, oh where, is my friend [child's name]?
Way down yonder at [name of school]!

HAPPY DAYS SONG

Familiarize youngsters with the days of the week with this song sung to the tune of "If You're Happy And You Know It."

If you're happy that it's [Monday], clap your hands.
If you're happy that it's [Monday], clap your hands.
If you're happy and you know it, then your face will surely show it.
If you're happy that it's [Monday], clap your hands.

Hokey-Pokey Shape Up

It's time to shape up youngsters' recognition of shapes with a few rounds of "The Hokey-Pokey"! In advance cut a variety of shapes from tagboard. To begin, give each child a shape cutout. When each student hears her shape named in the song, she performs the named actions. Each time you repeat the song, use a different shape name for the underlined word until each child has had the opportunity to participate. That's what it's all about!

(sung to the tune of "The Hokey-Pokey")

You put your [square] in. You take your [square] out.
You put your [square] in. And you shake your [square] about.
You do the hokey-pokey, and you turn yourself around.
That's what it's all about!

COLOR MARCH

Youngsters will wave these special flags with pride as they demonstrate their color-recognition skills. To prepare, make a class supply of flags in a variety of colors. To make each flag, staple a construction-paper triangle to a drinking straw. During circle time give each child a flag. Instruct students to listen for their flag colors to be mentioned in this song. When a color is named, each child with that color flag will stand and proudly march around as he displays his flag. Repeat the song, naming a different color each time, so that each child has a turn to march.

(sung to the tune of "The Ants Go Marching")

The [reds] go marching all around.
Hurrah! Hurrah!
The [reds] go marching all around.
Hurrah! Hurrah!
The [reds] go marching all around;
Then they stop to wave their flags around.
All the [reds] go marching around and around;
Then they stop and sit down. *(Boom, boom, boom.)*

A Terrific Transformation

Teach youngsters a simple, fun lesson on metamorphosis with this puppet. Hot-glue wiggle eyes and a pom-pom nose to the toe of a sock to represent a caterpillar; then turn the sock inside out. Hot-glue a decorated, butterfly felt cutout onto the foot part of the sock. To perform this chant with youngsters during circle time, slip the sock over your hand, caterpillar side out; then follow the suggestions provided for using the puppet with the rhyme. What a terrific transformation!

Caterpillar crawled to the top of a tree.   *Crawl puppet up one arm.*
"I think I'll take a nap," said she;
So under a leaf she began to creep.
She spun a cocoon and fell fast asleep.   *Turn back cuff of sock to create cocoon.*

After six long months in her cocoon bed,
Spring came to say, "Wake up, sleepyhead!"
Caterpillar awoke with a happy sigh,
"Look at me now—I'm a butterfly!"   *Turn sock inside out to reveal butterfly.*

Outside

Inside

THE MAGIC BAG

Bring some magic to your circle time with this neat little mystery bag. To prepare, decorate a large canvas bag with glitter paint pens, felt star cutouts, sequins, interesting buttons, and other notions. Secretly place a book, game, treat, or prop related to your unit of study in the bag each morning before circle time. When you're ready to reveal the bag's contents, wave your hand over the bag while chanting a series of magic words; then produce the special item. Youngsters will be caught in the spell—and you'll have their attention for your circle-time activity. Works like magic!

IMAGINATION BOX

Stir up youngsters' imaginations with this idea. Bring a decorative jewelry box to circle time. As you display the box, recite the chant shown. Invite the child named in the chant to remove the lid from the box, then to act out the imaginary item that she "finds" inside. Replace the lid, repeat the chant, and have the next child repeat the process, acting out his imaginary find.

Something is in our imagination box!
I wonder what that something could be.
[Child's name] thinks it's a [child names item].
Let's open the box and see.

MEOW!

Personal Treasures

Here's a neat twist to show-and-tell. Prepare a treasure box by spray-painting a large, lidded laundry detergent box with gold paint. After the paint dries, use glitter pens and sparkling stickers to decorate the box. Give each child an opportunity to take the box home overnight (with a note of explanation attached) and place a special item inside. When the child returns the box to school, invite her to show and tell about her treasure during circle time. If desired she might give clues to prompt her classmates to guess what her special item is before she reveals it.

If desired extend the use of your treasure box to incorporate basic concepts and your unit of study. Attach a note requesting that parents help their child find an item related to a specific concept or topic. For instance you might request that a child bring in an item of a certain shape or color. Or you might suggest that she find an outdoor item related to fall or spring to put in the treasure box.

JUKEBOX TUNES

With this little jukebox, you'll have ready-to-go tunes at your fingertips for circle time. To make a jukebox, cover an empty cereal box with solid-color Con-Tact® covering. Use permanent markers or paint pens to decorate the box with music notes. Cut a large slit in the top front of the box. Then write the title of each of your students' favorite songs on a separate notemcard. Add a simple picture clue to each card to help youngsters identify the song title; then slip the cards into the jukebox.

During circle time, give each of several children a jukebox coin (a poker chip or counter). Ask him to insert the coin into the jukebox and pick a song for the class to sing. After the child makes his selection, invite him to lead the group in singing a round of the song.

COOKING UP SOME FUN

This special, two-sided board will surely attract attention to your circle-time activities. To create a double-duty magnet/felt board, purchase a large, inexpensive metal cookie sheet. Hot-glue a sheet of felt to the back of the cookie sheet. Then use the felt-covered side of the board for flannelboard stories, fingerplays, and figures. Turn the board over to use magnetic figures and items during circle time. (Almost any item or picture can be backed with a piece of magnetic tape.) Invite youngsters to use the two-sided board to retell circle-time stories, and to practice the concepts and lessons reviewed during circle time. Your class will be cooking up some fun without even turning on the oven!

STORYTELLING WAND

A circle-time story will magically appear when this special wand is used to stir up the words. To make a wand, remove the cardboard tube from a pants hanger; then dip one end of the tube into glue. Roll the glue-covered end of the tube in glitter; then add a fluffy feather. After the glue dries—*Abracadabra!*—your storytelling wand is ready for use! During circle time, wave the magic wand over the heads of your students, reciting the magic chant shown. Then begin telling a story. Pass the wand around the circle. As each child receives the wand, she waves it over her head, then adds a line or event to the story in progress.

Bibbity, bobbity, boo. Bibbity, bobbity, bee.
Time for a story. One, two, three!

PUPPET PAL

Delight students each time you invite this clever puppet to your circle time. To make a Max the Mouse puppet, hot-glue felt ears, button eyes, yarn whiskers, and a pom-pom nose onto a brown or gray sock. Then cut off the top and bottom of an empty cereal box. If desired cover the box with gift wrap or decorative Con-Tact® covering. To use the puppet, simply slip it onto your hand; then slide your hand into the bottom of the box so that the puppet is hidden inside the box. At the appropriate time, tell youngsters that a guest has come to visit. Then slowly reveal

Max by sliding the puppet out of the top end of the box. After sharing his greeting, invite Max to tell a story, share a riddle, or sing a song with the class. Never underestimate the powerful pull of puppet play with little ones.

Surprise Boxes

Use the element of surprise to introduce new topics during circle time. Keep a variety of boxes on hand, such as a jewelry box, a decorative gift box, a hatbox, and a gift-wrapped copier-paper box. When you begin a new unit of study, place an item related to the topic in an appropriately sized box. During circle time show the class the box; then invite them to guess what might be inside. Give clues to help them guess the box's contents. After youngsters have exhausted their guesses, open the box to reveal the surprise. Then use the item to draw students' attention to the new topic of study. Surprise!

A SPECIAL BOOK

Who is *so* special? Share this unique book with youngsters to find out! Remove the pages from an old book, leaving the covers and binding intact. Cover the book covers with foil or shiny gift wrap; then title the book "So Special." Attach a small mirror to the inside of the back cover. During circle time tell students that you want to share with them a book about someone who is very special. Then pass the book to each child. As the child opens the book and peers at his reflection in the mirror, tell him that he is special; then name a few qualities about that child that make him special to you. If desired invite other class members to add their positive thoughts about the child, too. Who's *so* special? *Every* child is special!

THE NAME GAME

Dance youngsters into some name recognition with this simple idea. Print each child's name on a separate paper plate. Scatter the plates on the floor during circle time; then invite youngsters to dance to some lively music. When you stop the music, encourage each student to stand on the plate labeled with her name. Then collect the plates, randomly place them on the floor again, and start the music to play another round of this name game.

Do You See The Colors?

Color your circle time with this tune about colors. Each time you sing the song, replace the underlined word with the name of a different color. Appoint a child to sing the response, then find something of that color in the room. If desired expand the use of this song to include shapes and letters, too.

(sung to the tune of "The Muffin Man")

Do you see the color [red], the color [red], the color [red]?
Do you see the color [red] somewhere in this room?

Yes, I see the color [red], the color [red], the color [red].
Yes, I see the color [red] somewhere in this room!

PASS THE POTATO, PLEASE

Use this spud-passing game to prompt thinking in categorical terms. To make a potato, cut one foot from a pair of brown panty hose. Stuff the rest of the hose into the cutoff foot; then tie a knot in the open end and trim off the excess material. During circle time explain that you will announce a category, such as *animals, food, toys, vehicles,* or *things that fly.* Students will pass the stocking spud around the circle until you give the signal to "Stop." The child holding the potato at that time will name an item belonging to the designated category. Then, on the "Go" signal, students will resume passing the potato. Continue the game, periodically changing the category, for as long as student interest dictates.

MONSTER STOMP

Your little ones will stomp into basic concepts with this activity. Cover an empty powdered-drink-mix canister with construction paper. Draw a simple, silly monster (such as the one shown) on the canister. Next cut several construction-paper strips. On one end of most of the strips, draw a shape. On one end of the remaining strips, draw your silly monster. Put the strips in the canister programmed-side down. Then pass the can around at circle time. Invite each child to remove a strip and identify the shape on it. If the strip pictures a monster, the child yells, "Monster Stomp!" and all the students stomp around and act like big, scary monsters. On your signal the class sits down and resumes play until another monster is discovered.

Vary the game by programming sets of strips with colors or numbers.

Letter Hunt

A, B, C, D, E, F, G...can you find a match for me? Youngsters will practice important matching skills in this letter game. To prepare, cut 26 five-inch squares from each of two different poster-board colors. Print a different letter on each square so that you have an alphabet-card set in each color. Prior to circle time, place the letter cards of one color set around the room in plain sight. Then, during circle time, give each child one card from the other color set. Sing the alphabet song, replacing the ending with "We can sing the letter names. Now let's play the letter game!" At this time invite each child to find the letter matching the one she is holding. After all the matches have been found, ask each child to show and name her letter pair.

Cheers!

Use your circle time as an arena to reinforce and encourage youngsters for the many good things they know and do. Any time you want to applaud a child—and that will be often!—invite his classmates to join in with one of these cheery forms of recognition. Now for a round of applause...

- Clam Clap: Clap the thumb against any finger on the same hand.
- Opera Clap: Tap index fingers together.
- Ketchup Bottle Clap: Make a fist with one hand. Clap the other hand on top of the fist.
- Silent Applause: Wiggle fingers high in the air.
- Round Of Applause: Clap hands together in a circular motion in front of the body.

BE LIKE BEAR

Let Bear challenge your little ones' observation and imitation skills with this game. During circle time introduce youngsters to Bear, a flexible or jointed teddy bear. Explain that Bear wants to play a copycat game with the class. Then move Bear's arms, legs, and body into various positions. Invite youngsters to imitate each position that Bear models. After presenting Bear in a few rounds of simple poses, increase the complexity by adding an action to each of Bear's poses, such as jumping up and down or turning around. Conclude the game by having Bear—and the students—perform the actions in this short rhyme.

Dear Bear, dear Bear, sit on the rug.
Dear Bear, dear Bear, give yourself a hug!

THUMBS UP, THUMBS DOWN

Thumbs up for good listening! Invite youngsters to demonstrate their general knowledge in this listen-and-think game. Explain that each time you make a true statement about something, students will put their thumbs up. If your statement is false, children will give the thumbs-down signal. For starters use these examples; then make up your own statements relating to general knowledge, class rules, common courtesy, familiar stories, or even well-known facts about your community.

- Dogs have wings. *(Thumbs down.)*
- Bananas are yellow. *(Thumbs up.)*
- A refrigerator keeps food hot. *(Thumbs down.)*
- Chicks hatch from eggs. *(Thumbs up.)*

TIPS FOR TELLING TALES

Make storytime a favorite time for your little ones with these tips for adding a little razzmatazz to your read-alouds.

by Angie Kutzer

It's Storytime

Call your students over for storytime using the following rhyme. They're sure to enjoy the energetic transition and will settle down in no time for your storytime magic.

Gather Round

Come to the circle and sit down.
Shake your shoulders all around.

Hands up high, hands down low.
Wiggle your fingers, wiggle your toes.

Close your eyes and count to three...
One, two, three...
(Count aloud, slowly.)

Here's the book we're going to read.
(Show children the cover of the book.)

Read-Aloud Rituals

Set the mood for storytime by performing a ritual of some type before reading each day. Turn on a lamp, sit in a special chair, play soft background music, wear a unique hat, or use the poem from "It's Storytime" to signal youngsters that storytime is about to begin.

What's It All About?

Build interest and anticipation for your special story selections by introducing the books with props. For example, before reading *The Very Hungry Caterpillar* by Eric Carle (Philomel Books), show students a collection of the foods that will be mentioned in the story. If possible bring in a real caterpillar for little ones to observe. Props are also a great way to introduce unfamiliar objects or concepts. After discussing the props, invite youngsters to guess what the story might be about or whom the characters might be. Use the following suggestions for other popular titles to get you started; then use your imagination!

- *Lunch* by Denise Fleming (Henry Holt And Company, Inc.)—lunchbox, carrot, turnip, apple, mousetrap, and crayons

- *Goodnight Moon* by Margaret Wise Brown (HarperCollins Children's Books)—mittens, pajamas, socks, a clock, a red balloon, a comb, a brush, and a toy rabbit

- *In The Small, Small Pond* by Denise Fleming (Henry Holt And Company, Inc.)—toy pond animals, such as turtles, frogs, ducks, and insects; a cattail or another pond plant; and a container of water

- *Jump, Frog, Jump!* by Robert Kalan (Greenwillow Books)—a basket, a net, and a toy frog

Dressing The Part

For even more excitement, go a step beyond bringing props to introduce a story—actually *become* a character in the book! Come to the group dressed as a character with the storytime selection in hand. Children will love to hear Mother Goose reading her famous rhymes or the Gingerbread Man telling about his great adventure.

Children's Choice

While there will be times when you'll want to read specific books during storytime to correlate with a theme or time of year, consider having Children's Choice storytimes as well. Give each student a turn to bring a book from home to share with the class or to choose one from your classroom collection. If you have a large collection, fill a basket with several choices and have a student choose from the preselected group of books. You'll be amazed at their increased attention and desirable behavior when your children have a choice!

Could I Have A Volunteer?

Try some audience participation at storytime. Have students make sound effects, use instruments, perform motions, or dramatize characters as you read a story. For example, when you read a version of *The Three Billy Goats Gruff,* have volunteers tap wooden blocks each time a goat goes "trip-trapping" over the bridge. Add the swishy-swashy sounds and tiptoe movements to *We're Going On A Bear Hunt* retold by Michael Rosen (Simon And Schuster Children's) to really make the story come to life. Be creative! Almost any book has the potential for a stellar performance!

Be Our Guest

Create storytime suspense periodically with mystery-guest storytellers. Invite older children and adults to bring a favorite story to share with your little ones (or select appropriate stories for them). Consider having a high-school civic group adopt your class as book buddies. Or invite appropriate professionals to read to your group during specific theme units. For example, have a police officer read a safety favorite such as *Officer Buckle And Gloria* by Peggy Rathmann (G. P. Putnam's Sons). Or, during a study of weather, have your local news channel's meteorologist come by and read a weather story. Don't forget to include students' parents, too! The possibilities for storytelling guests are endless!

Perfectly Preschool Read-Alouds

Enhance storytime anytime with one or more of these appealing, age-appropriate books. Some feature repetitive text that invites youngsters to join right in. Some lend themselves to drama, encouraging little ones to imitate movements expressed in language. Some are easily adaptable to innovations and extensions. Some are just wonderful stories. But all are guaranteed kid pleasers!

Are You My Mother?
Written & Illustrated by P. D. Eastman
Published by Random House Books For
    Young Readers

Asleep, Asleep
Written by Mirra Ginsburg
Illustrated by Nancy Tafuri
Published by Greenwillow Books

Barnyard Banter
Written & Illustrated by Denise Fleming
Published by Henry Holt And Company, Inc.

Brown Bear, Brown Bear, What Do You See?
Written by Bill Martin, Jr.
Illustrated by Eric Carle
Published by Henry Holt And Company, Inc.

The Carrot Seed
Written by Ruth Krauss
Illustrated by Crockett Johnson
Published by HarperCollins Children's Books

Clap Your Hands
Written & Illustrated by Lorinda Bryan Cauley
Published by The Putnam Publishing Group

Dinosaurs, Dinosaurs
Written & Illustrated by Byron Barton
Published by HarperCollins Children's Books

Goodnight Moon
Written by Margaret Wise Brown
Illustrated by Clement Hurd
Published by HarperCollins Children's Books

Growing Vegetable Soup
Written & Illustrated by Lois Ehlert
Published by Harcourt Brace & Company

Guess How Much I Love You
Written by Sam McBratney
Illustrated by Anita Jeram
Published by Candlewick Press

Here Are My Hands
Written by Bill Martin, Jr., & John Archambault
Illustrated by Ted Rand
Published by Henry Holt And Company, Inc.

In The Small, Small Pond
Written & Illustrated by Denise Fleming
Published by Henry Holt And Company, Inc.

It Looked Like Spilt Milk
Written & Illustrated by Charles G. Shaw
Published by HarperCollins Children's Books

Jamberry
Written & Illustrated by Bruce Degen
Published by HarperCollins Children's Books

Jump, Frog, Jump!
Written by Robert Kalan
Illustrated by Byron Barton
Published by Greenwillow Books

Little Blue And Little Yellow
Written & Illustrated by Leo Lionni
Published by Mulberry Books

*The Little Mouse, The Red Ripe Strawberry,
    And The Big Hungry Bear*
Written by Don and Audrey Wood
Illustrated by Don Wood
Published by Child's Play (International) Ltd

Lunch
Written & Illustrated by Denise Fleming
Published by Henry Holt And Company, Inc.

Mouse Paint
Written & Illustrated by Ellen Stoll Walsh
Published by Harcourt Brace & Company

The Napping House
Written by Audrey Wood
Illustrated by Don Wood
Published by Harcourt Brace & Company

Peanut Butter And Jelly: A Play Rhyme
Illustrated by Nadine Bernard Westcott
Published by Puffin Books

Peter's Chair
Written & Illustrated by Ezra Jack Keats
Published by HarperCollins Children's Books

Piggies
Written by Don and Audrey Wood
Illustrated by Don Wood
Published by Harcourt Brace & Company

Pumpkin Pumpkin
Written & Illustrated by Jeanne Titherington
Published by Greenwillow Books

Quick As A Cricket
Written by Audrey Wood
Illustrated by Don Wood
Published by Child's Play (International) Ltd

Rosie's Walk
Written & Illustrated by Pat Hutchins
Published by Simon And Schuster Children's

The Runaway Bunny
Written by Margaret Wise Brown
Illustrated by Clement Hurd
Published by HarperCollins
    Children's Books

Silly Sally
Written & Illustrated by Audrey Wood
Published by Harcourt Brace & Company

Ten, Nine, Eight
Written & Illustrated by Molly Bang
Published by Greenwillow Books

Time For Bed
Written by Mem Fox
Illustrated by Jane Dyer
Published by Harcourt Brace & Company

The Very Busy Spider
Written & Illustrated by Eric Carle
Published by Philomel Books

The Very Hungry Caterpillar
Written & Illustrated by Eric Carle
Published by Philomel Books

The Very Quiet Cricket
Written & Illustrated by Eric Carle
Published by Philomel Books

We're Going On A Bear Hunt
Retold by Michael Rosen
Illustrated by Helen Oxenbury
Published by Simon And Schuster Children's

Where The Wild Things Are
Written & Illustrated by Maurice Sendak
Published by HarperCollins Children's Books

Who Said Moo?
Written by Harriet Ziefert
Illustrated by Simms Taback
Published by HarperCollins Children's Books

Whose Mouse Are You?
Written by Robert Kraus
Illustrated by Jose Aruego
Published by Simon And Schuster Children's

Clip Art For Circle Time

cloudy

rainy

snowy

sunny

Special Day

Birthday

DAILY NEWS

Gross-Motor Magic

This magical mix of gross-motor activities will have your little ones jumping, hopping, dancing, wiggling, and bouncing to the beat!

ideas contributed by Marie Cecchini and Linda Gordetsky

Creepy Crawlers

Youngsters will go buggy over this cooperative game! Divide students into pairs. Have one child in each pair stand behind her partner. Direct each pair to get into a crawling position. Instruct the child in back to grasp her partner's ankles. Play some slow music; then challenge the pairs to crawl forward, moving as one. Stop the music; then have the child in the front switch positions with the child in the back. Further challenge students by making groups of three or four children.

STUCK LIKE GLUE

Your little ones will be using their bodies and imaginations to get into these sticky situations. Divide youngsters into pairs. Invite each pair to use imaginary paintbrushes to brush glue over their bodies. Stand away from the group; then give directions, such as, "Stick your elbow to your partner's knee," or "Stick your hand to your partner's head." When each pair is stuck together, challenge them to walk to you; then wash away the glue by pouring an imaginary pail of water over the top of them. Now, that's some super glue!

MOVEMENT MESSAGES

Movement is the message your youngsters will hear when answering this call. Seat students in a group circle. Supply a child with a toy telephone. Using a second toy phone, place a call to the child; then leave a movement message for that child to give to another child in the group. For example, say, "Tell Tanner to jump three times." After the movement message has been completed, the child performing the movement is passed the phone and he receives the next message. Continue play until each child has had an opportunity to answer the phone and perform a movement.

> Tell Tanner to jump three times.

Walkin' Shoes

Your little ones will be putting their best feet forward in this fun movement activity. In advance enlist the help of parents to collect a variety of different kinds of shoes, such as bowling shoes, western boots, ballet slippers, tap shoes, and more. Place the shoe collection in a box. During a group time, invite a student to put on his choice of shoes. Ask him to show the group how a person wearing that kind of shoe would move. For example, a ballerina wearing ballet shoes may walk on tiptoe, or a cowboy wearing boots may move up and down like he is riding a horse.

Extend this into a whole-group activity by directing students to walk in a suggested way. Say something like "Pretend you are wearing clown shoes. Walk like a clown would walk." Or "Pretend you are wearing ice skates. Move like an iceskater." Your students will love walking in these imaginary shoes!

ANIMAL ANTICS

Your little ones will move like animals in this cooperative game. Prepare by cutting pictures of familiar animals from magazines. Glue each picture onto a sheet of tagboard; then laminate them for durability. Cut each picture in half using a different cutting line, such as a zigzag, straight, or curved line.

To play, provide each student with half of a picture. Encourage each youngster to find her partner by locating the child who has the matching picture half. When each child has found her partner, challenge the pair to work together to dramatize movements that could be made by their pictured animal. As the pair is moving, invite the remainder of the group to guess the name of the pictured animal.

ROAR!

Donnie

This music makes me feel happy.

And The Beat Goes On

Get youngsters moving and grooving to a musical beat. Collect a variety of rhythm instruments; then place them in a box. During a group time, name the instruments; then direct students to listen as you play each one. Encourage students to think about how each instrument's sound makes them feel, prompting them with descriptive words, such as *happy, sad, silly,* etc. Then invite a student to choose an instrument from the box. Have him play the instrument while the remainder of the group moves to the music. As the children are moving, snap a photo of each child; then write his completion to the sentence "This music makes me feel…" on a sheet of paper. Glue each child's photo onto his programmed paper. Compile the pages into a class book.

Limbo Like Me!

Everyone will want to play this limbo game similar to Simon Says. Ask a volunteer to hold one end of a broomstick while you hold the other end. Play some tropical music; then invite a child to be the limbo line leader. Challenge him to find a way to move under the broomstick without touching it, such as slithering, crawling, or hopping on one foot. Direct the remainder of the group to copy the leader's movement. When each child in the line has gone under, lower the stick. Have students continue to follow the leader under the stick. Play until a child touches the broomstick while going under. Then choose another limbo line leader.

HULA-HOOP® HUDDLE

Get ready for some Hula-Hoop® hysterics with this group game. Randomly place several Hula-Hoops® in an open area of your classroom. Invite students to march around the hoops as you play some music. Stop the music; then challenge each child to stand inside a hoop. Remove one hoop; then begin the music again. Continue play until there are no longer enough hoops to accommodate the group. What a happy hoopla!

Bouncing Balls

Invite your little ones to be bouncing balls when acting out the following poem:

I'm a little rubber ball,
(Squat on the floor.)

As round as round can be.
(Bend arms; rest hands on hips.)

Watch me bounce,
1…2…3!
(Jump up and return to a squatting position after each count.)

HERE TO THERE

Be prepared for lots of giggles and wiggles when you challenge students with this activity. Invite a small group of students to stand along a line in an open area of your classroom. Place a ball in front of each child. Direct each student to move the ball across a designated finish line some distance away, using a suggested body part. For example, have students move the balls using only their elbows. When each child has moved the ball over the finish line, direct him to move his ball back to the starting line using a different body part. What a workout!

FINE-MOTOR Fitness

Promote fine-motor fitness by adding some of these activities to your classroom centers. Your youngsters will be twisting, squeezing, pinching, and clipping as they exercise their small-motor muscles. Ready…set…let's work out!

by Lori Kent

FEED THE ALIEN

Your youngsters will practice hand-eye coordination and strengthen their finger muscles when they have a close encounter with this alien space creature. Remove the lid and label from an empty two-liter soda bottle. Use paint pens and other craft supplies to decorate the bottle to resemble an alien space creature. Place the bottle, a supply of marble moon rocks, and a pair of ice tongs on a tray; then place the tray in a center. Challenge a child to feed moon rocks to the alien by picking up marbles with the tongs, then dropping them into the bottle. For an added challenge, have the child count the moon rocks as he drops them into the bottle.

TRANSFER STATION

Tap into strengthening small hand muscles with this activity that is sure to cause a wave of excitement. Place two bowls and a sponge on a tray. Partially fill one bowl with water. Challenge a child to transfer the water from bowl to bowl by repeatedly dipping the sponge into the water, then squeezing it over the empty bowl. Have him continue dipping and squeezing until the water has been moved. Drip-drop!

CONFETTI COLLECTION

Put some punch into fine-motor practice with this creative center. Place colored construction-paper strips; a few bowls; and several seasonal, thematic, or round-shaped hole punchers in a center. A student makes confetti by holding a construction-paper strip over a bowl, then punching a series of holes into it. After each child has had several opportunities to make confetti, place the collected punches in your sensory table. Add bags of purchased confetti until the table is adequately stocked; then place some small scoops, spoons, cups, and containers in the table. Invite students to scoop and pour the confetti pieces.

RUBBER-BAND BOARDS

Inexpensive weaving looms (available at craft stores) are a great way for little ones to stretch their fine-motor skills. Place a few looms and a supply of colorful rubber bands in a center. To use a loom, a child loops a rubber band around a peg, stretches it across the loom, and then hooks it onto another peg. For your youngest preschoolers, provide fabric weaving loops to stretch across the loom. Youngsters will be delighted with the designs they create while building up their fine-motor muscles.

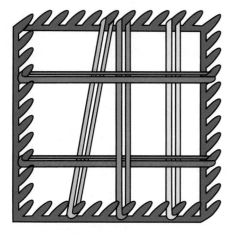

BOLT BOX

Your little mechanics will get down to the nuts and bolts of finger strengthening with this activity. Stock a toy toolbox with a few large and small nuts and bolts. Encourage a child to find the matches, then screw them together. When all the nuts and bolts have been paired, challenge the child to sort the bolts by size, then unscrew the pieces before returning them to the toolbox.

INSECT ZOO

Your little entomologists will go buggy for this center that strengthens finger muscles, classification, and sorting skills. Gather several jars with lids and a collection of at least three different types of small plastic insects. Store the insects in a basket. Remove the lids from the jars; then tape a different type of insect to the front of each jar. Place the jars, the lids, the basket of insects, and a pair of tweezers in a center. A child visiting this center picks up an insect with the tweezers, then drops it into the corresponding jar. When all the insects have been sorted, he screws the corresponding lid onto each jar. After viewing the insects, he counts the insects in each jar before returning them to the basket.

HOW DOES YOUR GARDEN GROW?

This center gets some green thumbs up for cultivating fine-motor skills. Cut out pictures of flowers from magazines and garden catalogs; then laminate them for durability. Hot-glue each picture onto a separate spring-type clothespin. Store the clothespin flowers in a basket. Place the basket and a length of plastic garden fencing in a center. To create a garden, a child clips her choice of flowers to the fence. As an added challenge, have her sort the flowers by color before clipping them onto the fence.

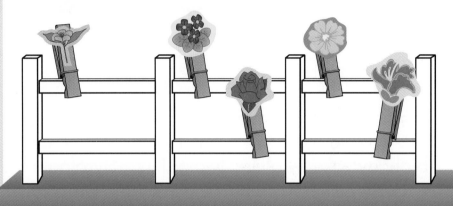

FUNNY FAMILIES

Plenty of giggles are in store when youngsters use their fine-motor skills to create this funny family of faces. To make a family of faces, insert a rectangle of felt into each of three embroidery hoops—one large, one medium, and one small. Trim away the excess felt from each hoop. Attach a self-adhesive Velcro® strip where each facial feature should be. Cut out eyes, noses, and mouths from magazines; then laminate them. Attach a Velcro® strip to the back of each one. Store the hoops and cutouts in a tub; then place the tub in a center. To create a family of faces, a youngster presses the desired features onto each hoop to create facial expressions.

Shoe Sort

Transform your dramatic-play center into a shoe store that will have fine-motor exercise all buckled up. Collect a variety of shoes with different closures, such as buckles, snaps, ties, hooks, and Velcro®. Place the shoes, shoehorns, a ruler, a mirror, and a small footstool in your dramatic-play center. Students are sure to enjoy measuring, fitting, and trying on the shoes; and the different types of closures will keep their fine-motor skills in step!

BIRTHDAY BLOWOUT

You won't have to send out invitations to get your little ones to come to this fine-motor center. Make a birthday cake by gluing two or three Styrofoam® circles together to create a cake shape. Decorate the cake with fabric, felt, ribbon, and trim pieces. Press several birthday-candle holders (available at craft or grocery stores) into the top of the cake. Remove the holders; then place a drop of glue in each hole. Replace the candle holders. When the glue is dry, place the cake and a supply of birthday candles in a center. To use the center, a child places a candle in each holder. For a variation, have a child pattern the candles or put a candle in the holder that is its color match.

HANGING OUT THE WASH

Your little ones will be proud to display their fine-motor fitness while hanging up laundry in this easy center. String a clothesline between two chairs. Place a quantity of spring-type clothespins and squares of colored felt near the clothesline. Invite your youngest preschoolers to clip the felt pieces to the clothesline. Challenge older students to clip the felt pieces on the clothesline in a color pattern. Red, blue, red, blue,…

OVER-AND-UNDER BASKETS

Little fingers will be sewing up some finger-strengthening exercise when creating these colorful baskets. To make one, a child weaves lengths of yarn, ribbon, or fabric strips through the holes in the sides of a plastic berry basket. When his weaving is complete, attach a pipe-cleaner handle to the basket. A-tisket, a-tasket, what a pretty basket!

DRIP-DROP POSIES

Youngsters will squeeze in lots of pincer-muscle practice while making these precious posies. Fill three plastic bowls with water; then add several drops of red, yellow, or blue food coloring to each bowl. Place an eyedropper in each bowl. Put the bowls and a supply of coffee filters on a work surface that has been protected with newspaper.

To make a flower, a child repeatedly drops different colors of food coloring onto a flattened coffee filter. When it is dry, gather the filter together in the center; then wrap one end of a green pipe cleaner around the gathered section as shown. If desired display these pretty posies in the baskets created in "Over-And-Under Baskets."

TOOTHPICK TOWERS

Your youngsters will be standing tall after constructing these toothpick towers that help build fine-motor skills. To make one, a child connects toothpicks and minimarshmallows together to make simple geometric shapes. He then uses additional toothpicks to connect the shapes together to form a tower. When his tower is complete, allow it to air dry until the marshmallows have hardened; then invite him to paint his tower with tempera paints.

SQUEEZE A SNACK

Here's a snack idea that your little ones are sure to grab on to. Into separate bowls place a variety of small snack items, such as Cheerios®, raisins, minimarshmallows, nuts, and fish crackers. Add a pair of small tongs to each bowl. Place the bowls and a class supply of paper cups in your cooking center. To prepare a snack, a child uses the tongs to place her desired snack items in her cup. For added challenge, tape a different numeral card from 1 to 5 on each bowl. A child then places the appropriate numbers of snacks in her cup. One, two, three. Snacktime is yummy!

TASTY NECKLACES

Your little ones are sure to sink their teeth into this fine-motor activity that strengthens finger muscles and hand-eye coordination skills. Stock a center with a quantity of o-shaped cereal and a class supply of string licorice. To make a necklace, a child strings a desired amount of cereal pieces onto his licorice. He then ties the ends together to make a nifty necklace that tastes as good as it looks.

JUICIN'

This center is the pick of the crop for strengthening hand muscles. Demonstrate for your youngsters how to use a citrus juicer by placing an orange half on top of a juicer; then squeeze and twist the orange to extract the juice. Place the juicer, two orange halves for each child, and a class supply of disposable cups in a center. A child visiting this center uses the juicer to extract the juice from two orange halves. He then pours the juice into a cup and drinks his delicious drink!

It's Rhythm-&-Rhyme, Moving-It Time!

Crank up the tunes and get grooving! Here's a collection of music and movement activities to set the mood for some "fun-tastic" learning!

ideas contributed by Carleen Coderre and Jean Feldman

RHYTHM RODS

These personalized rhythm sticks will prompt youngsters to rap and romp to their own beats. To make a set of rhythm rods, a child decorates two paper towel tubes with crayons, paint, or colored markers. Edge each end of each rod with a strip of colored vinyl tape to prevent the tubes from unraveling. Invite youngsters to create their own music by tapping the rods together like rhythm sticks, or using them like drumsticks on a tabletop, a chair seat, or the floor. Encourage student pairs to experiment with the different beats and tempos of various music styles, such as marches, rap, jazz, and rock-and-roll. It's rhythm time!

Symbolic Cymbals

These paper-plate cymbals will give youngsters the feel and excitement of using the real things—without the earsplitting noise level! Give each child two sturdy paper plates to decorate with markers or crayons. Using a real pair of cymbals, show youngsters how to clap the paper cymbals together to create a rhythm. Play some music with a steady beat; then have youngsters imitate your cymbal dance as you play the instrument in different positions, such as over your head, behind your back, to the right and left sides, and in front of your knees. Give each child an opportunity to play the real cymbals and lead the cymbal dance as you take the role of follower with the rest of the class.

SHAKIN' IT UP!

Youngsters will be bouncing to the beat with these shakers! For each child use a utility knife to cut a slit between the seams of a tennis ball. Show the child how to squeeze the ball to part the slit so that she can insert dried beans, popcorn kernels, small pebbles, or even a few small jingle bells into the ball. If desired hot-glue the slit together. Then invite the child to decorate her ball with glitter paint pens. To use, play or sing a lively tune to which youngsters can shake and bounce their musical balls. Hey, what's shakin'?

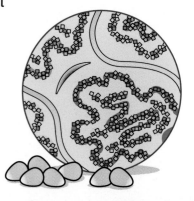

RHYTHMIC RAIN

Youngsters will experience the rhythm of the falling rain when they help create this colorful rain stick. In advance purchase a mailing tube at the post office. Have youngsters take turns hammering roofing nails at random into the tube. When the outside of the tube is dotted with nail heads, invite students to help cover it with colored, torn tissue paper dipped in liquid starch. After the tube dries, glue a lid to one end of the tube. Pour equal quantities of rice, aquarium gravel, popcorn kernels, and dried beans into the tube; then glue the lid onto the other end of the tube. To make the sound of rain, ask a child to slowly rotate the tube from end to end while the class sings songs about rain, such as "Rain, Rain, Go Away" and "It's Raining, It's Pouring."

JINGLE-BELL BRACELETS

These simple pieces of jewelry will have children jingling right along with any catchy tune. To make a bracelet, sew or tie several jingle bells onto a ponytail holder. Have each child slip the jingle-bell band onto her wrist or ankle; then play some rhythmic selections of music. Invite youngsters to shake their wrists or ankles, or to dance, while jingling to the beat of the music. Jingle bells! Jingle bells! Jingle all the way!

Nifty Noisemakers

There's nothing more fun than creating your own noisemakers for a special parade or production. In addition to making the instruments described on page 178 and on this page, here are a few more suggestions.

- String a few bells onto a length of yarn; then tie the ends together to create a jingling necklace or belt.

- Pour dried beans or popcorn kernels into a clean plastic soda bottle. Hot-glue the lid onto the bottle; then decorate the resulting shaker with paint pens.

- Cut wooden dowels into eight-inch lengths to create rhythm sticks. Squirt drops of different colors of craft paint into the lid of a shoebox; then roll the sticks back and forth through the paint. After the paint dries, use the colorful sticks to play colorful rhythms.

- Paint bulletin-board paper squares with glue; then sprinkle colored sand onto the squares. After the glue dries, attach the paper squares to wooden blocks to create sand blocks.

Self-Serve Center

Make music an accessible option to youngsters with this self-serve music center. Place a tape player and an assortment of tapes on a table. Attach a piece of green vinyl tape to the play button on the tape player and a piece of red vinyl tape to the stop button. Position a hat tree near the table on which to hang your rhythm instruments (purchased and child-made). Provide a box to hold the instruments that cannot be hung. Then introduce youngsters to the center, explaining how to operate the tape player and to care for the tapes and instruments. After a few rounds of full-service practice at the center, youngsters will be ready to go solo— or self-serve!

BODY MUSIC

Youngsters will be amazed to discover the musical instruments that are attached to their own bodies! Challenge students to explore the many different musical sounds they can make with the different parts of their bodies. First ask youngsters to create rhythmic sounds by breathing in different ways, then by clicking their tongues, smacking their lips, humming, and whistling. Then have them experiment with the many sounds their hands can make—clapping their hands together, snapping their fingers, and patting their hands against other body parts. Next encourage students to create different musical sounds with their feet. Finally invite youngsters to make music with their different body instruments while following the rhythms of some lively recordings. Now that's music!

THE BEAT GOES ON

This listening activity will give students some valuable practice in detecting rhythms and in following directions. To begin, play a musical selection with a steady, rhythmic beat. Begin a simple pattern to the rhythm of the music. For instance, you might clap your hands, then snap your fingers. Invite youngsters to join you in repeating the pattern. After a short time, begin another simple pattern, such as tapping your shoulders, then raising your arms. Continue in this manner throughout the selection, encouraging youngsters to watch and repeat each new pattern you introduce. Then, on the next round, you might increase the complexity of the pattern to three parts. If desired have students take turns creating patterns for the class to copy. This anytime activity has a beat that can't be beat!

Free To Fly

Freedom of expression is the way to fly in this activity. To prepare, tie two large scarves together. Explain that the scarves represent the wings of a bird, a butterfly, or any other flying creature that a child might want to imagine himself to be. Then play some peaceful, flowing music. Invite each child, in turn, to position the tied scarves across his back so that he can use them like wings. Encourage him to create his own flight pattern as he flies, flaps, flutters, and floats to express his interpretation of the music. Adjust the flight times of each student so that every child has an opportunity to fly.

Ribbon Rings

These colorful rings are the perfect dance companions and tools for movement exploration. To create a ribbon ring, tie several colorful ribbons in different widths and lengths to a shower-curtain ring or plastic bracelet. Then invite each youngster to rhythmically move her rings and her body to different styles of music. Or have youngsters mirror a leader as she moves with her ribbon ring to a simple rhythm, a musical selection, or no music at all. Students might also explore the movement of the wind usingtheir special rings.

Dancing Shoes

These special shoes can transform any child into a dreamy waltzer or a disco dynamo. To create a pair of dancing shoes, simply have a child personalize a pair of paper plates with markers or crayons. Then have him slip his feet into the imaginary shoes (stand on the plates). Play a musical selection and encourage each child to slide along the floor in his special shoes, keeping rhythm to the music. Challenge students to partner-dance as well as to try interesting slide-steps and backward and sideways moves. Be sure to play a variety of music as youngsters break in their imaginary dancing shoes.

The Circle Dance

What time is it? It's time to do the circle dance! Give each child an opportunity to show off his movement prowess while he's in the spotlight. To create the special stage, simply place a large plastic ring on the floor; then have your students form a larger, loose circle around the ring. Invite a child to stand inside the ring while you lead the class in singing this song. While you sing encourage the child in the ring to dance, move, or even act as silly as he wishes. Then call a different child to switch places with the first child, and repeat the song. Continue until each child has had a turn to do the circle dance.

(sung to the tune of "There's A Hole In The Bottom Of The Sea")

Oh, it's time to see the special circle dance!
Oh, it's time to see the special circle dance!
Oh, it's time! Oh, it's time!
Oh, it's time to see the special circle dance!

THE ZOO CREW

A real trip to the zoo might be in order after youngsters perform the zany actions to this song.

(sung to the tune of "Here We Go Round The Mulberry Bush")

Let's all go to the city zoo, the city zoo, the city zoo.
Let's all go to the city zoo to see what the animals do.

The kangaroo goes hop, hop, hop. Hop, hop, hop.
   Hop, hop hop.
The kangaroo goes hop, hop, hop. And we can do it, too!

Each time you repeat the song, replace the animal name and action with one of the following. Or make up your own animals and actions to insert into the song.

The elephant swings his trunk up high...
The monkey swings from tree to tree...
The lion roars and walks on fours...
The giraffe stretches his neck to eat...
The brown bear prances on two feet...

HOWDY, PARTNER

Promote social skills and cooperation with this lively activity. Instruct your class to form student pairs; then sing this song. As you sing have the partners perform the named action. After the last line, have youngsters find a different partner, then perform the action named in the next verse. Sing the song as many times as desired, inserting a different action—such as *tiptoe, jump, hop, gallop,* or *stomp*—each time you repeat the song.

(sung to the tune of "Skip To My Lou")

[Skip] around the room with me.
[Skip] around the room with me.
[Skip] around the room with me.
Won't you be my partner?

The Whole World IS A STAGE

Youngsters will have many opportunities to express their creative sides with these dramatic-play activities. From acting out songs to playing pirates, your youngsters will learn that in preschool, the whole world is a stage!

ideas contributed by Carrie Lacher

THIS IS THE WAY WE GO TO SCHOOL

Every child will have experiences to draw upon for this activity. During a group time, read aloud *This Is The Way We Go To School* by Edith Baer (Scholastic Inc.). Discuss the different means of transportation mentioned in the book; then ask students, "How did you get to school today?" Write their responses on a sheet of chart paper. Guide children in selecting classroom items to use as appropriate props to help them act out the different means of transportation listed on the chart. For example, arrange chairs in rows to create a bus. Transform a large cardboard box into a car. Or place a length of bulletin-board paper on the floor to resemble a sidewalk. When each child has had an opportunity to act out how he got to school, extend the activity by inviting youngsters to act out some of the other means of transportation from Baer's book.

PRESCHOOL EXPRESS

Grab a ticket and get on board for some dramatic-play fun that is sure to keep your little conductors on the learning track. Collect a variety of large cardboard boxes. Place the boxes on the floor in your group area. During a group time, show students photos of trains and locomotives, pointing out important features such as wheels and doors. Supply students with craft materials, such as markers, construction paper, scissors, and glue. Invite students to decorate the boxes to resemble train cars. When the cars are complete, line up the boxes end-to-end to create a long train. Make a dining car by adding some play food to one of the boxes; then add some stuffed-animal passengers to the other cars. Invite youngsters to climb on board and chug away on an imaginary train ride. Toot, toot! Off we go!

SONG DRAMA

Your little ones will be Broadway-bound after performing in this musical extravaganza! Write the words to some favorite songs on a length of bulletin-board paper; then post the chart near your group area. Sing the songs with your students; then brainstorm ideas about how the words to each one might be dramatized and what props may be needed. Write youngsters' responses next to the appropriate phrases on the chart. Then collect the needed materials using classroom supplies, family donations, or thrift-store purchases. After the props have been collected, encourage one small group of children at a time to dress up in their choice of play clothes. Encourage them to act out the lyrics of one song as the remainder of the group sings. Continue with the remaining groups and songs until your musical revue is finished. La-la-la-la-la!

Row, row, row your boat.

POET'S CORNER

Introduce your youngsters to the magic of poetry by having them dramatize their own poems. Program a sheet of paper with the poem framework shown; then duplicate a page for each student. During a group time, brainstorm a list of different things students can pretend to be, such as an elephant, a princess, a tree, etc. Then, working with each individual student, write her responses as she completes each sentence. After completing her poem, encourage her to act it out, using props if she desires. When each child has had an opportunity to create a poem and dramatize it, place the poems in a box labeled "Poetry Play." During center time encourage students to select their own or other poems from the box to dramatize.

I am a cat .
I can arch my back .
I can meow .
I feel soft .
I smell like fish .
I am playful .
I am orange .
I am a cat .

I am a [person, place, or thing].
I can [movement].
I can [sound].
I feel [texture].
I smell [scent].
I am [emotion].
I am [color].
I am a [repeat first line].

ALL IN THE FAMILY

Family fun will take center stage when you add a family prop box to your dramatic-play area. Cover a large cardboard box with bulletin-board paper. Cut pictures of family members and family groups from magazines; then glue them onto the box. Collect an assortment of men's, women's and children's dress-up clothes and shoes. Include a baby doll, baby clothes, a blanket, and a bottle in your collection. Place all the items in the box. Introduce the items in the family prop box to your students; then place the box in your dramatic-play center. Soon your little ones will be role-playing family situations. There may be no place like home—but this center comes close!

SET THE SCENE

Add new dimension to your little ones' dramatic play with simple backdrops. Use a black marker to draw an outline of a scene, such as a row of houses, on a length of bulletin-board paper. Don't worry about your art ability; your little ones will think you're a great artist! As you draw, encourage students to suggest details for you to add, such as flowers, mountains, and trees. When the outline is complete, invite your students to color in the scene using markers, crayons, or paints. Attach the backdrop to a wall in your dramatic-play center. When you are ready to change the focus of the center, roll the paper into a scroll; then secure it with a rubber band. Draw a new scene to coordinate with your current theme or encourage youngsters to explore a different topic in their dramatic play. Keep the scrolls for use by next year's class or perhaps for a repeat performance of a favorite theme.

FANTASY HATS

These fantasy hats are sure to capture your little ones' fancies. Make a hat for each child by cutting an 18-inch circle from white bulletin-board paper. Roll the circle into a cone; then secure the edge with tape. Have each student embellish his hat using a variety of craft supplies, such as glitter, stickers, and ribbons. Invite students to wear their hats with chosen dress-up items when they play in your dramatic-play center.

TREASURE TROVE

Ahoy, matey! Your little pirates will love hunting for this treasure! Cover a lidded or hinged cardboard box with wood-grained Con-Tact® paper to resemble a treasure chest. Make silver and gold nuggets by placing small stones into a resealable sandwich bag to which a squirt of metallic paint has been added. Shake the bag until the stones are covered with paint; then spread them onto newspaper to dry. Make coins by gluing gold or silver foil giftwrap to sheets of construction paper, then cutting circles from the paper. Place the nuggets and coins into the box along with a variety of beaded necklaces and craft jewels. Place the treasure chest in your dramatic-play center. Your youngsters will soon unlock the wealth of creative opportunities this treasure box holds!

FASHION CATALOG

Fashion fever will strike your students when you place this couture catalog in your dramatic-play center. To make a catalog, take a photo of each student wearing his choice of clothing items from your dramatic-play center. When the film has been developed, write each child's description of how he is dressed on the bottom of his photo. For example, a child might pretend to be dressed as a fireman, a ballet dancer, or a mom. Place the photos into a small photo album. Show the album to your students, noting how each child is dressed. Then place the album in your dramatic-play center for children's reference. For a timely twist, take photos of children wearing seasonal items of clothing; then place those pictures in the catalog. This photo album is sure to spark little ones' interest and keep those imaginations working!

ballerina   cowboy

COOL COMBOS

For a dramatic change of pace, combine other classroom centers with your dramatic-play center. For example, add a water table and invite youngsters to wash dishes or doll clothes. Or provide a collection of building blocks for making baby beds and furniture. Or place a basket of favorite books in your dramatic-play center and encourage little ones to "read" to doll babies or act out the stories.

Invite youngsters to suggest creative ways to combine different centers with the dramatic-play center. You'll be surprised at what their active imaginations will cook up!

BABY DAY

Your little ones will coo with delight when they spend a day being babies. In preparation for your scheduled Baby Day, send home a note with each child requesting that parents send in a baby picture of their child. Mount the pictures onto a sheet of tagboard; then write each child's name under her photo. Hang the poster on a wall near your group area. Place baby blankets, bottles, baby toys, doll-sized diapers, and dolls in your dramatic-play center.

On the scheduled day, invite a mother and baby to visit your classroom. Remind students of the delicacy of babies and stress gentle hands and soft voices. Challenge youngsters to remember what it was like being a baby. Then have students guess the name of the baby in each photo on the baby poster. During center time, invite students to role-play mommies, daddies, and babies. Complete your Baby Day by serving snacks in clean, sanitized baby-food jars and baby "sippy" cups. Then, during rest time, invite youngsters to lie down on baby blankets spread on the floor as you play a tape of soothing lullabies. Night, night, babies.

CANINE CAPERS

Your little pups will be putting on the dog in this activity. Prepare a doggie headband for each child by cutting out two ear shapes from white construction paper. Staple the ears onto a construction-paper headband. Invite each student to color his headband using the colors of his choice. When he is finished, fit the headband to his head; then staple the ends together. Use face paints to add canine facial features and spots to each child's face.

Have students wear their headbands as they howl along to "How Much Is That Doggie In The Window?" or any favorite song about dogs. Then encourage your little ones to act out doggie behaviors from tail waggin' to hole diggin'. Hot-diggety-dog!

Exploratory ART

Invite little ones to explore and create with these ideas for process art.

ideas contributed by Tricia Daughtry, Holly Dunham, and John Funk

Smash Painting

This art idea will be a smash with your preschoolers! Set out tempera paints, paper, margarine-tub lids, and a few toy hammers or mallets. Invite a child to drip a bit of paint onto his paper, place a margarine-tub lid over the paint, and tap the lid. Have him lift the lid and observe how the paint has moved. Invite him to use other paint colors and repeat the process as many times as he desires.

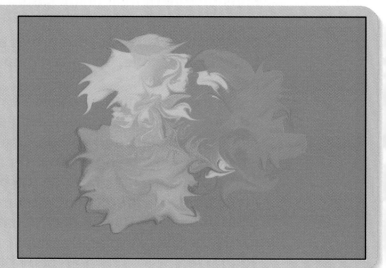

Putt 'n' Paint

Encourage little ones to visit the greens—and blues and reds and yellows—with this innovative painting technique! In advance, round up some old golf balls and a putter from a child's plastic set of golf clubs. Cover a sidewalk or blacktop area with newspaper. Lay a long length of bulletin-board paper on top of the newspaper. Finally prepare a few shallow pans of tempera paint in various colors.

To paint, a child dips a golf ball into a color of paint and sets it down on one end of the paper. He taps the ball with the putter to make a paint trail down the paper. When every child has had an opportunity to putt 'n' paint, display your class's creative effort in a hallway or as a bulletin-board background.

Carpet-Square Prints

Looking for a new art idea? Look down—on the floor! Carpet squares will provide interesting textures for paint prints. Visit your local carpet or home-improvement store, and ask for some carpet samples. Try to gather a few different textures, such as berber, sculptured, and plush carpeting. Use a utility knife to cut the samples into smaller, more manageable squares or rectangles. Set out large sheets of construction paper or pieces of bulletin-board paper and shallow trays of tempera paint. Encourage youngsters to press the carpet samples into paint, then onto paper. Invite them to compare the prints created by different textures of carpeting.

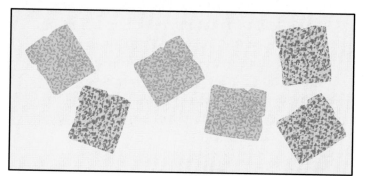

Egg Roll

This alternative to traditional marble painting is perfect to use for Easter or during a unit on eggs. In advance, hard-boil an egg for each child. Place a sheet of drawing paper in a box lid. Drizzle a little tempera paint on the paper; then invite a child to lay his egg in the box lid. Have him gently tilt and rock the box lid to make the egg roll through the paint. Continue by adding other paint colors until the child is satisfied with the design. When finished, he'll have both a painting and a colored egg!

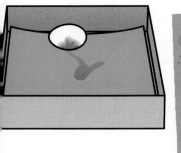

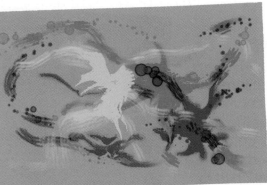

Wrap It Up

Here's an art supply that makes both a great painting surface *and* a great painting tool: bubble wrap!

* Use a length of bubble wrap in place of fingerpainting paper.

* Clip a piece of bubble wrap to your easel.

* Make a print from a painted bubble-wrap design by pressing a sheet of drawing paper over it.

* Create a bubble-wrap mitt. Just wrap a length of bubble wrap around a child's hand and staple it to fit snugly. Then invite the child to use the bubble-wrap mitt to daub paint onto paper to create a design.

Texture Zoo

Most preschoolers adore animal art. Show yours how to create a zoo full of animals using interesting textured materials. Set out pieces of materials in all kinds of textures, such as fake fur, corrugated cardboard, satin, cotton batting, sandpaper, and corduroy. Also provide glue, scissors, and craft materials, such as pipe cleaners, wiggle eyes, buttons, and construction-paper scraps. Cut a strip of sturdy tagboard for each child.

As each child visits the art area, have him choose a few textured pieces to glue onto his tagboard strip. Then have him use craft materials to turn each piece of textured material into a creature. Your students' creativity will amaze you as they add eyes, noses, ears, and even tails to their critters. When all the glue has dried, display the strips side by side along a wall. "Zoo-tiful!"

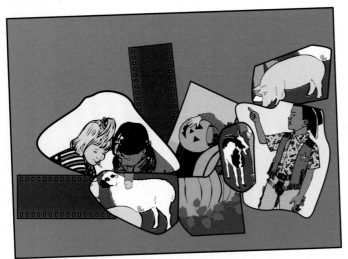

Photo Collage

What to do with all those not-so-great photos from that last roll of film? Invite your young artists to use them for a collage. Photos and negatives will provide new cutting and gluing experiences. Set out a supply of discarded photos and negatives, glue, scissors, and paper. (Do not use instant photos for this project.) Encourage children to cut and glue the photos and negatives to make designs of their choice.

Gorgeous Gift Wrap

Don't toss those wrapping-paper scraps! Recycle them into beautiful works of art. Provide children with gift-wrap scraps, scissors, glue, and construction paper. Invite a youngster to tear or cut the gift wrap as she desires, then glue the pieces onto a sheet of construction paper. Provide diluted tempera paint or diluted colored glue, and invite the child to paint over her collage design.

Art On A Theme

Encourage little ones' classification skills as you gather supplies for a thematic collage. Here are a few ideas to get you started. No doubt you and your students can think of other art themes.

Kitchen Art

- pieces of sponges
- pieces of scrub pads
- pieces of towels/dishrags
- food labels
- plastic wrap
- aluminum foil

Office Art

- rubber bands (whole and in pieces)
- paper clips (various sizes and colors)
- clear and colored tape
- sticky notes
- brads
- index cards
- adhesive labels

Sewing Art

- buttons
- pieces of rickrack
- pieces of elastic
- pieces of Velcro®
- pieces of lace
- fabric scraps
- zippers

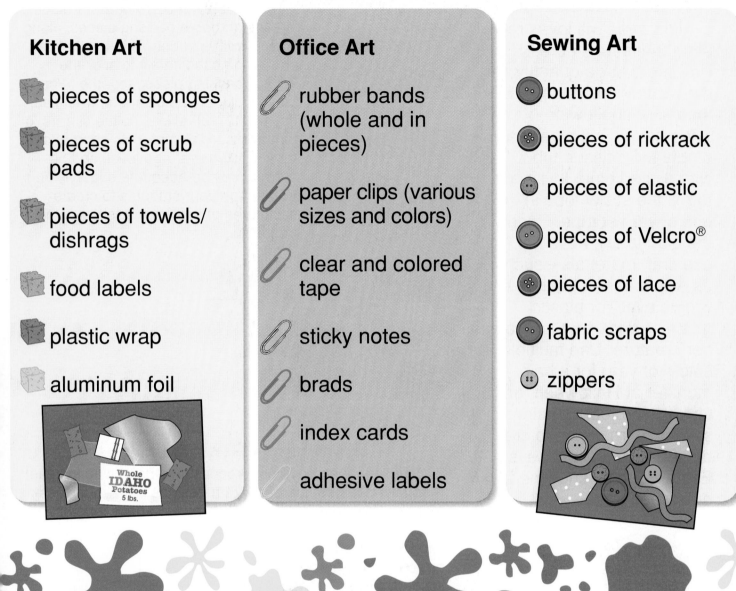

Jar Art

Turn a collage into a three-dimensional project in a flash! Instead of having youngsters glue collage items onto a sheet of paper, invite them to glue items onto a clean, empty jar. Baby-food jars are great for this, or you can supersize the artwork by having little ones use peanut-butter or pickle jars.

Hairy Monsters

Little ones will love creating these fun figures. Prepare a large quantity of cut yarn pieces and place them in a shallow box. Then have a child paint an empty toilet-tissue tube with diluted glue. Invite her to roll the sticky tube in the box of yarn scraps. Once the glue is dry, have her use craft materials—such as pipe cleaners, buttons, wiggle eyes, or plastic gems—to add features to her creature. Use multiple colors of yarn for a hairy monster at Halloween, or vary the project by using specific yarn colors to create Thanksgiving turkeys, Easter rabbits, snowmen, or leprechauns.

Stick With Styrofoam®

Gather up those annoying packing peanuts and put them to good use! Set out a supply of Styrofoam® or biodegradable packing pieces, along with a variety of items that can be used safely to stick the packing pieces together. You could include pipe cleaners, twist-ties, tiny twigs, craft sticks, coffee stirrers, or toothpicks. (Use materials appropriate for your students' age level, and be sure to provide adequate supervision.) Encourage your students to create sculptures of their own designs with the materials.

Starched-Yarn Designs

Don't get hung up about process art—hang it up instead! Display these neat starched-yarn designs from your classroom ceiling. To make one, dip yarns of various lengths, colors, and thicknesses into liquid starch. Then arrange these pieces inside a plastic lid lined with waxed paper. Let the design dry at least overnight. (It may take a few days to dry, depending on the thickness of the yarn and how saturated it becomes. If necessary, turn the design over partway through the drying time.) When the design is stiff and dry, remove it from the waxed paper. Use fishing line to hang it from the ceiling.

Hot-Glue Designs

Give youngsters experiences with making rubbings with this easy-to-prepare project. Simply heat up your hot-glue gun; then use it to make designs on paper. Create a random design, or actually trace over a picture with the hot glue. Set the papers aside to cool and dry. Then tape the designs to an art table, and set out a supply of copy paper and peeled crayons. A child may lay a sheet of copy paper over a hot-glue design and rub across the paper with the side of a crayon. Ooh, it's magic!

Refrigerator-Magnet Masterpieces

For another fun rubbing project, gather up some interesting refrigerator magnets. Check around your house and at garage sales, or ask parents to send some in. Look for magnets in definite shapes or with raised details that will make interesting rubbings. Set out the magnets, a few cookie sheets, copy paper, and peeled crayons. To make a rubbing, a child arranges the magnets of his choice on a cookie sheet and then lays a sheet of paper over the magnets. He rubs with the side of a crayon to make a unique picture.

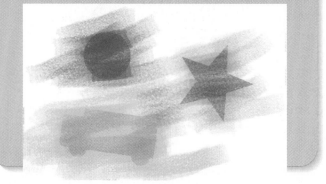

Art-Center Additions

Keep little ones interested and excited about your art center by changing the available materials on a regular basis. Of course, you'll want to keep the basics (paint, crayons, play dough, and paper) available at all times. But look for new and different things to pique your young artists' interests. Have you tried any of the following?:

- cotton swabs
- packing peanuts
- cotton balls or batting
- Easter grass
- gift-wrap stuffing
- shape-punched confetti
- Styrofoam® balls and cups
- whole and cut-up toilet-tissue tubes and paper-towel rolls
- drinking straws
- paint additions, such as spices, salt, or glitter

RECIPES
FOR ARTS AND CRAFTS

BAKING DOUGH

2 cups flour
1 cup salt
water

Mix the dry ingredients; then add enough water to create a workable dough. Invite children to sculpt figures or roll and cut the dough with cookie cutters. Bake the dough at 300°F for 1 to 1 1/2 hours (depending on the thickness of each figure). Finished products can be painted.

MILK PAINT

evaporated milk
food coloring

Divide one or more cans of evaporated milk evenly among several containers. Add a few drops of a different color of food coloring to each container and mix until the desired shades are achieved. Have youngsters paint with this mixture on construction paper to create a creamy, pastel look.

MAGIC CRYSTALS

2 cups water
2 cups Epsom salts
food coloring (optional)

In a saucepan, combine the water and Epsom salts, and bring to a boil. Stir the mixture and allow it to cool. If desired, add a few drops of food coloring. Have students paint with this mixture on construction paper. The paint will dry to create clear or colored crystals.

DECORATIVE DYE

1 tablespoon rubbing alcohol
food coloring
rice or pasta

In a small, tightly lidded container, put one tablespoon of rubbing alcohol and a few drops of food coloring. Place rice or pasta into the mixture and seal the lid. Shake the container gently for one minute. Spread out the dyed objects on paper towels or newspaper until dry.

TEACHER-MADE PLAY DOUGH

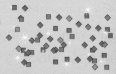

1 cup flour
1/2 cup salt
2 teaspoons cream of tartar
1 cup water
1 teaspoon vegetable oil
food coloring

Mix the dry ingredients together. Then add the remaining ingredients and stir. In a heavy skillet, cook the mixture for two to three minutes, stirring frequently. Turn the dough onto a lightly floured surface and knead it until it becomes soft and smooth. Mix up a separate batch of dough for each color desired. Store the dough in an airtight container.

COLORED GLUE

food coloring
white glue

Add a few drops of a different color of food coloring to each of several empty squeeze bottles. Gradually add glue, using a drinking straw to stir the glue until it's evenly tinted.

EXTRA-BRIGHT TEMPERA PAINT

2 cups dry tempera paint
1 cup liquid soap (clear or white works best)
1 cup liquid starch

Mix the paint and soap; then add starch and stir. If the mixture becomes too thick, add more liquid soap. Store the paint in a coffee can with a plastic lid.

BUBBLE MIXTURE

1/4 cup dishwashing liquid
1/2 cup water
1 teaspoon sugar
food coloring (optional)

Mix the dishwashing liquid, water, and sugar together in a container. If color is desired, mix in a few drops of food coloring.

CORN SYRUP PAINT

light corn syrup
food coloring

Divide one or more bottles of corn syrup evenly among several containers. Add a few drops of a different color of food coloring to each container and mix until the desired shades are achieved. This paint requires a few days of drying time.

NUTTY PUTTY

3 1/2 cups peanut butter
4 cups powdered sugar
3 1/2 cups corn syrup or honey
4 cups powdered milk
chocolate chips (optional)

Mix all ingredients except chocolate chips. Divide mixture into 15 to 20 portions, place into plastic bags, and refrigerate. After students wash their hands, have them mold and shape the dough on waxed paper. Use chocolate chips as decorations if desired. Students may eat their creations.

KOOL-AID® DOUGH

2 1/2–3 cups flour
1/2 cup salt
1 package unsweetened Kool-Aid®
1 tablespoon alum
2 cups boiling water
3 tablespoons corn oil
1 cup additional flour

Mix the first six ingredients into a dough. Using some or all of the additional flour, knead the dough until it reaches the desired consistency. Store the dough in an airtight container.

EASY PAPIER-MÂCHÉ

liquid starch
cold water
newspaper torn into strips

Mix equal parts of liquid starch and cold water. Dip the newspaper strips into the mixture before applying to a form of chicken wire or rolled newspaper.

SALT PAINT

2 teaspoons salt
1 teaspoon liquid starch
a few drops of tempera paint

Mix the ingredients together. The salt gives a frosted appearance to the paint.

COLORED GRITS

liquid tempera paint
grits

In a large bowl, mix the ingredients, being careful not to let the grits get too wet. Spread the mixture onto cookie sheets to dry for a day or two, stirring occasionally. Use as you would colored sand.

SHINY PAINT

1 part white liquid glue
1 part liquid tempera paint

Mix the ingredients. This paint will retain a wet look after it has dried.

SCIENCE INVESTIGATIONS

Young children are eager to learn and explore their environment. Capitalize on their natural curiosity while teaching some of the skills that real scientists use. Observing, comparing, classifying, and communicating are all important science process skills—and very appropriate for the preschooler who wants to learn about the world!

ideas contributed by Ann Flagg

OBSERVATION AND COMMUNICATION

Begin by teaching youngsters to use their five senses to gather information about the world. Observation is the foundation of all other science skills. And language development will happen naturally as children communicate and explain what they observe.

> I thought the white stuff was the same. But I tasted it and one was salt and the other one was sugar.

ACTIVITY 1

To prepare, duplicate the five-senses cards on page 205. Cut apart the cards and laminate them, if desired. Then place a bowl of sugar and a bowl of salt in front of a small group of children. Ask, "Do you think these two substances are the same? How can you find out?" Show the children the five-senses cards and lead them to use each of their senses one at a time to explore the substances. Ask the children first to listen to, then look at, then touch, then smell, and finally taste the salt and the sugar. Have each child state his findings in his own words.

PRESCHOOL SCIENCE TIP:

Begin your observation activities with a question and purpose that will keep children focused. Complete an observation activity in ten minutes or less to ensure success.

ACTIVITY 2

Gather three pairs of identical objects and two paper bags for this activity. (If desired, use objects that reinforce your current theme.) Place one item from each pair in one bag, and the matching items in the other bag. Then show the bags to a small group of children. Ask, "Can you find two objects that match using only your sense of touch?" Ask a volunteer to reach one hand into each bag and try to pull out a matching pair of objects without looking.

Vary this activity to address the sense of hearing by placing an object in a shoebox. Seal the box shut with tape. Have a small group of children pass the box around, shaking it to try to determine the identity of the object inside. Encourage each child to make a guess before opening the box to reveal the object.

ACTIVITY 3

In advance, program a sheet of paper with the words "I am touching Goop! Goop is _____!" Duplicate the page for each child in your class. Then cut each page into an abstract blob shape (taking care not to cut off any words).

Then follow the recipe below to make a batch of Goop. Give a small amount of Goop to each child and allow plenty of time for free exploration. Then encourage observations and communication by creating a class book of your preschoolers' impressions. Give each child a cut-out page and write her dictation on the blank line. If desired, have youngsters illustrate their ideas.

I am touching Goop! Goop is <u>smooth</u>!

GOOP

- food coloring
- 6 tablespoons water
- 10 tablespoons cornstarch

Add a few drops of food coloring to the water. Sprinkle the cornstarch into the water slowly. Mix until the Goop has an even consistency. It should run through your fingers, but feel solid if you slap the mixture. Adjust the amounts of water and cornstarch until you achieve the correct consistency. Store the Goop in an airtight container.

COMPARISON AND COMMUNICATION

Comparison involves using observation skills to find similarities and differences. Preschool children will be able to compare and contrast tangible items more easily than ideas and concepts. Communication skills will develop as youngsters explain the similarities and differences they observe.

ACTIVITY 1

In advance, purchase or ask parents to donate a bag of apples. Cut several apples into slices, so that you have enough for each child to have one slice. Prepare a language experience chart by duplicating the five-senses cards on page 205, then cutting out the cards and gluing them onto a sheet of chart paper. When you are ready to begin, distribute an apple slice to each child. Ask youngsters to use all five senses to examine the apple slices. Record their observations on your chart. Then use the recipe on this page and the remaining apples in your bag to prepare some applesauce. Give each child a taste of the warm applesauce and record their observations as they again use their five senses. Ask youngsters to explain how the cooked applesauce differs from the apple slices. How are the apple slices and applesauce the same?

Apple Slices		Applesauce
see	My slice is red on the outside. Tim	It looks kind of brown and white. Kia
hear	Apples are crunchy. Keisha	It's quiet. Laurie
touch	The apple skin feels smooth. Greg	

CHUNKY APPLESAUCE

- 5–6 apples, cored
- 1/2 cup water
- 3 tablespoons honey

Chop the apples and place the chunks in a saucepan with the water and honey. Boil, stirring occasionally, until the apples are soft. Remove from heat, let cool, and serve warm.

ACTIVITY 2

Partially fill your water table, several dishpans, or several buckets with tap water. Invite a small group of children to play in the water and observe it. Record their statements when you ask, "What do you know about water?" Then scoop some of the water into a container and tell the children you are going to place it in the freezer. Once the water is frozen, unmold it from the container into the empty water table or an empty dishpan. Ask, "What do you know about ice?" and record youngsters' answers as they observe and touch the giant ice cube. Reread the students' statements about water, and ask them to compare and contrast the ice and water.

Water is soft, but the ice is hard.

ACTIVITY 3

Basic graphing is a wonderful way for children to get a visual picture of a comparison. Graphs also integrate basic math skills and vocabulary (*more, less, same*) into a science lesson.

Simple horizontal and vertical bar graphs can be created on a chalkboard, a wall, or the floor of your classroom. Use the chalkboard, a length of bulletin-board paper, or even a shower curtain liner for a graph. Make graphing fun by using lots of different materials to create graphs (see "Great Graph Markers"). What to graph? Almost anything! See the list below to get you started.

THINGS TO GRAPH

- Children's favorites (breakfast foods, holidays, colors, etc.)
- Children's birth months
- Children's hair colors or eye colors
- Number of people in children's families
- Types or features of children's clothing (pants/skirts, zippers, buttons, etc.)
- Types of housing children live in (house, apartment, mobile home, etc.)
- Kinds of pets children own
- Number of seeds found in various fruits
- Results of a sink/float activity
- Yes/No questions (such as "Do you like peanut butter?" or "Do you have a sister?")

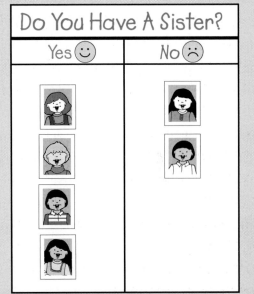

GREAT GRAPH MARKERS

- Real objects (fruit, shoes, crayons, etc.)
- Children's photos
- Sticky notes (quick and easy)
- Seasonal or thematic shape cutouts
- Linking cubes in towers
- Beads on strings
- Personalized shoeboxes in stacks
- Clothespins (clipped to the sides of a chart)

PRESCHOOL SCIENCE TIP:

When creating a graph, mark off same-sized spaces or place graph markers with identical spaces between them. Preschoolers who don't yet have the ability to compare numbers will be looking for the longest line or tallest tower, and can be misled if graph markers aren't placed appropriately.

CLASSIFICATION AND COMMUNICATION

Classification involves grouping and sorting according to common characteristics. Preschoolers will be able to practice this skill using concrete objects. As children group objects together and sort them out, encourage them to verbalize their reasoning.

ACTIVITY 1

Designate a table in your classroom as the Collection Center. Ask the children to help you create a collection by finding objects in your classroom or outdoors, or by bringing in items from home. You can make a collection of anything! Consider collecting signs of fall, signs of spring, toys with wheels, seeds, rocks, or insects. When a youngster places an item in the Collection Center, ask her to explain why it belongs in the collection.

After you've built a collection, invite the children to observe the characteristics of the various objects, and then sort them. Specify a characteristic by which to sort, such as *rough rocks/smooth rocks* or *toys with two wheels/toys with four wheels.* More advanced youngsters may be able to choose a sorting characteristic on their own.

ACTIVITY 2

An exploration of magnets will provide the perfect opportunity to practice classification skills. Gather some strong magnets and a variety of items, some that will be attracted by a magnet and some that will not. (See the lists on this page.) Label two Styrofoam® trays: one with a happy face and the word "Yes," and one with a sad face and the word "No." Invite the children to experiment with the magnets and the items. Have them sort the items as they work, placing the items on the appropriate trays.

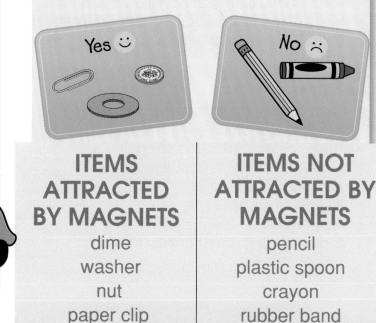

ITEMS ATTRACTED BY MAGNETS	ITEMS NOT ATTRACTED BY MAGNETS
dime	pencil
washer	plastic spoon
nut	crayon
paper clip	rubber band

PRESCHOOL SCIENCE TIP:

Small items such as those used for Activity 2 can be a choking hazard for preschoolers. Try placing tiny objects in a sealed glass jar. Invite children to place a strong magnet on the outside of the jar to test the attraction.

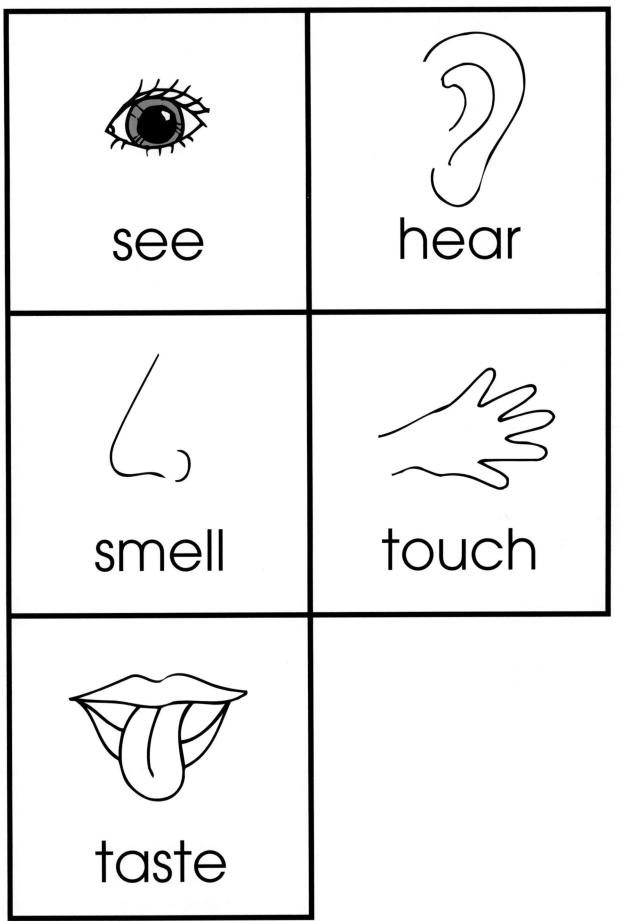

see

hear

smell

touch

taste

THE NATURE NICHE

Carve a niche into your schedule for nature investigations with these hands-on ideas. Then head outdoors for some enticing and exciting explorations!

ideas contributed by Lucia Kemp Henry and Mackie Rhodes

A Bug's-Eye View

Here's a fun way to engage youngsters in some grassy explorations. While outdoors, instruct each child to lie on his stomach and pretend to be a bug crawling through the grass. Ask him to examine the grass carefully as he crawls around, noting the many different things along the ground and on the grass blades. After returning to your classroom, have each child illustrate his observations and then glue a thinly stretched layer of Easter grass over his drawing. Display the title "A Bug's-Eye View" on a bulletin board; then exhibit each picture with the child's dictation on the display. Creep. Crawl. Create!

Casey

I saw a rock and a catepillar.

HOOP IT UP!

Ring up some valuable observation skills with this outdoor activity. Gather several plastic hoops, each in a different color; then cut out a large bulletin-board-paper circle corresponding to each hoop color. Position each hoop in a different outdoor space. For instance, one hoop might be placed in the grass, another in an area of soil, and another against a large tree trunk. Divide your class into the same number of groups as there are hoops; then have each group examine the area encompassed by its assigned hoop. Write students' observations on the corresponding circle cutout. Afterward have the class compare their observations of the outdoor areas.

IN THE GRASS:
—dirt under the grass
—ants crawling
—2 beetles
—little white flowers

Rock-A-Doodle-Doo!

Youngsters will crow about all the interesting discoveries they make when they play this game. Explain that while the class takes a nature walk, you will occasionally call out, "Rock-a-doodle-doo!" On this signal, an appointed group of students will locate and then carefully lift a small to medium-sized rock from its site. Without disturbing the area, the group will call out all its findings under the rock, such as worms, roots, bugs, or dead leaves. Then a group member will gently replace the rock. The class resumes its nature walk until you give the signal for another group.

A Tree In Season

Use this year-round activity to document the seasonal changes of a tree while creating a special portfolio of each youngster's fine-motor skills. To begin, select a tree on or near your school campus—preferably one that exhibits lots of interesting changes throughout the year. At the beginning of the school year, introduce your class to the special tree. Ask students to carefully observe and then illustrate the tree. Write each child's dictated observations on her page. At least once a month, have students return to observe the tree; then repeat the process above. At the end of the year, sequence and bind each child's illustrations between two construction-paper covers. Title the book "A Special Tree"; then share the book with the child's parents at the end-of-the-year conference, noting the child's progress in his fine-motor *and* observation skills. Like the tree's seasonal changes, the child's skill progression will be quite noticeable.

Maria 11-16-99

The tree has colors today!

Leaf Sort

What sort of fun can be had in this detail-oriented sorting activity? "Leave" it to youngsters to find out! To prepare, have students collect a large variety of fall leaves, either on your school's campus or at home. Place all the leaves into a basket; then attach a leaf representing each leaf type in the collection—such as oak, maple, or birch—to a separate box. Invite a small group to sort the leaves by type into the appropriate boxes. Then have them sort each leaf set by color onto corresponding sheets of construction paper. Finally have the group sort each color set by size. After sorting the leaves, challenge each youngster in the group to select a leaf, then describe it using a combination of attributes. For instance, the child might describe her leaf as "a big yellow oak leaf." Little ones will really fall for this idea!

oak

Creature Feature

Bring the small creatures of nature into the limelight with this activity. During a nature walk or any outdoor excursion, instruct students to observe as many different small creatures as possible, such as worms, beetles, flies, spiders, and ants. (You might provide hand lenses for students to use.) Then gather youngsters together for this movement exercise. To begin, call out the name of a creature discovered by your students. Ask each student who observed that creature to raise his hand. Then shine a flashlight at each of those students, one at a time. While shining the light on a child, have him imitate the movements of the creature; then instruct him to stop when you move the light onto another child. It's time for your critters to shine!

Nature Necklaces

These nature necklaces will provide a nifty way to practice matching and sorting skills. To make a necklace, hot-glue a nature item—such as a leaf, an acorn, a miniature pinecone, or a small stone—onto a tagboard circle. Punch a hole in the circle; then string a length of yarn through the hole to create a necklace. Give each child a necklace to wear while on an outdoor excursion. Ask the child to find an item to match the item on his necklace. During group time, invite each child to share his find with the class.

To use the necklaces in a sorting activity, simply hang several necklaces—each with a different item—on a corkboard. Position a box for each item under the corresponding necklace. Then give a child a collection of nature items to sort accordingly into the boxes.

Brainstorm Bonanza

On a nice warm day, warm up youngsters' imaginations with this idea. First have youngsters collect a large variety of nature items, such as sticks, small rocks, leaves, acorns, and flowers. During group time, show a sample of each nature item. Ask students to identify the item, then tell something about it. After sharing what they know about the item, invite youngsters into the world of imagination. Ask them to tell some things they might be able to do with the item. Give some thoughts of your own to get students started. For example, suggest that sticks can be used to build small houses, acorns might make a good substitute for marbles, and leaves can be used to tickle toes! After youngsters brainstorm some uses for nature items, take them and the collection of nature items outdoors for some imaginative play.

Shadow-Box Blocks

Build student interest in nature with the addition of these nature blocks to your block center. To create nature blocks, cut a few empty toaster-pastry boxes in half. Tape together any open or loose flaps. If desired, cover each box-half with colored construction paper or decorative Con-Tact® covering. Then hot-glue a small nature item inside each box. Place the shadow-box blocks in your block center. Encourage youngsters to use these blocks, in combination with the other blocks, to create structures and imaginative play scenes. Youngsters will amaze you with their natural creativity!

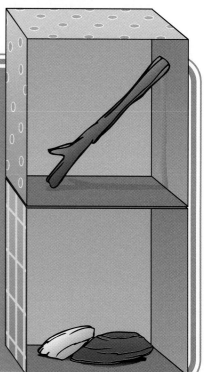

A Balancing Act

Estimating and counting are key elements in balancing out this small-group activity. To prepare, have students gather a collection of pinecones and acorns. Divide the class into several small groups; then give each group a pinecone. Invite each group, in turn, to place its pinecone on a simple balance scale; then challenge youngsters to estimate the number of acorns they believe will be needed to balance the scale. Write each member's estimate on a sheet of paper. Have each group member add an acorn, repeating the rounds until the scale is balanced; then have the group chorally count the acorns as a volunteer removes them one at a time from the scale. Did any student estimate correctly? Whose estimate was too high? Too low? After comparing the results for that group, repeat the activity with the next group.

Moving Right Along

If youngsters have spent any amount of time outdoors, they are certainly aware of the many movements of nature. Ask youngsters to share what they know about different outdoor things and how they move, such as leaves falling, sticks floating in water, snowflakes blowing in the wind, or a spider crawling on a twig. Write their comments on chart paper; then invite youngsters to engage in some creative movements of their own. To begin, read a child's comment from the chart. Ask youngsters to interpret that movement in their own expressive ways. For example, a student might pretend to be a leaf falling straight down from a tree or floating round and round before landing on the ground. Or he might be a spider crawling very slowly or quite rapidly up a twig. Ready? Let's move!

Water Wonders

Prompt students to explore the properties of certain items in water. Place a collection of nature items—such as sticks, pinecones, rocks, flowers, shells, and leaves—in a dishpan near your water table. Encourage small groups of students to use these items during their waterplay time. Challenge them to guess whether or not each item will float before it is placed in the water. After experimenting with the different items, invite each youngster to share her findings with her group. Ask her to give her explanation about why an item did or did not float.

Hmmm…wonder if this sweet-gum ball will float?

Our Three Environments

Help your class explore our three environments—land, water, and air—with a nature walk or a discussion supplemented with book or magazine pictures. On three separate sheets of chart paper, one labeled for each environment, write a student-generated list of things observed in that environment. Then place three sheets of construction paper on the floor: green for land, blue for water, and white for air. Whisper the name of a nature item (or creature) to a student volunteer; then have her stand on the paper representing the environment in which her item might be found. Ask the child to announce her item to the class; then invite students to decide whether that item might also be found in another environment. For instance, the child might choose the water (the blue paper) if her item were a duck, and the class might decide that a duck can also be found on the land and in the air. Continue in this manner until every child has had a turn.

Just Imagine...

Imaginations will soar...or crawl...or even float with this silly pretend activity. To begin, ask youngsters to close their eyes and listen carefully as you name an absurd imaginary scenario about an item found in nature. After a brief period of silence for thinking, invite youngsters to open their eyes and share their silly thoughts with the class. Here are a few absurdities to give you a jump start:

- What if rocks grew on trees?
- Pretend all flowers can fly.
- Imagine worms can bounce!
- What if sticks could climb trees?
- What if each raindrop turned into a cricket?

A Land Of Imagination

Youngsters' familiarity with nature's land environment will make this sand-table simulation a real winner. To prepare, place a collection of plastic land critters, various craft items such as Easter grass and shell pasta, and lots of land nature items near your sand table. Instruct small groups of students, in turn, to plan and design a land environment using the available materials and their own knowledge. When they have finished, ask youngsters to describe and explain the different details of their environment, such as grassy areas or rocky mountains. Then invite the group to engage in some imaginative play in their environment. Repeat this process with each small group. Land ho!

Try this year-round idea to emphasize nature every month of the year. To create a nature tree, position a large, bare branch upright in a large clay pot (be sure the drain-hole is sealed); then fill the pot with rocks. If desired, pour mixed plaster of paris into the pot and allow it to dry thoroughly. Have students help you use these nature-related suggestions to make ornaments for your tree each month.

JANUARY Hot-glue three sweet-gum balls together to resemble a snowman. Spray-paint the snowman using a small spray bottle filled with white washable tempera paint. Hot-glue a yarn-loop hanger to the snowman.

FEBRUARY Cut a circle shape from bread. Spread the shape with a thick coat of beaten egg white; then press birdseed onto the bread. Let the bread dry thoroughly before adding a yarn hanger. Be sure to place your tree outside for the birds to enjoy!

MARCH Place a few lima beans into a resealable plastic sandwich bag lined with a moist paper towel. Hang the bag from the tree using an ornament hanger. Watch for the beans to sprout!

APRIL Use an iron to press a fresh, new leaf between two sheets of waxed paper. Cut around the leaf; then hang the cutout on the tree with an ornament hanger.

MAY Cut a flower picture from a plant or gardening catalog. Glue the cutout onto a piece of construction paper; then loosely cut around its outline. Attach a yarn-loop hanger.

JUNE Use a potato-peeler to shave the bark off a small stick. Hot-glue tissue-paper wings to the stick to create a butterfly or another flying creature; then attach a yarn-loop hanger.

JULY Cut out a tagboard fruit or vegetable shape. Paint this cutout with a glue color corresponding to the food it represents; then add a few actual seeds from that food. Attach a yarn hanger to the cutout.

AUGUST Paint a seashell with tempera paint; then embellish it with colored sand. Hot-glue a yarn hanger to the shell.

SEPTEMBER Cut a few apples into thin slices and allow the slices to dry out. String the dried apple slices onto a length of yarn; then tie the yarn ends together. Add the garland to your tree.

OCTOBER Glue a pressed fall leaf onto a black or blue tagboard circle. Attach a yarn hanger to the circle.

NOVEMBER Glue a pattern of acorns and seedpods onto a tagboard strip. Punch a hole in one end of the strip; then hang the strip with an ornament hanger.

DECEMBER Decorate a pinecone with glitter or glitter pens; then twist a pipe-cleaner hanger around the pinecone.

The Magic Of MANIPULATIVES

This unit brings you a bounty of creative, hands-on ideas for manipulatives. So go ahead—make your classroom a place for free exploration and fun!

ideas contributed by Gayla King and Betty Silkunas

Blocks

- In advance collect old blankets or several yards of fabric. Cut the fabric into a variety of sizes. Place the fabric pieces in the block area. Encourage students to build houses, forts, castles, or playhouses in the center; then invite them to drape the fabric pieces over the blocks to make walls and roofs.

- Use wide, colored tape to lay out a series of roads on the floor or carpet near your block area. Leave room between roads for students to build block houses and buildings. Then have your little ones "drive" toy vehicles on the roadways.

- In advance use three different blocks to build a short tower in the block area. Have each child who visits the center duplicate the same tower. Then pair students. Have one student in the pair use four blocks to make a tower. Have his partner examine the tower and use four of the same blocks to make a matching tower. Have the students switch roles and continue until each child has had several turns building the model tower.

- Have each student use classroom blocks of two or three different sizes to make a patterned design.

- Provide each child with a matched set of hand-sized blocks. Have him tap the blocks together in a rhythm. Then play a recording of upbeat music and have youngsters parade around the room playing their rhythm blocks.

- Place funnels, cone-shaped paper cups, and tagboard crowns in your block area. Encourage each student to don a crown; then have her use the funnels, paper cups, and blocks to create a castle with turrets.

- Place pairs of socks of different colors, sizes, and patterns in a laundry basket. Place the laundry basket in a center. To use the center, a child matches the pairs of socks, then rolls each pair into a ball.

  - Have each child cut off the cuffs from a pair of old ribbed socks. Have him glue craft items—such as yarn, pom-poms, buttons, sequins, and glitter—onto the cuffs to make nifty bracelets or armbands.

  - Encourage each child to bring a new, clean sock to school. Have each child personalize and decorate his sock; then mount his sock near his cubby or on a classroom wall. Fill the socks with stickers, snacks, and pencils on special occasions or class party days.

- Place large spoons, a classroom supply of tube socks, a laundry basket, and a large bowl of dried beans in a center. To use this center, a child half-fills a sock with dried beans. Then assist each child in tying a knot at the top of his sock and then folding over the excess cuff to make a beanbag. Have each youngster toss his beanbag into the laundry basket from specified distances. Or pair students and have them toss a sock beanbag back and forth.

- On a wall, mount a clothesline at students' eye level. Fill a small laundry basket with socks in many sizes. Place the basket and a supply of spring-type clothespins near the clothesline. Encourage students to hang the socks on the clothesline from smallest to largest.

  - Partially fill each of several socks with a different item, such as rice, marbles, sand, pebbles, beans, popcorn kernels, and keys. Knot the top of each sock. During circle time, pass the socks around one at a time. Ask youngsters to feel each sock. Have each child describe the way it feels and guess what the contents may be.

- Show students how to use socks as nonstandard units of measurement. Then place an assortment of same-sized socks at a center. Have youngsters use the socks to measure items in your room such as desks, tabletops, shelves, and doors.

Goldfish® Crackers

- Draw five fishbowls on a large sheet of construction paper. On each fishbowl draw a different set of fish from one to five. Place the paper and a bowl of Goldfish® crackers in a center. To use this center, a child counts the fish in each set and practices one-to-one correspondence by placing a cracker on each fish pictured.

- Add a few drops of blue food coloring to softened cream cheese. Have a student spread some of the tinted cream cheese on a large rice cake to represent water. Then have him press several Goldfish® crackers onto the cheese for a yummy under-the-sea snack.

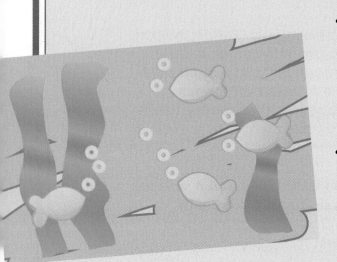

- Stock an art center with a supply of paintbrushes, paints, glue, tissue paper, yarn, white construction paper, Goldfish® crackers, and o-shaped cereal. Encourage each student to use the materials to create an underwater scene.

- Pair your students. Provide each student pair with a small bowl of crackers and two paper plates. Have each child put a handful of crackers on his plate. Have the pair count the crackers on each plate. Then have the pair determine which plate has more crackers on it and which has fewer.

- Provide each child with a pretzel stick, a plastic spoon with a dollop of peanut butter, and a small paper cup half-filled with fish crackers. Have each child dip the end of his pretzel stick into the peanut butter. Then have him use the pretzel as a fishing pole to "catch" a fish cracker to eat. Allow each child to continue in this manner until he eats all of his crackers.

- Pair students. Provide each student pair with a large, folded sheet of construction paper and a cup of crackers. Have one child in the pair unfold the paper and arrange a set of crackers on one half of the construction paper. Then have the other child in the pair create the same set on the other half of the paper.

- Place cups, a large bowl of crackers, and several plastic containers (such as milk jugs and jars) in a center. To do this activity, a child fills a cup with crackers. Then he pours the crackers into a plastic container. Have him count and tally how many cups it takes to fill the container.

- Reinforce size-seriation skills with this activity. Purchase a set of heart-shaped cookie cutters in graduated sizes. Trace the hearts onto a sheet of tagboard. Place the tagboard, the cookie cutters, and red play dough in a center. Have students who visit the center use the cookie cutters to cut the dough and match each heart shape to the corresponding heart on the tagboard.

- Encourage each student to trace cookie cutters onto a sheet of paper. Then have him paint the designs.

- Add glitter to a supply of play dough. Place the play-dough and star-shaped cookie cutters in a center for students to use to cut sparkling designs.

- Assist each youngster in making a simple sandwich. Have each child cut his sandwich with the cookie cutter of his choice.

- Place a supply of fish-shaped cookie cutters and slotted spoons at your water table. Have students use the slotted spoons to "catch" the fish.

- In advance purchase small, medium, and large bear-shaped cookie cutters. Cut out a small-, medium-, and large-sized chair, bed, and bowl from construction paper. Next add oatmeal to your favorite homemade play-dough recipe. Place the dough, cutouts, and cookie cutters in a center with a copy of *Goldilocks And The Three Bears*. To use this center, a child looks through the book and then uses the cookie cutters to cut three different-sized bear shapes from the dough. Then he matches each bear to a corresponding-sized chair, bed, and bowl.

- Place a set of geometric cookie cutters and a supply of play dough in a center. Encourage each child who visits the center to create shapes from the cutters of his choice. Assist each child in making trains, cars, trucks, or large machines from the shapes.

Craft Sticks....

- Help little ones improve fine-motor skills with this activity. Provide each child with a craft stick and play dough. Encourage each child to roll her play dough into a snake shape, then use a craft stick to cut the roll into pieces.

- Place a supply of craft sticks and plastic farm or zoo animals in a sand table. Encourage your little ones to insert the sticks in the sand to make fences and pens for the animals.

- Stock a center with different colors of play dough and matching-colored craft sticks. Encourage children who visit the center to roll each color of dough into a ball. Then have him insert the corresponding craft stick into each ball of dough.

- Give this fun musical activity a jingle. For each child, hot-glue a large jingle bell to a craft stick. Then encourage your little ones to jingle and jangle these marvelous musical instruments!

- Supply each child with a ball of play dough and several craft sticks for free sculpting.

- At snacktime, provide your students with craft sticks to help them spread icing, peanut butter, or any other creamy substance.

- This game of dominoes reinforces visual discrimination. To make dominoes from craft sticks, use a fine-tip marker to draw a line across the middle of each of 28 craft sticks. Attach a sticker or glue a small picture to each end of each craft stick (using seven basic pictures or stickers). Place the dominoes in a center. Have students spread the sticks, picture-side up, on a table or floor. Have them match the pictures and place the sticks end-to-end. Have students continue in this manner, matching pictures at either end of the path.

- Youngsters will love making these creepy-crawly caterpillars. To make a caterpillar, glue one medium-size pom-pom to one end of a craft stick. When the glue dries, glue two small wiggle eyes on it. Then glue small pom-poms to the remainder of the craft stick.

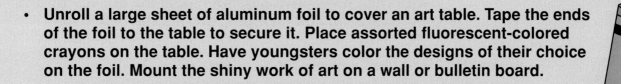

- To reinforce color recognition, give each small group of youngsters a basket of assorted crayons. Have them cooperatively sort the crayons by color.

- Unroll a large sheet of aluminum foil to cover an art table. Tape the ends of the foil to the table to secure it. Place assorted fluorescent-colored crayons on the table. Have youngsters color the designs of their choice on the foil. Mount the shiny work of art on a wall or bulletin board.

- In advance collect old and broken crayon pieces. Have youngsters peel the paper wrappings off all of the crayon pieces. Sort the pieces by color; then melt them. Pour the hot wax into each portion of an ice-cube tray. Freeze the tray for four to five hours. Pop out each section and you've got crayon cubes!

- For each child, secure a rubber band around two or three different-colored thin crayons. Provide him with a sheet of paper and have him create a multicolored design.

- Provide each child with a square of fine sandpaper and assorted crayons. Have each child color the rough side of the sandpaper with the color or colors of his choice. Use the resulting sparkling squares of color as a bulletin-board background or border.

- Hot-glue crayons on tagboard strips in different-colored patterns. Using cor-responding-colored crayons, have your youngsters dupli-cate the same patterns on a tabletop. Then encourage your students to make pat-terns of their own.

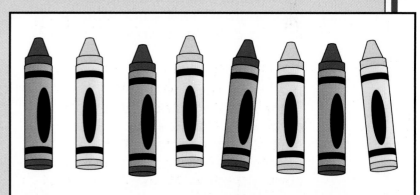

- To help little ones compare nonstandard units of measure, provide each child with a crayon and two other objects, such as a paintbrush, craft stick, or key. Have each child choose one of the objects and align it with the crayon. Have him determine which object is longer and which is shorter. Then have him use another object to compare to the crayon.

Beanbags................................

- Head outdoors and have your little ones experience a beanbag obstacle course. Make a row of beanbags in an open area, spacing the bags five feet apart. In turn have each student run in a zigzag formation around the beanbags. Then have each student repeat the activity by hopping, skipping, and galloping around the beanbags.

- Make beanbags from various types of fabrics such as corduroy, satin, faux fur, burlap, and flannel. Place the bags in a center for your students to feel and use for free exploration.

- Program several sheets of tagboard with different shapes of various colors. Tape the tagboard sheets on the floor. Then call out a shape or color, and have each child in a small group toss a beanbag onto the corresponding shape or color.

- Have your students estimate how many beanbags will fit into each of several containers, such as a bread box, a small laundry basket, a shoebox, and a backpack. Fill one of the containers with beanbags; then have your youngsters count with you to see how many actually fit. Continue in the same manner using a different container.

- Pair up your students and have them place a beanbag between their tummies. Have them try to walk from one specified place to another without dropping the beanbag. Then have them place the beanbag between their ears and walk without dropping the beanbag. Encourage student pairs to come up with other cooperative ideas using the beanbags.

- Place beanbags and several containers—such as large baskets, flowerpots, hatboxes, sand buckets, wagons, and large gift bags—in an open space. Then have students take turns tossing beanbags into the containers from specified distances.

- Have your little ones use inclined planes for beanbag races. In advance, lean two wooden planks near a toy shelf or table. Place a basket of beanbags near the shelf or table. Have two students at a time use the beanbags and slide them down the planks for a beanbag race.

Cotton Balls

- Here's an activity to help little ones improve their fine-motor skills. Place two baskets, a supply of cotton balls, tweezers, salad tongs, and spring-type clothespins in a center. Have youngsters visiting the center use the tools provided to transfer cotton balls from one basket to the other.

- Help your little ones develop the important skill of patterning. Provide each student with pastel-colored cotton balls, glue, and a tagboard strip. Have each child glue cotton balls on the tagboard to make a pattern.

- For each child, staple together two cutouts identical in shape and size, leaving an opening on one side. Encourage each child to decorate her shape. Have each child stuff cotton balls inside the opening; then staple the opening closed.

- Supply each small group of students with spring-type clothespins, cotton balls, paint, and large sheets of construction paper. Have each child in the group clip a cotton ball in a clothespin. Encourage each child to dip the cotton ball into paint and create the design of his choice.

- Fill a plastic tub with cotton balls. Place the tub, plastic shovels, and pails in a center. Have students who visit the center use the shovels to shovel the "snow" into the pails.

- Have each little bunny in your room make his own bunny tail. Provide each child with glue, cotton balls, and a round tagboard cutout. Have him glue the cotton balls on his cutout. When the glue dries, pin a bunny tail on each of your students. Then have each student pretend to be a bunny and have him hop, put his paw on his nose, and wiggle his tail. Next have a student volunteer demonstrate a bunny movement while the other children copy the movement and follow along.

Toy Vehicles

- Your little ones will be trackin' down some fun with this idea. Tape a piece of bulletin-board paper to a tabletop. Place several toy vehicles and paint atop the table. Have each child in a small group select a vehicle, dip its wheels in paint, and "drive" his vehicle on the bulletin-board paper. Encourage each student to examine the tracks that each vehicle made.

- Place a variety of toy vehicles in a center. To use the center, a child sorts and classifies the vehicles by type, size, and color.

- Supply a small group of students with a variety of toy vehicles. Have the group line up the vehicles from smallest to largest.

- On a vinyl tablecloth, use a permanent marker to draw roadways. Then glue small, plastic toys to represent houses, farms, schools, parks, and restaurants on the tablecloth. Place the table cover and a variety of toy vehicles in a center. Students who use the center will have fun driving buses, cars, and trucks all around town.

- Add several different toy boats to your water table. Have two children at a time have boat races or pretend to sail their boats to a tropical destination.

- Stock your block area with dump trucks or other toy trucks just right for hauling. Also stock your center with cargo items that youngsters can load onto and unload from the trucks, such as clothespins, marbles, buttons, and seashells.

- Place toy trucks and jeeps in your sand table or sandbox. While at the center, encourage your youngsters to pretend that the vehicles are dune buggies and drive their vehicles on the beach dunes.

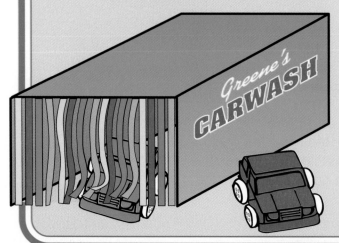

- Give your youngsters a chance to wash toy vehicles in a pretend car wash. To make a car wash, remove the two end panels from an opened shoebox. To one end attach four-inch lengths of bright-colored ribbon. Place the car wash and several mini cars in a center, and encourage students to drive their vehicles through the pretend water tunnel.

- Cover a shoebox lid with checkered cotton fabric. Cut out some small food items from old magazines. Laminate the cutouts if desired. Place the lid, cutouts, and bear counters in a center with a copy of *The Teddy Bears' Picnic* by Jerry Garcia and Dave Grisman (HarperCollins Children's Books). To use this center, invite a child to look through the book; then encourage him to use the food cutouts and the bears on the tablecloth to have his own teddy bear picnic.

- Hot-glue small strips of elastic to a supply of bear counters. Place the resulting bear finger puppets and a cassette recording of upbeat music in a center. Have each child in a small group place a bear on his index finger, listen to the music, and make his bear dance.

- This math idea will provide lots of counting fun. In advance collect five berry baskets. Turn the baskets upside down; then program each basket with a numeral from 1 to 5. Place the baskets and a supply of bear counters in a center. To use this center, encourage a child to place the correct number of bears in each corresponding "bear cave." If desired, also have each child numerically sequence the bear caves.

- Get your little ones in the mood for counting with this hands-on activity. Have each child in a small group take a handful of bear counters and place his bears on a paper plate. Have each child count how many of each color he has on his plate. Then have him count how many bears he has in all.

- For a fun circle-time activity, fill a sock and a small basket with colored bear counters. Have a student volunteer take out one bear from the sock; then have him find a matching colored bear in the basket. Have several other children point out objects in your classroom that are the same color. Continue in this manner until each color has been matched.

- Place two different-colored bears at students' eye level in the front of your room. Ask your students to carefully examine them. Then have them close their eyes. Take one bear away. Ask your students to open their eyes and guess which colored bear is missing. Continue in this manner, adding one more different-colored bear each time.

More Manipulatives

Here's a handy reference guide listing additional manipulatives you may want to consider using in your classroom. Busy hands are happy hands!

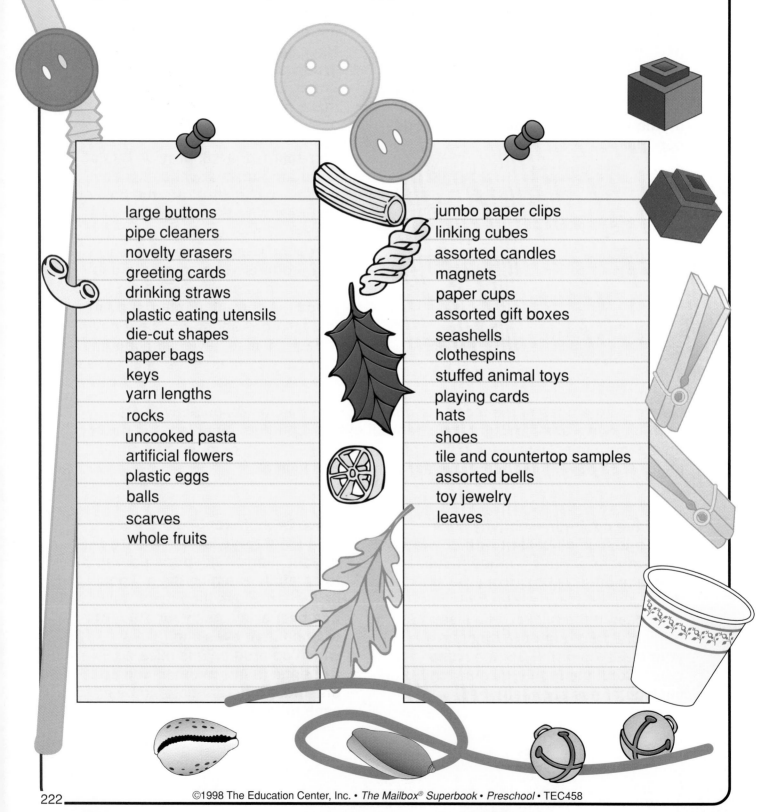

large buttons
pipe cleaners
novelty erasers
greeting cards
drinking straws
plastic eating utensils
die-cut shapes
paper bags
keys
yarn lengths
rocks
uncooked pasta
artificial flowers
plastic eggs
balls
scarves
whole fruits

jumbo paper clips
linking cubes
assorted candles
magnets
paper cups
assorted gift boxes
seashells
clothespins
stuffed animal toys
playing cards
hats
shoes
tile and countertop samples
assorted bells
toy jewelry
leaves

A Self-Esteem Sundae

Build your youngsters' confidence and self-satisfaction with this refreshing sampler of activities. Each one is guaranteed to yield two scoops of self-esteem topped with a smile (and a cherry, of course!).

ideas contributed by Barbara Backer and Angie Kutzer

Set Up For Success

You'll find tons of self-esteem wherever you find successful children. Activities that ensure success include open-ended arts and crafts, free exploration with blocks and manipulatives, a discovery table filled with science wonders, and dramatic play. Choice is also a big esteem-builder, whether it involves choosing a center or simply choosing which crayon to use. Set up your classroom with success in mind, making sure that there are plenty of achievable challenges. Then watch as the self-esteem encircles your class like whipped cream on a sundae!

What's In A Name?

A lot of self-esteem! Displays that include your students' names are real confidence boosters. Consider creating a door display reflecting your current theme of study. Here's a list of some popular themes, along with ideas for your door. A self-esteem opportunity is knockin'—let it in!

apples—tree with personalized apples

bears—bear tracks with personalized pawprints

circus—clown holding personalized balloons

dinosaurs—cave scene with child-decorated dinosaur cutouts; each dinosaur is personalized as "[Child's name]-o-saurus"

fall—colorful leaves scattered around personalized pumpkins

space—personalized rockets going toward a moon cutout

Easter—a large basket cutout filled with personalized eggs

My Family And Me

Want to make your classroom burst at the seams with self-esteem? Then invite each of your youngsters to bring in a family photo to share with the group. Tape each photo to a large sheet of bulletin-board paper. After each child shares information about his family, write down a few family-fact highlights beside his photo. Title your display "I Love My Family And My Family Loves Me!" Each youngster is sure to be pumped with pride!

Erica has one brother named Alex and a new baby brother named Ian. Her mom is an artist and her dad is a dentist.

Joseph has one older brother named James. James and Joseph play baseball on the same team. Joseph's mother's name is Anita. She is a scientist.

Kate's parents own a toy store. She has one older brother named Todd.

Look At Me!

Provide an assortment of mirrors in your classroom to encourage exploration with facial expressions and body gestures, and to help children feel comfortable and confident about themselves. Invite a pair of students to share a mirror and make comparisons about each other. Reinforce the unique and special qualities of each child. Then use a mirror to play "Mirror, Mirror" on page 238 during circle time. Try placing a full-length mirror in your dramatic-play area along with a couple of hand mirrors so that children can see how they look from behind. Include a mirror or two in the art area to encourage youngsters to create self-portraits. For added effect cover a bulletin board with aluminum foil to showcase these fabulous faces! Look in the mirror; what do you see? A totally terrific, wonderful me!

Guess Who?

Dish out individual scoops of self-esteem by describing each child's unique attributes and special abilities. Turn these descriptions into riddles for the rest of the group to solve. For example, "This child has long, brown hair. She likes to build with blocks. She can cross the monkey bars. She always uses good manners. Her sister's name is Katrina. Who is she?" Be ready for spoonfuls of smiles and giggles as children hear about themselves in such a positive manner.

What's Cookin'?

Nothing gives children more confidence and self-respect than being able to do "grown-up" things. Set up a cooking center in your classroom and provide simple no-cook recipes for your little ones to prepare on their own. Make step-by-step pictorial recipe cards for them to follow similar to the ones shown here. Then stand back and let your little chefs get to work. Mmm, mmm, good!

Puzzle Power

Foster even more self-esteem in your little ones with these personable preschool puzzles. Mount enlarged photocopies of children's individual snapshots on pieces of tagboard. Laminate them if desired. Then cut each picture into several pieces according to your children's abilities and store each puzzle in a separate, resealable plastic bag. This activity provides *two* scoops of self-esteem—one for the child who succeeds at completing a puzzle, and one for the person whose picture is recognized. Now that deserves a sugar cone and sprinkles!

I Can Do It!

Teach your youngsters this adaptation of the traditional tune of "B-I-N-G-O." Before each round of the song, encourage a different child to name an activity that he can do; then insert that phrase into the verse.

There are a lot of things that I
   can do all by myself; oh...
I can [comb my hair],
I can [comb my hair],
I can [comb my hair],
Without a grown-up's help. Yea!

Hear Ye! Hear Ye!

Celebrate your youngsters' new accomplishments while boosting their self-esteem at the same time! Reproduce the patterns on page 228 on construction paper. Color the medallions and cut them out. If desired make them extraspecial by embellishing them with glitter and sequins. Attach each medallion to a different tagboard headband. When a child in your classroom deserves a cheer, put one of these headbands on her and have her go to another classroom to share her good news. Encourage other teachers to send their successful students to your classroom to receive smiles and cheers as well.

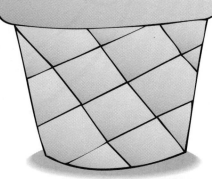

We All Scream For Self-Esteem!

Here are a few wonderful literature selections that will flavor your efforts in building your little ones' self-esteem. It's a triple scoop of fun!

Hooray For Me!
Written by Remy Charlip & Lilian Moore
Published by Tricycle Press

Just Because I Am:
A Child's Book Of Affirmation
Written by Lauren Murphy Payne, M.S.W.
Published by Free Spirit Publishing Inc.

Glad Monster, Sad Monster:
A Book About Feelings
Written by Ed Emberley & Anne Miranda
Published by Little, Brown And Company

Medallion Patterns
Use with "Hear Ye! Hear Ye!" on page 227.

©1998 The Education Center, Inc.

©1998 The Education Center, Inc.

Getting To Know ME

Help little ones learn important personal information with these activities.

ideas contributed by Carrie Lacher and Lori Kent

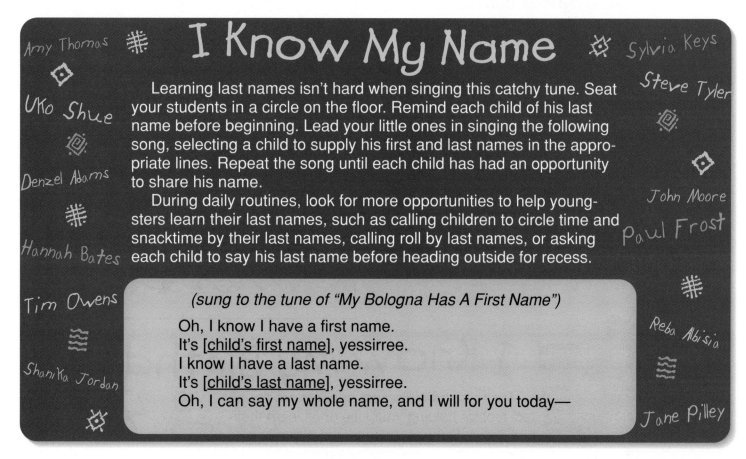

I Know My Name

Learning last names isn't hard when singing this catchy tune. Seat your students in a circle on the floor. Remind each child of his last name before beginning. Lead your little ones in singing the following song, selecting a child to supply his first and last names in the appropriate lines. Repeat the song until each child has had an opportunity to share his name.

During daily routines, look for more opportunities to help youngsters learn their last names, such as calling children to circle time and snacktime by their last names, calling roll by last names, or asking each child to say his last name before heading outside for recess.

(sung to the tune of "My Bologna Has A First Name")

Oh, I know I have a first name.
It's [child's first name], yessirree.
I know I have a last name.
It's [child's last name], yessirree.
Oh, I can say my whole name, and I will for you today—

Amy Thomas
Sylvia Keys
Steve Tyler
Uko Shue
Denzel Adams
John Moore
Paul Frost
Hannah Bates
Tim Owens
Reba Albisia
Shanika Jordan
Jane Pilley

I Know My Parents' Names

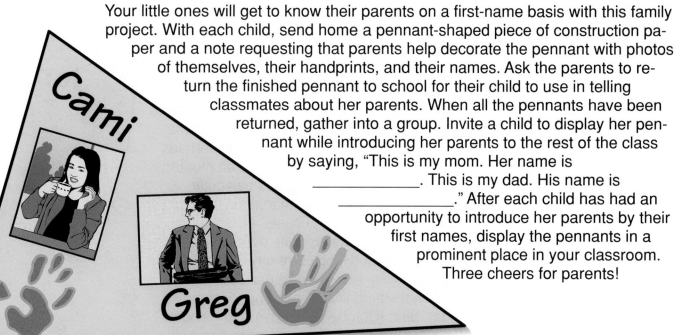

Your little ones will get to know their parents on a first-name basis with this family project. With each child, send home a pennant-shaped piece of construction paper and a note requesting that parents help decorate the pennant with photos of themselves, their handprints, and their names. Ask the parents to return the finished pennant to school for their child to use in telling classmates about her parents. When all the pennants have been returned, gather into a group. Invite a child to display her pennant while introducing her parents to the rest of the class by saying, "This is my mom. Her name is _____. This is my dad. His name is _____." After each child has had an opportunity to introduce her parents by their first names, display the pennants in a prominent place in your classroom. Three cheers for parents!

Cami
Greg

I Know Where I Live

Help each of your little ones learn the name of her street with this project that gets parents and children working together. Cut a class supply of poster-board strips in a color that matches the street signs in your community. Print each child's street name on a separate strip. Make a holder by cutting a slit into one end of a paper-towel tube. Insert a child's street sign into the holder. Place the holder on a table; then have the child sit on the floor below the street sign to give the appearance that the sign is taller than the child. Take a photo of each child sitting under her street sign. Glue the photo to a copy of the parent note on page 232. As each child is able to state this information at school, acknowledge her street-name savvy with a small treat, such as a sticker or stamp.

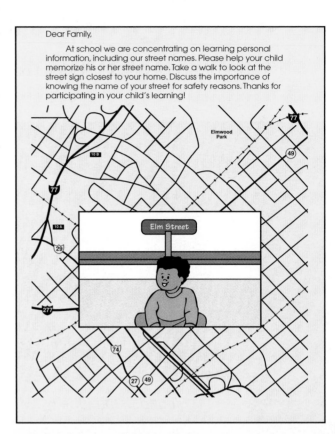

Dear Family,
    At school we are concentrating on learning personal information, including our street names. Please help your child memorize his or her street name. Take a walk to look at the street sign closest to your home. Discuss the importance of knowing the name of your street for safety reasons. Thanks for participating in your child's learning!

I Know My Birthday

Kim Wells
March 12

These birthday-present puppets are the perfect tool for helping your little ones learn their birthdates. Cut a class supply of three-inch squares from colored poster board. Write each child's first name, last name, and birthday on a separate poster-board square. Help each student count a number of stickers to indicate her age; then have her attach the stickers and a mini gift bow to the top of her square so it resembles a present. Glue a craft stick to the back of the completed square.

Alex Bruce
June 11

Have little ones bring their birthday puppets to your group area. Review each child's birthdate, emphasizing the different months (and perhaps sorting the children into groups by birth month). Next explain that when you call a particular month, all the children born in that month may jump up and show their puppets. After you've called out all the months, invite everyone to sing several rounds of "Happy Birthday To You," inserting the name of a different month each time you reach the third line of the song ("Happy birthday, dear [October] birthdays,") and encouraging those children to jump up once again.

Personal Information Passport

Name _Duncan Jerrett_

Parents' Or Guardians' Names

Debbie

Dennis

Street _Sea Island Court_

Birthday _September 7_

I Know All About Me!

This culminating project is sure to get your little ones' seal of approval. Reproduce a class supply of the passport cover and information sheet on page 233. To make a passport for each child, fold a piece of blue construction paper in half; then glue the passport cover to the front. If desired, add an official-looking gold-seal sticker to the cover. On the inside, glue the duplicated personal information sheet to one side; then glue the child's photo on the opposite side. Invite each child to dictate his full name, parents' names, street name, and birthday. Write this information on the corresponding lines inside the passport.

Use the passports for the activities described in "Show What You Know!" Then, after a few days, encourage each youngster to take his Personal Information Passport home and show off his knowledge to his family.

Show What You Know!

Give each youngster a chance to show off the personal information she's learned. Keep the Personal Information Passports (made in "I Know All About Me!") handy in your classroom for a few days. During transition times—such as on the way to the playground, on the way to circle time, or as children choose and go to centers—choose a child's passport and quiz her on a bit of personal information, such as her last name or her birthday. Use a rubber stamp to stamp the inside or back of her passport each time she correctly relates some personal information. When every child has several stamps in her passport, send the passports home to spark discussions with parents.

My birthday is May 14th!

Dear Family,

At school we are concentrating on learning personal information, including our street names. Please help your child memorize his or her street name. Take a walk to look at the street sign closest to your home. Discuss the importance of knowing the name of your street for safety reasons. Thanks for participating in your child's learning!

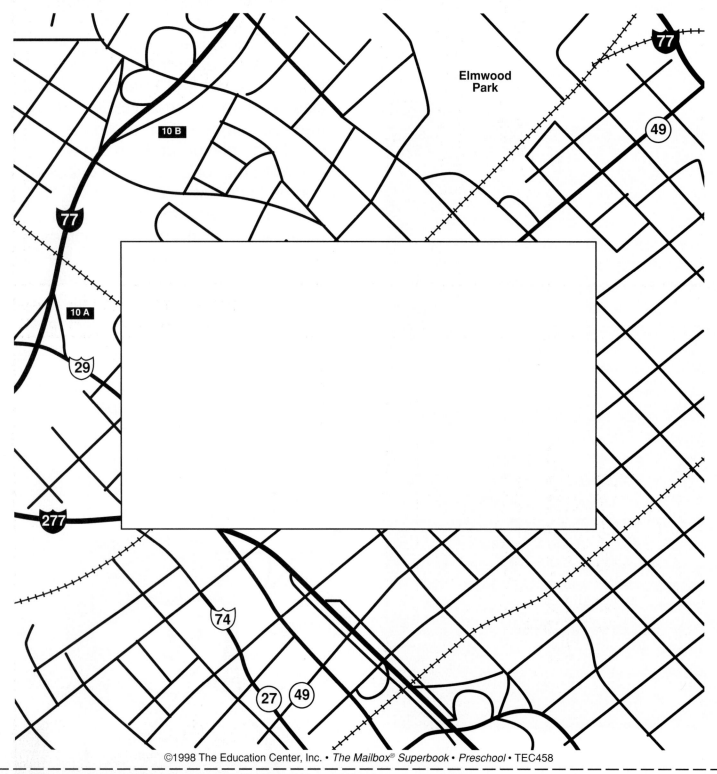

©1998 The Education Center, Inc. • *The Mailbox® Superbook* • *Preschool* • TEC458

Note To The Teacher: Use with "I Know Where I Live" on page 230.

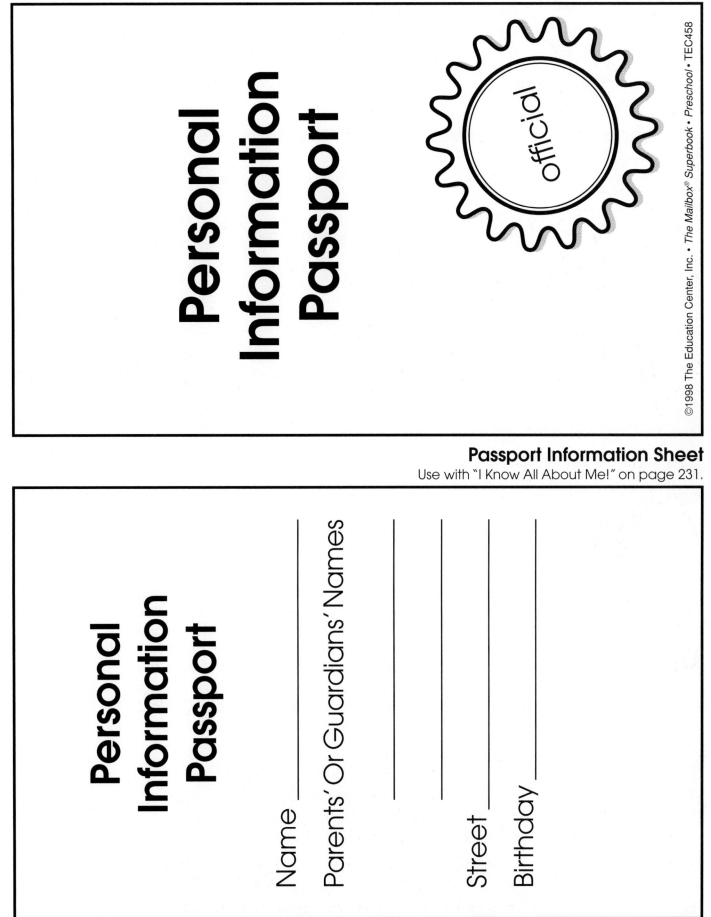

Personal Information Passport

official

©1998 The Education Center, Inc. • *The Mailbox® Superbook* • *Preschool* • TEC458

Personal Information Passport

Name

Parents' Or Guardians' Names

Street

Birthday

Time To Share

Sharing is simple with the help of these activities. In no time at all, you'll have a classroom filled with a fair share of kindness and cooperation.

ideas contributed by Lisa D. Cowman

TO SHARE OR NOT TO SHARE

That is the question your youngsters will answer when they participate in this activity. In advance, reproduce a class supply of coloring pictures. Working with a small group, give each child a picture and one crayon, making sure that each child's crayon is a different color. Instruct your little ones to color their pictures. When youngsters request additional crayons, tell them that the only crayons available are the ones you've given out. Lead them to the idea of sharing or trading the crayons by saying something like "You need a brown crayon? Hmmm...I see Carrie has one." Soon your little ones will discover for themselves that sharing is a colorful solution!

Share-A-Song-O

Your little ones will be sharing smiles when they participate in this simple circle-time game. Gather your youngsters into a circle. Then ask one child to stand in the center of the circle and hold a favorite classroom item, such as a stuffed toy or a manipulative. Lead your little ones in singing the following song. As you end the song, invite the child in the center to hand the toy to another child and join the circle. The child given the item moves to the center of the circle. Continue playing until each child has had an opportunity to share the toy.

Share
(sung to the tune of "Bingo")
There was a child, a special child, who liked to share with others.
S-H-A-R-E,
S-H-A-R-E,
S-H-A-R-E,
And [child's name] was [his/her] name-o!

SHARE A STORY

Your little ones will better understand the value of sharing after listening to one of these stories.

The Rainbow Fish
Written and illustrated by Marcus Pfister
Translated by J. Alison James
Published by North-South Books Inc.

It's Mine!
Written and illustrated by
Leo Lionni
Published by Alfred A. Knopf
Books For Young Readers

Stand And Share

Encourage your youngsters to put their sharing skills into practice with this game, which is similar to Heads-Up, Seven-Up. Obtain five matching pairs of different-colored manipulatives such as buttons or counting bears. Have your little ones sit on the floor; then choose five children to stand in front of the group. Give each of these children a pair of matching manipulatives. Instruct the seated children to close their eyes and hold their hands out in front of them. To play, each standing child shares one of his manipulatives by quietly slipping it into the hand of a seated child. He then returns to the front of the class and hides the remaining manipulative behind his back. When the five children have shared, they call out, "Stand and share," as a signal to the rest of the children to open their eyes. The children who have received a manipulative stand, and each guesses which child shared with him. When everyone has guessed correctly, invite the guessers to share the manipulatives in the next round of play. Continue to play until all children have had an opportunity to share.

Treasures To Share

Sharing and responsibility are the treasures your little ones are sure to find after digging into this activity. Send home copies of the letter on page 237, requesting that each child bring in a small, inexpensive toy. Decorate a shoebox and its lid to resemble a treasure chest; then reproduce a class roster and tape it to the inside of the lid. As each child brings in her treasure, label it with her name and place it inside the box. (If a child cannot bring an item from home, allow her to choose a small item from the classroom to include in the treasure chest.) When all of the children have contributed items, show them the contents of the treasure chest; then send the treasure chest home with a different child each night. Each day when a child returns the box, cross her name off the list. Your little ones will be all the richer for sharing their treasures with others.

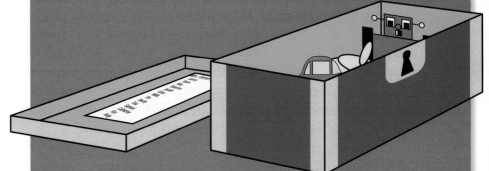

GOOD CHOICES

Now that your little ones have practiced sharing, follow up with this activity that gives them the opportunity to make good sharing choices. Discuss with your students health reasons why some things are not appropriate for sharing. As you name each of the following items and others, ask students to show you the thumbs-up sign if the item is appropriate for sharing or the thumbs-down sign if the item is not appropriate for sharing. Then ask children to suggest items for the rest of the group to evaluate with thumbs-up or thumbs-down signals.

- crayons
- your toothbrush
- books
- facial tissue
- toys
- medicine
- a drink from your cup
- a new game
- your apple

The Sharing Quilt

Piece together your little ones' thoughts about sharing with this group project. Spread a paper tablecloth flat. Using a marker, draw dotted lines that resemble stitching on the tablecloth, dividing it into as many equal-size squares as there are children in your class. Cut a class supply of construction-paper squares that are slightly smaller than the tablecloth's squares. Invite each child to cut out magazine pictures of things that could be shared, then glue the pictures onto a construction-paper square to make a collage. Glue each child's collage onto the tablecloth; then label each child's square with his name. Display the quilt on a wall or bulletin board titled "We Care—We Share."

Lori   Jayne   Todd
Elizabeth   Kevin   John

Time To Share

Remembering to put sharing skills into practice is easy when wearing these fun necklaces. Reproduce a class supply of the sharing-clock pattern (page 237) onto tagboard. Have each child color and cut out a clock. Punch a hole near the top of each clock; then lace a length of yarn through the hole and tie the ends together. Encourage around-the-clock sharing by having your little ones wear these necklaces during cooperative art activities, center times, and anytime a reminder is needed to share and share alike.

Dear Family,
 We have been learning about sharing. To help us understand the value of sharing, we are preparing a treasure chest to send home with a different child each night. Please help us fill our chest by sending in a small, inexpensive toy, such as those packaged in fast-food meals. We will return the toy when each child has had an opportunity to take the treasure chest home. Be on the lookout! Our chest of treasures will be coming to your home soon.
 Thank you for sharing in your child's learning!

©1998 The Education Center, Inc. •
The Mailbox® Superbook • Preschool •
TEC458

_____
teacher

Sharing Clock
Use with "Time To Share"
on page 236.

What time is it?

Time to share!

©1998 The Education Center, Inc. • TEC458

WE'RE UNIQUE!

Help your preschoolers understand the abstract concepts of equity and diversity with this creative collection of ideas. Then listen as your youngsters squeal, "Eureka! We're 'unique-a'!"

ideas contributed by Lisa D. Cowman

Mirror, Mirror

Bring a mirror to circle time and invite your youngsters to participate in this rhyming game. Pass the mirror around the circle as you chant the rhyme below. When the word *see* is said, direct the child who is holding the mirror at that time to keep it, look in it, and complete the second line of the rhyme by himself, naming a feature such as *two ears, red lips, freckles,* or *brown hair.* Then repeat the rhyme and continue passing the mirror until everyone has had a turn.

Mirror, mirror, what do you see?
I see [blue eyes] looking at me.

I see blue eyes looking at me.

ALL WRAPPED UP

Put the same number of pennies into each of two different-sized boxes. Wrap one of the boxes in the comics section from the newspaper. Wrap the other box in festive gift wrap with a ribbon and bow. Ask your students to compare the boxes. Take a vote on which one you should open first. Have a student volunteer open each box and count the pennies. Once your youngsters realize that the boxes hold the same thing, explain to them the parallel between themselves and the gifts: While everyone looks different on the outside, we all hold the same value.

THE SAME GAME

Gather your little ones around for this visual-discrimination game. Choose two students to stand in front of the group. Direct the other students to discover the pair's similarities. For example, they both might have brown hair, be wearing short sleeves, have on tennis shoes, or be tall. List students' responses on the chalkboard. Repeat this procedure with several different pairs of students; then count the items on the lists to see which list is the longest. If desired, repeat the game on another day using students' differences.

Brown hair
Black noses
Long bodies
Wagging tails

Different Strokes For Different Folks

Use this activity as a follow-up to "The Same Game." Have each child look through a magazine and cut out pictures of people who look different from her. Encourage her to tell you what's different about each person; then have her tell you something she likes about each person. Explain to the group that even though people look different, they are all special in their very own way. Extend this idea by having each child glue her cutouts to a mural titled "All Different, All Special."

SHARE AND COMPARE

Help youngsters uncover commonalities among themselves with this activity. Divide your class into pairs. Give each child a copy of page 241. Help each child write her name and her partner's name on her paper; then have the children color in the appropriate spaces. Provide each pair with an inkpad to make thumbprints. When the comparisons are complete, have each pair share its results with the rest of the group. Is the pair more alike or more different? Can they still be friends? You bet!

INK PAD ORANGE

Let's Be Friends

Now that your little ones have discovered many ways that people are alike and different, share a feel-good book about equality and diversity. Two excellent choices are *We Are A Rainbow* by Nancy María Grande Tabor (Charlesbridge Publishing, Inc.) and *All The Colors Of The Earth* by Sheila Hamanaka (William Morrow And Company, Inc.). After the story, celebrate with song. Teach your children "The Friendship Song" shown here.

The Friendship Song

(sung to the tune of "Jesus Loves The Little Children")

There are oh, so many children,
All kinds of children in the world.
Shades of yellow, brown, and white,
With big smiles that are so bright.
There are oh, so many children in the world!

There are oh, so many children,
All kinds of children in the world.
Different colors of our skin,
Doesn't mean we can't be friends,
With the oh, so many children of the world!

Me	You
My name is	Your name is
_____.	_____.
My hair color	Your hair color
My eye color	Your eye color
My thumbprint	Your thumbprint

Note To The Teacher: Use with "Share And Compare" on page 240.

I CAN DO IT BY MYSELF!

These activities provide just the practice needed for your little ones to develop independence with self-help skills such as dressing and serving.

ideas contributed by Linda Gordetsky and Angie Kutzer

I Can Pour

Here's a circle-time game that pours on the fun. Seat youngsters outside in a group circle. Give one child a cup filled with water, beans, rice, sand, or another pourable material. Give each of the remaining children an empty cup. Direct the child with the filled cup to pour the contents into the cup of the child on his left. Continue until the contents have been returned to the original cup. When your group can successfully pass the contents around the circle, add the following song to the game. Lead the group in singing the song as each child pours the contents of his cup into another child's cup.

Just Watch Me Pour
(sung to the tune of "Miss Mary Mack")

Just watch me pour, pour, pour
This to a friend, friend, friend.
[His/her] name is [child's name], [child's name], [child's name].
[He'll/she'll] pour again-gain-gain.

I Can Serve

Use this small-group activity time and again to serve up some spooning and scooping practice. Seat a small group of youngsters around a table. Give each child a plastic plate. Fill a serving bowl with play-dough balls, nonmenthol shaving cream, or fingerpaint. Put a spoon in the bowl. Have the children pass the bowl from child to child so that each child can serve herself a ball of dough or a spoonful of the substance. When everyone has been served, invite each child to enjoy some sensory play with the material on her plate. Vary the activity on another day by putting a different substance in the bowl.

I Can Make A Sandwich

Invite children to make peanut-butter sandwiches to practice spreading and slicing. Then have them make these praiseworthy flip books. For each child, duplicate the sandwich patterns on page 245 twice onto white construction paper. Cut out the shapes; then number them and program them with the words *put, spread, spread,* and *slice* as shown. Have each child color page 2 brown and color page 3 purple. Have him cut page 4 in half. Stack the pages in the order shown, so that page 4 is on top. Bind the slices together near their tops as shown to create a flip book. To read the book, a child flips page 1 to the top of the stack and reads the pages in sequence.

I can __put__ .
1

I can <u>spread</u>.
2

I can <u>spread</u>.
3

I can _slice_ .
4

I can slice .
4

...d.
3

I can <u>spread</u>.
2

1

I Can Dress

Children will practice dressing with success when you play this fun game of musical clothing. In advance, fill a tote bag with articles of clothing that have a variety of fasteners such as buckles, snaps, buttons, and ties. Be sure to include one item for each child. To play, seat the children in a circle on the floor. Direct them to pass the bag from child to child as music plays. When the music stops, the child holding the bag should select one item from the bag to put on. Assist the child or have a friend from the circle assist the child in putting on the item. Continue play until each child has had an opportunity to select and put on an article of clothing.

I Can Do Lots Of Things At Home!

Since your youngsters are growing up, there are lots more things they can do at home. Consider sharing *Now I'm Big* by Margaret Miller (Greenwillow Books) with your class to help them realize things they can do by themselves now that they are growing up. Make a class list of things your children are proud that they can do. Then sing the following song, inserting a different task each time you repeat the verse.

You Are Growing Up
(sung to the tune of "If You're Happy And You Know It")

You are growing up; now you can [brush your teeth].
You are growing up; now you can [brush your teeth].
You are growing up, it's true. We're so very proud of you!
You are growing up; now you can [brush your teeth].

"I Can" Awards

Who can zip, button, or tie? Everyone will know with these awards that are as cute as a button. To prepare a set of awards for each child, duplicate page 246 onto construction paper. Color or have the child color the awards. Laminate them for durability; then cut them out. Punch holes in the zipping and tying awards and cut a slit in the buttoning award as indicated. When a child has mastered zipping, use a safety pin to attach the appropriate award to a zipper on his clothing. Thread a child's shoelaces through the holes of the tying award; then have the child retie his laces into a bow. Attach the buttoning award to a child's clothing by sliding a button through the slit.

Praise, Parents, Praise!

Here's a gentle way to remind parents to give their children praise for becoming more independent. Send home a copy of the song above, along with a list of tasks each child may be learning to do or may already be able to do independently. Parents are sure to appreciate your helping them sing their children's praises!

I can comb my hair.

I can pick out my clothes.

I can match socks.

I can serve food.

I can clean my room.

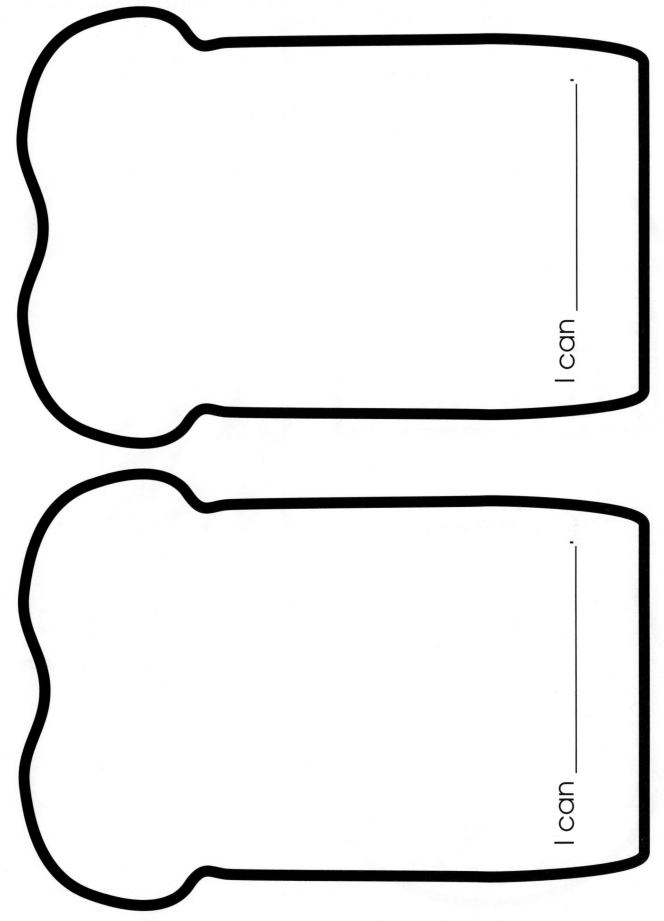

I can _____

I can _____

Awards
Use with "'I Can' Awards" on page 244.

I can tie!

I can button!

I can zip!

LET'S RECYCLE!

Use these earth-friendly ideas to model environmentally sound practices and turn everyday trash into useful classroom treasures.

ideas contributed by Lori Kent

EGG CARTONS

Egg-Cup Puppets

Put some fun into storytelling with these easy-to-make egg-carton puppets. To make a puppet, cut an egg cup from an egg carton. Use craft items such as pom-poms, tissue paper, wiggle eyes, markers, glitter, construction-paper scraps, and yarn to decorate the inverted egg cup to resemble a favorite character from a story, fingerplay, or poem. Glue a craft stick to the back of the cup. Encourage youngsters to use the puppets to help retell their favorite fingerplays, stories, or poems.

Egg-Carton Boats

Your little ones will love sailing these egg-carton boats at your water table. To make a boat, cut a Styrofoam® egg carton into a four-cup section. Tape a triangle cutout to a toothpick; then insert the toothpick between the egg-carton cups as shown. Place several boats and small toy people at the water table. Bon voyage!

Nature-Walk Container

Head outdoors with your students to gather some treasures from the natural world around them. In advance, provide each child with an empty egg carton; then have him walk around your school or center grounds. Encourage him to look for items such as leaves, twigs, grass, tree bark, and small rocks; then have him place the items in his carton. After returning to your room, have each youngster sort his items by type, color, or shape. If desired, provide each child with a sheet of cardboard and glue; then have him glue his items to the cardboard to make a nature collage.

And The List Goes On...

- Turn an empty, cardboard egg carton upside down. Through the top of each egg cup, cut a hole large enough to insert supplies such as scissors, crayons, and pencils.

- Cut apart the egg cups from several egg cartons. Cut a small hole in the bottom of each cup. Place the egg cups and lengths of yarn in a center. Have each child who visits the center string a yarn length through a few cups for an "eggs-traspecial" necklace!

- Cut apart individual egg cups from a supply of egg cartons. Use the cups for a multitude of class functions, such as dispensing student portions of glue, party snacks, or edible manipulatives such as Gummy bears. Store game pieces, game markers, and dice in the cups. Or use them at an art center to organize craft supplies such as sequins, beads, and pom-poms.

Lunch Bags & Grocery Bags

Flap Books

This fun book-making idea will have your little ones eager to put pencil to page. For each child, cut off the top of several paper lunch bags. Stack the bottom portion of each bag so that all of the flaps are on the right. Then staple the bags on the left side. Provide each child with a paper-bag book and markers. Encourage him to fold back the flap and draw a picture so that only half of the picture will show when the flap is down. Have each child hold up one page of his book and have the class guess what the picture might be.

Grocery-Bag Kites

Watch your students soar to new heights when making grocery-bag kites. In advance, collect a classroom supply of paper grocery bags. To make a kite, fold down the top edge of the opened bag twice. Decorate the bag with drawings, stickers, or small seasonal cutouts. Then punch two evenly spaced holes on each side of the folded area. Thread a 12-inch length of string through each of the four holes and tie it in place. Take your youngsters outdoors and have them hold the string and run—allowing the bag to fill with air. Let's go fly a kite!

It's In The Bag

Your little ones will have seriation skills in the bag with this activity. In advance, fill several lunch bags with items that vary in weight, such as feathers, packing peanuts, cotton balls, dried beans, sand, and pebbles. Each bag should have only one kind of item. Fold the top of each bag; then staple the bag shut. Place the bags at a math center. To use the center, a child holds each bag and feels its weight. Then he places the bags in order from lightest to heaviest.

And The List Goes On...

- Program the outside of each of several lunch bags with a different numeral. Place the bags and a quantity of sandwich-shaped cutouts in a center. Have each child who visits the center place the corresponding number of sandwich shapes in each bag.

- Provide each child with a grocery bag. Assist him in folding the top of the bag to the outside several times to resemble a hat. Then supply each child with craft items—such as glue, glitter, tissue paper, and faux jewels—to decorate his hat.

- Place a few snacks in a lunch bag for each child. Then take your youngsters and a blanket outdoors to have a picnic.

- Tape a large grocery bag to each end of your art table. Have your youngsters use the bags to dispose of paper scraps.

Baby-Food Jars

Gift Jars

Here's a nifty, creative gift jar for someone special. In advance, collect a classroom supply of baby-food jars with lids. Then provide each child with a large cup of snack items such as jelly beans, candy hearts, pretzels, or M&M's®. Using craft glue, assist each child in covering the top of a lid with one kind of snack item. When the glue dries, spray a few coats of varnish on the lid; then let it dry overnight. Have each child fill the jar with the left-over snacks from his cup; then secure each child's lid to his jar. To complete the project, tie a length of ribbon around the jar. The recipient of this special gift is bound to be pleased!

Crystal Creations

Entice your students with this gem of a science project. Supply each child with a clean baby-food jar. Assist him in measuring one tablespoon of water and one tablespoon of Epsom salts into the jar. Stir in 1/4 teaspoon of blue, yellow, or red food coloring. After a few days, encourage your youngsters to examine their jars. They'll be amazed to see colored crystals forming!

Root Watchers

Plant seeds of enthusiasm with this activity, and your little ones will become active root watchers. Provide each child with an empty baby-food jar, a 2 1/4" x 7" strip of construction paper, crayons, and a wet paper towel. Have each child use the crayons to decorate his construction-paper strip with pictures of things that grow from seeds. Then assist each child in lining the inside of his jar with the paper towel. (If necessary, stuff the inside of the jar with crumpled paper to help the paper towel stay pressed against the jar.) Help each child slide two or three bean seeds between his jar and the paper towel. Pour one inch of water into each child's jar. Assist him in taping his construction-paper strip around the jar; then place the jar in a warm location. Encourage your students to examine their jars and to add water when necessary. After a week, unwrap the jars. Your youngsters will be fascinated to see their beans growing roots and sprouts.

And The List Goes On...

• Use baby-food jars to store liquid tempera paint at your art center.

• Punch holes in the lids of several baby-food jars. Fill each jar with a different color of glitter. Place the jars in your art area for youngsters to use for craft projects.

• Have your little ones use baby-food jars for short-term insect viewers. Punch a few holes in the lids of a classroom supply of jars. Provide each child with a jar. Then take your youngsters outdoors for an insect hunt.

Cardboard Tubes

Center Props

Build new interest in your centers with these nifty props made from cardboard tubes. In advance, reproduce a variety of simple patterns that correspond with your current theme. Have each child choose a pattern; then have him color it. Assist each child in cutting out his pattern; then mount it on a cardboard tube as shown. If desired, glue each tube to a cardboard base for sturdiness. Place the theme-related props in your puppet or block area for your little ones to use for free exploration.

Snappy Shakers

Create some sound excitement when students make these snappy shakers. Provide each child with a toilet-tissue tube. Encourage each child to use markers, crayons, and stickers to decorate his tube. Insert several crepe-paper streamers in one end of each child's tube; then staple the opening shut. Next have each child partially fill his tube with rice or beans. To complete the project, have each student insert several streamers in the opened end of the tube; then staple the opening shut. Encourage your little ones to shake their snappy shakers to an upbeat musical selection.

Art-Project Protectors

When you use this idea, your youngsters will get their works of art home with ease. Provide each child with a large cardboard tube. Encourage him to decorate his tube. Then label each child's tube with his name. Each time a student completes a large painting or picture, have him roll his art and slide it into his cardboard tube. Students' protected projects will be ready for transport.

And The List Goes On...

- Have each child use a cardboard tube to make a kazoo. Provide each child with a toilet-tissue tube, a sheet of waxed paper, and a rubber band. Have each student place the sheet of waxed paper over one end of the tube and secure it with a rubber band. Encourage each child to hum through the open end.

- Stock your sand table with cardboard tubes that vary in size. Encourage students who visit the center to use the tubes for funnels and sand chutes.

- Place several cardboard tubes, shallow pans of paint, and paper in your art area. Have each child who visits the area dip one end of a cardboard tube into a pan of paint, then press it onto a sheet of paper. Have him continue in this manner until he has a desired design.

- Have each child dip one end of a cardboard tube into a bowl of bubble solution. Then have him blow through the other end to make oodles of bubbles.

Plastic Containers

Picture-Perfect Tubs

Youngsters will love these personalized storage tubs. In advance, collect a class supply of large margarine tubs. Take a photograph of each child. Cut out and glue each photo to a margarine lid. Cover the lid with clear Con-Tact® paper if desired. Secure each lid on a margarine tub. Provide each child with her personalized tub and have her use it to store her small classroom supplies, such as crayons, scraps of paper, and scissors.

Molly

Drips Be Gone

Try this neat idea for storing paint and catching paint drips. In advance, collect several plastic yogurt containers with lids. Through the top of each lid, cut a hole large enough to insert a paintbrush. Using permanent markers, color each yogurt lid to correspond to one color of paint you'll be using. Then fill each container with a different color of paint and put the matching-colored lid on each container. Place each container in an easel tray in your art area. Insert a paintbrush through the hole in each container. No more drips!

Strawberry • Banana

YOGURT

And The List Goes On...

- Use margarine tubs to store individual portions of play dough for each child.

- Stock your math center with plastic containers that vary in size. Have youngsters who visit the center stack and count the containers.

- Use yogurt containers as individual juice sippers. Collect a classroom supply of clean, lidded yogurt containers. Cut a small cross (+) in the center of each lid. Label the outside of each container with a child's name. Fill each container with juice; then secure the lid. Insert a straw through the cross, and each child will be ready for sipping!

- Store yarn neatly to eliminate messy tangles. Cut a cross (+) in the center of a margarine-tub lid. Put a ball of yarn in the tub; then pull one end of it through the slits in the lid. Replace the lid. Your youngsters will be able to pull out just the right amount of yarn without any tangles.

Super Slate

Recycle rectangular baby-wipe containers into individual slates for your students' use. To make a slate, cover the lid of an empty baby-wipe container with a sheet of self-adhesive chalkboard paper (available at a teacher-supply store). Trim the excess paper as needed. Inside the tub, place a piece of chalk and a square of felt. Place the individual slates in an art area or a writing center. To use the slate, a student writes or draws a picture with the chalk, then wipes the slate clean with the felt.

Berry Baskets

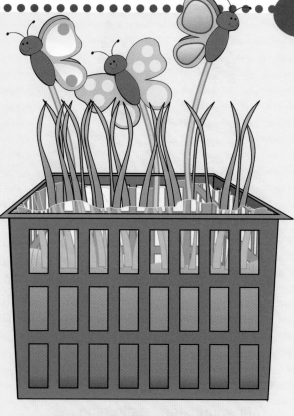

Counting Blueberries

Are your little ones getting into counting these days? If so, use this "berry" good idea to reinforce counting skills. In advance, place cotton balls in a resealable plastic bag with blue powdered tempera paint. Shake the bag to coat the cotton balls; then place them on a paper plate. Label the outside of five berry baskets with a different numeral from 1 to 5. Place the baskets, the paper plate, and a pair of tongs in a center. When a child visits this center, have him arrange the baskets in numerical order. Then have him use the tongs to place the corresponding number of cotton-ball "blueberries" in each basket.

Berry-Basket Storage

Here's a tip to help you get your supplies organized. Collect several berry baskets. Mount a piece of magnetic tape to one side of each basket. Mount the berry baskets on one side of your filing cabinet. Use the baskets to store lightweight classroom supplies, such as erasers, pencils, and stickers.

Butterfly Baskets

Your students will be all aflutter when making these creative butterfly baskets. To make one, line a plastic berry basket with plastic wrap; then half-fill it with potting soil. Sprinkle grass seeds atop the soil and place another thin layer of soil atop the seeds. Place the basket in a warm location. Using a spray bottle, water the seeds daily. After the grass grows approximately two inches, mount butterfly stickers or cutouts to one end of several pipe cleaners, and insert them in the soil. Display each child's basket in your classroom to help make springtime spirits soar.

And The List Goes On...

- Place several berry baskets and small plastic animals at your sand table. Encourage youngsters to use the baskets for fun zoo props.

- Stock your art area with play dough and several berry baskets. Encourage your little ones to use the baskets to make interesting designs in the play dough.

- Provide each child with a berry basket and several pieces of yarn. Assist each child in weaving the yarn through the sides of his basket. If desired, attach a pipe cleaner to the basket for an easy handle.

STYROFOAM® MATERIALS

Cut, Stuff, Tie, And Toss!

Your little ones will have fun tossing these lightweight balls indoors or out. In advance, collect several pairs of clean discarded pantyhose and a supply of Styrofoam® packing peanuts. Measuring from the toe of each pair, cut off a 12-inch length of nylon. Then stuff each piece with packing peanuts. Tie a knot at the top of the fabric; then cut off the excess material. Encourage your youngsters to use the balls for circle-time games, outdoor play, or free exploration.

Stacking Patterns

Your youngsters' patterning skills will really stack up when they give this creative activity a try. In advance, use two or more different-colored permanent markers to color the rims of a supply of Styrofoam® cups. Place the cups in a center. To use this center, a child stacks the cups to make a color pattern. Then have him "read" his pattern to a classmate. To vary the activity, add different-colored cups to the center.

Ink-A-Dink

Transform Styrofoam® meat trays into super stamps for youngsters to use again and again. In advance, trace simple geometric shapes or patterns that correspond with your theme unit on a clean meat tray. Using an X-acto® knife, cut out the shapes. Then glue each cutout onto a thick square of cardboard or a wooden block. Place the stamps, a shallow pan of diluted tempera paint, and sheets of construction paper and bulletin-board paper in a center. To use this center, have a child dip a stamp into the paint, then press it onto a sheet of paper. The completed designs can be displayed on a wall or bulletin board, or used for gift wrapping.

And The List Goes On...

- For each child, trace a simple shape onto a clean meat tray; then cut out the shape. Punch holes around the edges of each cutout. Have each youngster use a shoestring to lace around his shape.

- Convert Styrofoam® meat trays into durable stencils. To prepare a stencil, trace a simple shape onto a clean meat tray. Cut along the outline using an X-acto® knife. To use a stencil, a child places it on a sheet of art paper. Then he traces the outline of the stencil with a crayon and colors in the shape.

- Place meat trays at your water table and encourage little ones to use them as barges.

SEASONAL & HOLIDAY

This display is as easy as apple pie! Cover a bulletin board with a green plastic tablecloth and a fall-leaves border. Cut a large basket shape from a piece of cardboard. Use a black marker to draw lines on the shape to make it resemble a bushel basket; then staple it to the bottom of the bulletin board. Have each child use red, green, or yellow paint to sponge-paint a construction-paper apple shape. When the paint is dry, attach the apples above and around the basket. Finish the display with the title "Apple Appeal."

Cut a tree shape from brown bulletin-board paper and staple it to one side of a bulletin board. Cut out a supply of construction-paper leaves; then label each leaf with a different title from your classroom book collection. Pin the leaves to the tree. During storytime have a student pick a leaf from the tree. Read the corresponding book; then pin the leaf to the right side of the board to form a pile.

Who Said "Boo"?

Complete this spooky display with a little help from your youngsters. Give each child a construction-paper mask shape. Have her decorate her mask with markers, pom-poms, ribbon, sequins, colored glue, buttons, or other craft materials. Staple the *tops* of the masks to a black background. Tape each child's photo to the background under her mask. Encourage children to guess who's under each mask, then flip it up to find out. Boo!

Get lots of gobbles and grins when youngsters make these turkeys. To make a turkey, paint a toilet-paper tube brown. Trace and cut out two hand shapes from colorful construction paper. Staple the hand cutouts to the tube to represent feathers. Then staple a brown circle to the tube to make the turkey's head. Glue on two oversized wiggle eyes and a yellow paper beak. Finish the gobbler by drawing a red wattle under the beak. Display the turkeys with a scattering of straw and some miniature pumpkins.

Create a snow scene using blue and white bulletin-board paper as shown. Have youngsters add paper snowflakes and cotton snow on paper building rooftops. Next have each child put on his snow gear and lie on the floor as if he were making a snow angel. Take a snapshot of him. (Do not use instant film.) Cut the photos closely around each child's body as shown. Have each child use an angel template (cut a bit larger than the photo cutouts) to sponge-paint a blue angel on the snow. When the paint is dry, staple each photo atop a different angel.

Divide a bulletin board into thirds by covering it with gift wrap representing each of these three holidays: Hanukkah, Christmas, and Kwanzaa. Add the title and subtitles to the board. Then give each child a candle cutout. Have her color her candle to represent her favorite holiday. Personalize each candle. Then invite each child to pin her candle to the corresponding area of the board.

Our Class Cares!

Cut out a large heart from bulletin-board paper. Decorate the edges of the heart with lacy doilies. Write "Our Class Cares!" on the heart. When you (or another adult) observe a caring act—such as sharing, using a kind word, or helping a friend—invite the caring student to either stamp, sticker, or sponge-paint a smaller heart onto the heart shape. When the heart is filled, invite your youngsters to enjoy a class treat of heart-shaped cookies.

Who's Lucky?

Encourage each child to decorate a personalized shamrock cutout with an assortment of green craft materials, such as sequins, buttons, dyed pasta, and ribbon. Staple the tops of the shamrocks to a bulletin board so that they can be flipped up. Each morning, before students arrive, hide a small leprechaun cutout under one of the shamrocks. Invite children to guess where the leprechaun is hiding. Designate that shamrock's lucky owner as your helper for the day.

Have each child paint a basic shape cutout half red and half brown. Provide the child with two hole reinforcers to use for the robin's eyes and half of a rubberband to resemble a worm. Direct the child to cut a beak from yellow paper and glue the worm to it. Then have her glue the eyes and beak to the brown part of the robin. If desired, cover the words in the board's title with birdseed. Tweet, tweet!

Cut a length of pastel bulletin-board paper to fit a classroom board. Have each child create a chick by using the bottom of a plastic cup to print a yellow circle onto the paper. Direct him to glue an orange craft-foam beak and two wiggle eyes onto the circle to resemble a chick. Have him add legs with an orange marker. Then glue a yellow craft feather onto each chick. Have each child create an eggshell by using the open end of a plastic cup to print bright colors of paint onto a construction-paper egg cutout. When the paint is dry, puzzle-cut the eggs to resemble broken eggshells. Glue the eggshells to the pastel paper and add the title to complete the board.

Cover a bulletin board with three strips of paper to represent land, water, and sky. Then instruct each child to find pictures in magazines of objects found on land, in water, or in the sky. Have children tear or cut out the pictures; then glue them to the appropriate places on the board. Add the title in large block letters. Hooray for Earth Day!

Have each child bring in a photo of his mother or female caregiver. Cut a large vase from bulletin-board paper. Use a marker to write the title on the vase. Cut out a class supply of colorful construction-paper flowers. Cut a hole in the center of each flower. Tape each photo to the back of a flower so that the picture is showing through the hole. Use crepe paper to represent stems, and add a few construction-paper leaves.

Cut a large circle from white poster board. From yellow bulletin-board paper, cut a number of sun rays equal to the number of students in your class. Invite a few children to fingerpaint the center of the circle with red paint. Then add some yellow paint and have another group of children fingerpaint. Continue adding yellow paint until the whole circle is painted. After the paint dries, staple the circle to a bright blue background. Write each child's name and favorite summer word on one of the sun rays; then attach them all around the circle. Add the title to complete the display.

Jim corn on the cob

Jeri hot

Kirk watermelon

Joey fireflies

Kevin peaches

Here Comes Summer!

Donald suntan

Cathy cookouts

Holli swim

Kerrie pool

Jeremy ice cream

Charlie shorts

Tina beach

Have each child bring in a photo of his dad or male caregiver. Cover a board with aluminum foil. Make two sticks of dynamite by taping two short pieces of rope to the ends of two red tagboard rectangles. Staple these to the board as shown, then add a yellow spiked gift bow to the end of each piece of rope. Title the board; then attach the photos. If desired, staple yellow or gold starburst cutouts between the photos.

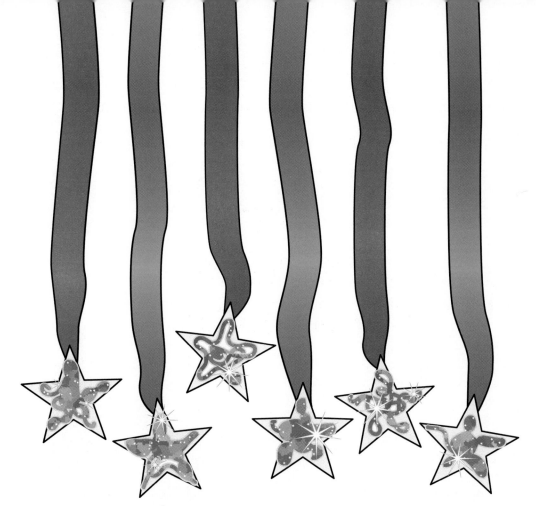

Duplicate a large star pattern on white construction paper for each child. Have her cut out her star, then use glue to make a design on one side. Help the child sprinkle glitter to cover the glue design. When the glue dries, turn the star over and ask the child to create another glue-and-glitter design on the back. Tape each star to the end of a red or blue streamer, then hang the streamers from your classroom ceiling for a dazzling patriotic display.

Cut a length of light brown bulletin-board paper to fit one of your classroom boards. Before covering the board with it, print each child's footprints on the paper with brown paint. After the paint dries, have children use large paintbrushes to spread diluted glue around the footprints. Sprinkle sand onto the glue; then staple the paper to the board and add the title. To complete the display, hot-glue some real seashells to it.

ARTS And CRAFTS All Year

Celebrate through the year with these seasonal craft projects that even little hands can create.

ideas contributed by Bonnie Cave, Linda Ludlow, and Allison Ward

FALL

"SPOOK-TACULAR" HALLOWEEN TREES

"Haunting" around for a Halloween craft? This ghoulish project is sure to provide some spooky fun! Using chalk or oil pastels, draw a leafless tree and a moon on a large, black construction-paper rectangle. Lightly spray the tree with hairspray to prevent smearing. Next gently pull apart several cotton balls; then glue them to the paper. Add a pair of small wiggle eyes to each cotton ghost. Boo!

GOODNESS! IT'S A GLIMMERING GHOST!

The fun has just begun with these ghosts that glimmer day and night. In advance, collect a class supply of plastic tumblers or large cups with slick surfaces. Protect a work surface with waxed paper. To make a ghost, dip a 15-inch square of cheesecloth into a mixture of one part glue and one part water. Squeeze the cloth to remove as much of the liquid as possible. Drape the cheesecloth over an upside-down tumbler. While the glue mixture is wet, sprinkle the ghost with clear glitter. Allow the ghost to dry overnight. The following day detach the fabric from the cup. Glue on wiggle eyes; then use fishing line to suspend the ghost from your ceiling. To have a ghost hunt, turn off your classroom lights. Have youngsters use flashlights to search for glimmering ghouls.

I am thankful for my mom.

Marissa

GREAT GOBBLER PLACEMATS

Circles and triangles make up these placemats that youngsters can use at a class feast or family dinner. To assemble a placemat, a child glues colorful construction-paper triangles to the back of a large brown circle to represent feathers. She then glues a yellow circle, two black circles, a red triangle, and an orange triangle onto the brown circle as shown to resemble the turkey's head. Write on the placemat as the child dictates a thankful thought; then personalize the placemat. These decorative turkey placemats sure do make a terrific Thanksgiving table decoration!

FALL LEAF BANNER

Follow up a leaf hunt by making autumn banners. To make a banner, fold a three-foot length of waxed paper in half; then unfold the paper. Brush one-half of the paper with a layer of thinned white glue. Arrange pieces of torn tissue paper and several leaves over the glue. Cover the project with the remaining half of the waxed paper. Sandwich the project between newsprint; then press it with an iron on low heat. Fold a 9" x 12" sheet of construction paper lengthwise; then unfold the paper. Brush glue over the paper; then center a three-foot length of yarn in the crease. Refold the paper, tucking one narrow end of the waxed-paper project inside. Tie the yarn ends and suspend the resulting banner for all to see.

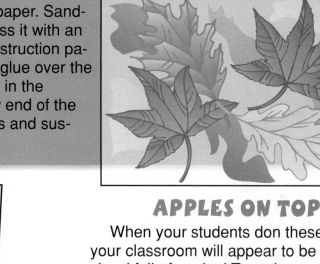

APPLES ON TOP

When your students don these hats, your classroom will appear to be a fall orchard full of apples! To make an apple hat, turn under the edge of a paper lunch bag several times. Sponge-paint the outside of the bag with red, yellow, or green paint. When the paint is dry, glue a green paper leaf shape to the top of the hat (the bottom of the bag). Punch a hole through the folded layers of the bag on both sides; then tie an 18-inch length of yarn to each side. To secure a child's hat on her head, tie the yarn beneath her chin.

HANDFULS OF LEAVES

It won't be a mystery who makes these fall trees because they'll have youngsters' fingerprints all over them! To prepare, put a damp sponge in each of three separate trays; then squirt red, yellow, or orange paint over each sponge. To make a fall scene, have each youngster paint a tree onto a large piece of art paper. Have her press her fingers into a paint-filled sponge, then onto the paper. She repeats this process to fill the tree and ground with leaves, wiping her fingers each time she changes paint colors. What an awesome autumn project—lots of leaves with no raking necessary!

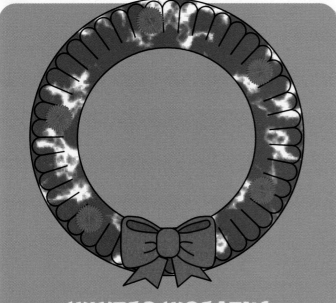

WINTER WREATHS

If you're looking for a craft that will make each child proud of his creative efforts, then these wreaths are winners. To make a Christmas wreath, cut out a paper plate's center. Have a child paint the rim of the plate green using a brush or sponge-painting technique. When the paint is dry, invite the child to spruce up his wreath by decorating it with gold, red, or green glitter glue; red dot stickers; or red pom-poms. Add a paper or fabric bow to the wreath. Punch a hole near the top of the wreath; then add a length of yarn for hanging.

To make a winter wreath, paint the plate rim blue. Splatter-paint the wreath white or decorate it with glitter, artificial snow, or cotton.

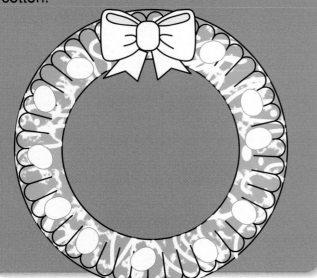

GINGERBREAD ORNAMENT

Youngsters will run, run as fast as they can to make these cinnamon-scented ornaments. Mix an amount of cinnamon and red glitter into a bottle of white glue so that the glue is tinted but still fluid. Squeeze the glue onto a large, paper gingerbread-cookie shape to decorate it. When the glue is dry, punch a hole near the top of the shape; then add a ribbon loop for hanging. Now catch those gingerbread ornaments as fast as you can and hang them on a class tree!

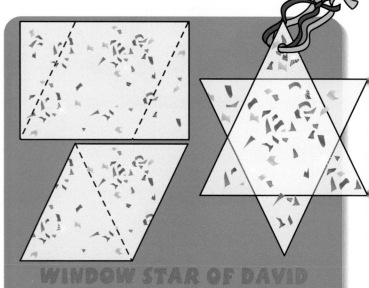

WINDOW STAR OF DAVID

This window decoration will shine during the days and nights of Hanukkah. To make one, cut two same-sized rectangles from clear Con-Tact® covering. Peel the backing off of one rectangle; then lay it sticky-side-up on a table. Sprinkle foil confetti onto the shape. Peel the backing off the second rectangle; then gently press it over the first shape. Trim the rectangle to form a parallelogram as shown. Then cut the parallelogram in half to form two triangles. Glue the triangles together to form the Star of David. Punch a hole near the tip of one triangle; then tie on lengths of blue and gold curling ribbon for hanging.

NEW YEAR'S PARTY HAT

Ten, nine, eight…count down to New Year's fun with these festive party hats. To make one, use a variety of art supplies—such as markers, crayons, stickers, feathers, glitter, and confetti—to decorate a paper half-circle that measures 12 inches on the straight side. To the bottom center of the undecorated side, tape icicle tinsel (used to decorate Christmas trees). Roll the half-circle into a cone shape, making sure that the tinsel hangs out from the point of the cone. Staple the paper in place. To complete the hat, punch a hole on each side; then tie an 18-inch length of yarn to each side. Help each child tie on his party hat; then, as a group, count down to begin a New Year's class party!

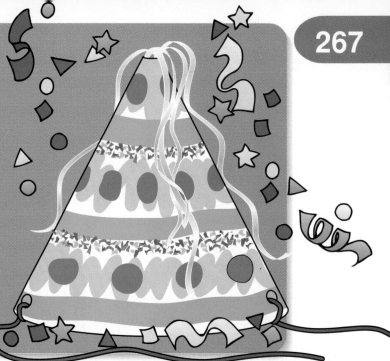

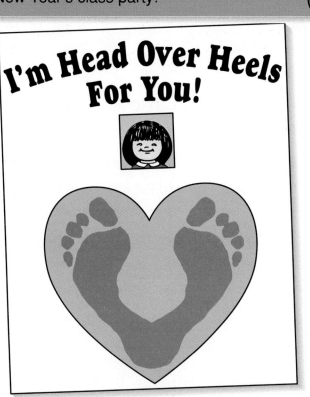

I'm Head Over Heels For You!

HEAD OVER HEELS

Step right up for a valentine project that you'll fall head over heels in love with! In advance take a close-up picture of each child; then have the pictures developed. Mix a small amount of dishwashing liquid with red tempera paint in a shallow pan. Place paper towels and a dishpan of warm, soapy water nearby. To make a valentine, ask a child to dip her bare feet into the paint. Have her press her feet one at a time onto a pink paper heart so that the heel prints overlap. Assist the child as she washes her feet. When the paint is dry, glue the heart onto a large piece of paper. Add the child's photo and the message shown. Who could resist such a sweet sentiment?

SNOWFLAKE CHARMER

Make these necklaces as keepsakes of a snowy day. Paint three snap-apart craft sticks white. When the paint is dry, stack and glue the sticks—one atop the other—to form a snowflake. Glue sequins or pearls onto the snowflake. Tie the center of a length of white yarn near the tip of one of the sticks; then tie the ends of the yarn together to complete the necklace.

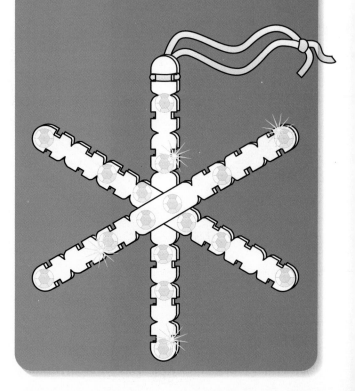

SHAMROCK NECKLACE

The rainbow of colors and the shamrocks on this necklace may bring you enough luck to find a pot of gold! Use markers to color each of six rigatoni noodles—one purple, one blue, one green, one yellow, one red, and one orange. Cut a double shamrock shape as shown from green construction paper. Fold the cutout over the center of a 30-inch length of yarn; then glue it together over the yarn. If desired, add green, gold, or multicolored glitter to the shamrock. Thread three noodles onto the yarn on each side of the shamrock. Tie the yarn to complete the necklace; then begin looking for gold. Good luck!

Everlasting Easter Eggs

The Easter Bunny loves decorating eggs, and so will your little ones. Shape a ball of Crayola® Model Magic® nontoxic, air-drying modeling compound into an egg shape. Allow the egg to dry overnight. Use markers, watercolor paints, or a sponge-painting technique to decorate the egg. If desired glue on sequins or jewels, or add glitter glue to the egg. Moms will want to display these unique eggs for years to come.

A-TISKET, A-TASKET

These baskets are so sweet—especially when they've been filled with Easter candies! Fold two identically sized construction-paper circles in half. Glue the circles together so that the sides overlap and two points meet to form a basket as shown. Glue a construction-paper strip to the inside of the basket for a handle. Decorate the basket with markers or stickers. Fill the basket with Easter grass and goodies. A-tisket, a-tasket, what a lovely basket!

MOTHER'S DAY HYACINTHS

Give Mom a pretty pot of hyacinths in honor of her special day. In advance spray-paint a supply of popped popcorn light blue, pink, yellow, or lavender. Allow the paint to dry. Cover a work surface with waxed paper. Put Aleene's™ Tacky Glue in a small container. To make a pot of flowers, color a craft stick green. Lay the stick on the paper. Repeatedly dip pieces of popcorn into the glue; then press them onto the top half of the stick to resemble a hyacinth. When the glue is dry, peel off the waxed paper; then add several more popcorn pieces to the opposite side of the stick. Put a small lump of clay into the bottom of a small plastic cup; then press the craft stick into the clay so that the flower stands upright. Dip the ends of several construction-paper leaves into glue; then tuck them into the cup around the flower. Complete the pot by adding a Mother's Day message.

Happy Mother's Day!

GROWING CATERPILLAR

This crafty caterpillar promotes creativity *and* counting skills! To make one, sponge-paint the desired number of small paper plates. When the paint is dry, poke two pipe cleaners through the rim of one of the plates and twist them into place. Use markers to add facial features below the pipe-cleaner antennae. To assemble the caterpillar, arrange the plates side by side, slightly overlapping the plates' edges. Use brads to fasten the plates together. Or, as a variation, punch two holes on opposite sides of each plate's rim so that a child can connect the plates with brads. When assembled properly, the caterpillar will fold into a stack. Invite each child to count as he watches his caterpillar grow plate by plate!

RAINY-DAY WATERCOLORS

This simple project is inspired by April showers. After looking at pictures of spring flowers, use watercolor markers to draw simple flowers on a piece of white construction paper. Paint water over the drawings, watching as the colors blend into a rainy-day garden.

HAPPY FATHER'S DAY

Each dad who receives this card will be surprised to find out that he had a hand in making it! For each child, fold a light-colored sheet of construction paper in half. Send the paper and a marker home with each child, along with a note requesting that the child's dad (or male caregiver) trace the outline of his hand on the front of the card. When the card is returned, write "Happy Father's Day" on the front of it and the poem shown on the inside. Encourage the child to write his name and draw a picture of his dad in the card. Then assist him in pressing a paint handprint onto the front of the card inside the outline of his dad's hand.

Happy Father's Day

Hand in hand
all through the day,
You help me work
and help me play!

Sam

FIRECRACKER, FIRECRACKER

Boom, boom, boom! An explosion of fun is in store when youngsters make these firecracker paintings. Arrange newspapers on the ground outside. To paint, put a large sheet of black construction paper on the newspaper. Dip a paintbrush in red, white, or blue paint; then splatter-paint the black paper. Using a different brush for each color of paint, continue painting in this manner to create a shower of fireworks. While the paint is wet, sprinkle on glitter. Oh, say, can't you see these patriotic paintings on display!

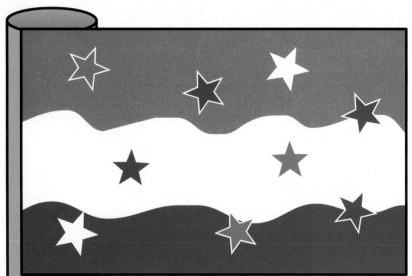

STAR-SPANGLED BANNERS

These bright banners let you know that red, white, and blue are the colors of the season. Using patriotic paint colors, paint a design on a white construction-paper rectangle. When the paint is dry, add star stickers if desired. Tape the banner to a paper-towel tube. Wave those flags with pride!

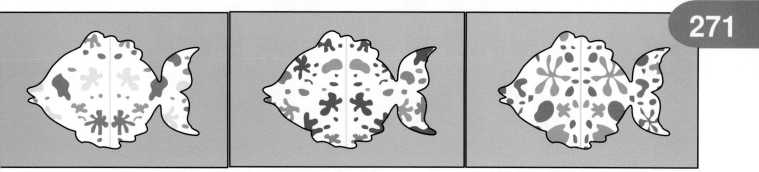

FISHY ART

To make this unique fish painting, fold a sheet of construction paper in half. Unfold the sheet. Using paintbrushes, drop several colors of paint onto one-half of the paper. Refold the paper; then gently press the sides together. Unfold the paper once more. Allow the paint to dry. Cut a simple fish shape out of an identically sized sheet of blue construction paper. Glue the remaining blue frame on top of the painted sheet. Display these projects together on a wall (patchwork style) to create a lovely school of fish.

A SLICE OF SUMMER

After serving a watermelon treat, wash and dry the seeds for use on this sensory project. Just before painting, mix enough watermelon-flavored drink mix into red fingerpaint so that it smells like the real thing. Fingerpaint on a fingerpainting-paper circle. Drop watermelon seeds onto the wet paint. When the paint is dry, mount the circle onto a slightly larger green construction-paper circle.

SUMMER GARDENING

This painting idea comes fresh from the garden. In advance collect vegetables and prepare them for painting. For example, slice a broccoli stalk in half, trim the bottom off a carrot, and slice a green pepper in half. (For best results, let the cut vegetables dry for a short period.) Pour appropriate colors of paints into shallow tins. To begin, draw lines to create several rows on a length of brown bulletin-board paper. Next paint prints in the rows using your choice of vegetables. Now that's an open-ended art idea that's freshly picked and freshly painted!

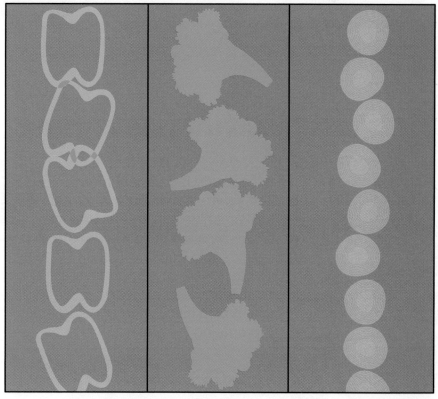

SEASONAL SONGS, POEMS, AND FINGERPLAYS

Enhance circle time or anytime with this just-right collection
of rhythm and rhyme for your favorite holidays and seasons.

contributed by Lucia Kemp Henry

FALL LEAVES ACTION POEM

The leaves on the trees blow in the breeze   *Sway from side to side.*
And they all fall down, down, down.   *Slowly "fall" to the floor.*
The leaves are blowing down to the ground   *Stand up and wave arms.*
As they whirl and twirl all around.   *Twirl in a circle.*
The leaves on the ground pile up so high   *Raise hands above head.*
'Til no more are left in the trees or the sky!   *Shake head "no"; show empty hands.*

If desired, have youngsters hold large construction-
paper leaves as they perform the poem.

ANIMALS IN AUTUMN

Six black crows get fat eating corn.
Five mice scurry on a frosty morn.
Four red squirrels hide nuts in a tree.
Three chipmunks stop and look at me.
Two brown beavers build their home all day.
And the little wild goose will soon fly away.

Use this poem as an introduction to a
circle-time discussion about animals
preparing for winter.

PUMPKIN SONG

(sung to the tune of "Twinkle, Twinkle, Little Star")

Pumpkin, pumpkin, big and round;   *Hold arms out wide.*
Pumpkin, pumpkin, on the ground.   *Stoop down and touch floor.*
Pumpkin, pumpkin, orange and fat;   *Pat stomach with both hands.*
Pumpkin, pumpkin, look at that!   *Point ahead with eyes wide.*
Pumpkin, pumpkin, my oh my!   *Smile.*
I can't wait for pumpkin pie!   *Rub tummy.*

WINTER WEATHER CHANT

It's cold outside!
The wind does blow.
The rain falls down.
The clouds drop snow.

It's warm inside!
The fire is bright.
The cocoa's hot.
Your hugs feel right!

It's cold outside—
Too cold to play.
It's warm inside;
Let's stay in all day!

After reciting this chant, have young-sters tell you different ways to get warm on a cold day.

I'M A LITTLE CANDLE

(sung to the tune of "I'm A Little Teapot")

Verse 1: I'm a little candle dressed in white,
Wearing a hat of yellow light.

Chorus: When the night is dark, then you will see
Just how bright my light can be!

Verse 2: I'm a little candle straight and tall,
Shining my light upon you all.

Repeat chorus.

Verse 3: I'm a little candle burning bright,
Keeping you safe all through the night.

Repeat chorus.

Use this song for Advent, Hanukkah, Christmas, or Kwanzaa.

GIFTS OF LOVE

I couldn't buy a gift for you 'Cause I am very small.	*Put hands in pockets; shake head "no." Point to self.*
But I can give you some things— The greatest gifts of all!	*Shake head "yes." Hold hands out as if giving gift.*
I can give you kisses. I can hug you, too.	*Blow kisses. Hug self.*
I can give a friendly smile And tell you, "I love you!"	*Smile and wave. Say "I love you" in sign language.*

VALENTINE SONG
(sung to the tune of "Merrily We Roll Along")

Won't you be my valentine,
Valentine, valentine?
Won't you be my valentine?
Here's a **heart** for you.

Won't you be my valentine,
Valentine, valentine?
Won't you be my valentine?
Here's a **card** for you.

Won't you be my valentine,
Valentine, valentine?
Won't you be my valentine?
Here's a **hug** for you.

Repeat the song as many times
as desired, substituting other
gifts or gestures for
the boldfaced
words.

ST. PATRICK'S DAY

Before teaching youngsters this call-and-response rhyme, prepare several green construction-paper cutouts of various objects, such as a leaf, a frog, a bug, and a kite. Hold up the cutouts one at a time and repeat the chant, having youngsters replace the boldfaced word each time.

Teacher, showing **leaf** cutout:
    Have you seen
    Something green
    On St. Patrick's Day?

Students:
    Yes, we have seen
    A **leaf** that's green
    On St. Patrick's Day.

SPRINGTIME SONG

(sung to the tune of "Did You Ever See A Lassie?")

Hello, spring! It's good to see you,
To see you, to see you.
Hello, spring! It's good to see you!
It's springtime again!

Hello, **leaves**! It's good to see you,
To see you, to see you.
Hello, **leaves**! It's good to see you!
It's springtime again!

Hello, **buds**! It's good to see you,
To see you, to see you.
Hello, **buds**! It's good to see you!
It's springtime again!

Repeat the song, if desired, asking students to name other springtime objects to substitute for the boldfaced words.

WATCH THE RAIN

(sung to the tune of "London Bridge")

Watch the rain come falling down,
Falling down, falling down.
Watch the rain come falling down.
Watch the rain fall.

Watch the rain fall on the **grass**,
On the **grass**, on the **grass**.
Watch the rain fall on the **grass**.
Watch the rain fall.

Repeat the verse as many times as desired, substituting other appropriate words—such as *trees, leaves,* and *birds*—for the boldfaced word.

MOMMY (OR DADDY)

(sung to the tune of "Daisy, Daisy")

Mommy, Mommy,
You know that I love you.
You're my mommy—
Nobody else will do!
Oh, Mommy, when we're together,
We have the best time ever!
Oh, Mom, it's true:
I do love you!
Mommy, nobody else will do!

Use this song in celebration of Mother's Day. To use the song for Father's Day, simply substitute *Daddy* for *Mommy* throughout the song.

LET'S GO OUTSIDE

Let's go outside.	*Pretend to open door.*
It's summertime!	*Jump up and down and smile.*
We'll play at your house	*Point to an imaginary friend.*
And then play at mine.	*Point to self.*
Let's go outside.	*Pretend to open door.*
It's nice and hot.	*Fan face with hand.*
We'll get the hose	*Pretend to spray hose.*
And splash a lot!	*Make splashing motions with hands.*
Let's go outside.	*Pretend to open door.*
The sun is bright.	*Circle arms overhead to imitate sun.*
Let's play all day	*Skip or run in place.*
'Til we say, "Good night!"	*Wave good-bye.*

Here's a handy collection of seasonal and holiday group activities that will add spark to your curriculum all through the year!

ideas contributed by LeeAnn Collins

FALL FOLLIES

Fill your classroom with these swirling, twirling colorful leaves that will welcome fall with lots of smiles. Cut a class supply of leaf shapes from colored construction paper. Tape a craft stick to the back of each leaf. Then use the leaves with the activities listed below.

- Play lively classical music and invite each child to dance around in a designated area, performing some creative movements with his leaf.

- Play a game similar to Simon Says by giving directions to children who are holding specific-colored leaves. For example, "Red leaves, stand up," "Orange leaves, jump up and down," and "Yellow leaves, wiggle your noses."

- Direct each child in a small group to choose a leaf. Create a graph with the leaf choices. Compare to see which color is the group favorite.

"BOO-TIFUL" PATTERNS

This patterning activity will make your little pumpkins grin like jack-o'-lanterns! To prepare, duplicate onto orange construction paper a class supply plus several extra of the patterning card on page 281. Cut out each card, fold it along the dotted line, and tape the open side together. Give each child one of the two-sided cards. Then use the extra cards to create a simple pattern on the floor. Have students help you read the pattern aloud. Then invite each student, in turn, to place his card on its correct side to extend the pattern. If desired add difficulty to the activity by making cards in two different colors. Bat, bat, pumpkin, bat, bat…

FINDING FEATHERS

"Gobble, gobble, gobble!" Can your students help the turkey find his lost feathers? Have several children stand in a row in front of the rest of the group. Direct the group to close their eyes while you distribute a feather to each of two or more standing children (depending on how difficult you want to make the game). Have all the standing children cup their hands behind their backs, so that it appears that all are hiding feathers. Have the children in the seated group open their eyes; then invite volunteers to try to guess who is holding a feather. If a child guesses correctly, have her change places with the feather holder. When all of the feathers have been found, it's time for another round. Continue until every child has had a turn to stand in front of the group.

Let It Snow!

Practice counting, comparing, and predicting while discussing winter activities with your youngsters. To prepare, duplicate the pictures on page 282, color them, and cut them out. Glue each picture to the center of a separate small paper plate. Ask your students what activities they like to do in the snow and make a list of their responses. Display the paper plates in front of your group; then give each child a spring-type clothespin. Have him attach his clothespin to the plate showing his favorite winter activity. Stop periodically as children are voting and discuss which activity has the most or fewest votes. About halfway through the voting, ask your students to predict which activity will come out on top. Count the votes together after everyone has had a turn. Were the predictions correct? Let it snow!

HAPPY HOLIDAYS

Celebrate the season with this visual-discrimination activity. Gather a collection of winter holiday objects—such as an ornament, a menorah, a candle, a star, a dreidel, and a small wrapped gift. Arrange these objects on a tabletop for your group of students to see. Direct students to close their eyes while you remove an object. Invite youngsters to take turns guessing which item is missing. Have the correct guesser remove an object in the next round of play. For an added challenge, arrange the objects in a row. Give students a minute to study the lineup. Then cover the objects with a cloth and see who can remember which objects were first, second, third, and so on.

My Rhymin' Valentine

Encourage youngsters to make a rhyme every time with hearts and body parts! Cut out a class supply of small, felt hearts. Give each child a heart cutout. Then have each child find a valentine partner. Instruct the children to listen to the word you say, then put their hearts on their partners' body part that rhymes with that word. For example, if you say, "bear," a child should put his heart on his partner's hair. If you say, "egg," he should put his heart on his partner's leg. It's really true that it's more fun with two!

tree

RAIN, RAIN, RAIN

On a rainy, spring day, introduce this musical raindrop activity. To prepare, duplicate a copy of page 283 onto blue construction paper for each child. Have the child cut out his raindrops (or precut them for younger preschoolers), then arrange the drops in front of him. Call out a size and instruct the child to hold up his corresponding raindrop. Then sing the following song and have each child "rain" the appropriate raindrop.

(sung to the tune of "She'll Be Coming 'Round The Mountain")

I'm a teeny, tiny raindrop in a cloud.　　*(Sing quietly.)*
I'm a teeny, tiny raindrop in a cloud.
I'm a teeny, tiny raindrop,
I'm a teeny, tiny raindrop,
I'm a teeny, tiny raindrop in a cloud.

I'm a medium-sized raindrop in a cloud.　*(Sing in a normal tone of voice.)*
I'm a medium-sized raindrop in a cloud.
I'm a medium-sized raindrop,
I'm a medium-sized raindrop,
I'm a medium-sized raindrop in a cloud.

I'm a great big raindrop in a cloud.　　*(Sing loudly.)*
I'm a great big raindrop in a cloud.
I'm a great big raindrop,
I'm a great big raindrop,
I'm a great big raindrop in a cloud.

SCRAMBLED EGGS

Scrambled eggs are good for breakfast, but not for Easter! Mix up a class supply of colored, plastic eggs so that each egg's two parts are different colors. Put the eggs in a basket. Explain to your little ones that the Easter Bunny has had an accident; then show them the basket of eggs. Ask students if they think they could work together to help him out. Instruct them to switch the egg tops and bottoms so that the basket is full of solid-colored eggs for the Easter Bunny to hide. Congratulate them for completing the task and working together well. Then, later in the day while your students are not in the room, put a few jelly beans in each egg and hide the eggs around your classroom. Write a thank-you note from the Easter Bunny and tape it to the handle of the empty basket. When your bunny helpers return to the classroom, read the note aloud and invite them to find the hidden eggs. Hippity-hoppity! Easter's on its way!

Dear Friends,
Thank you for helping me get my eggs in tip-top shape for Easter. I've hidden an egg for each of you to find. Happy hunting!

Love,
The Easter Bunny

Use with " 'Boo-tiful' Patterns" on page 278.

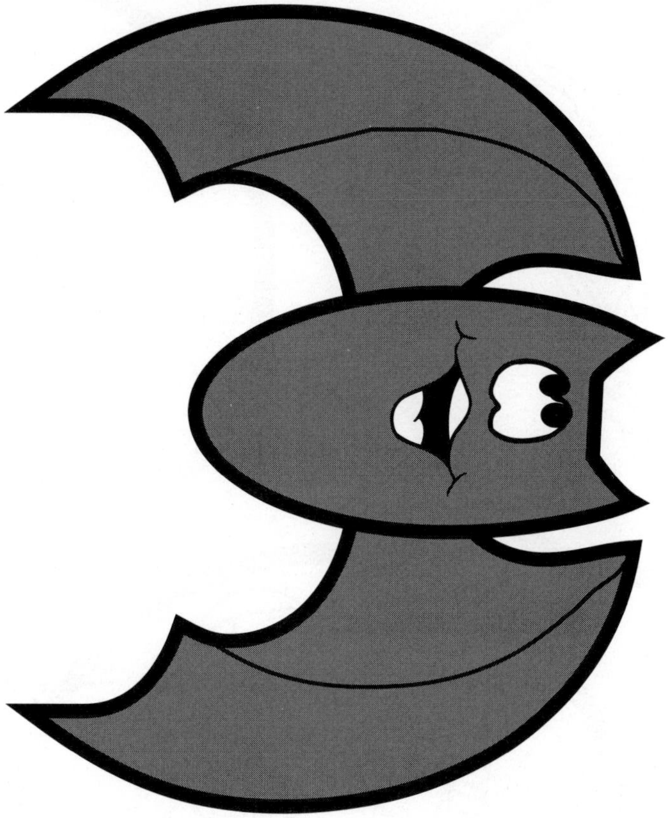

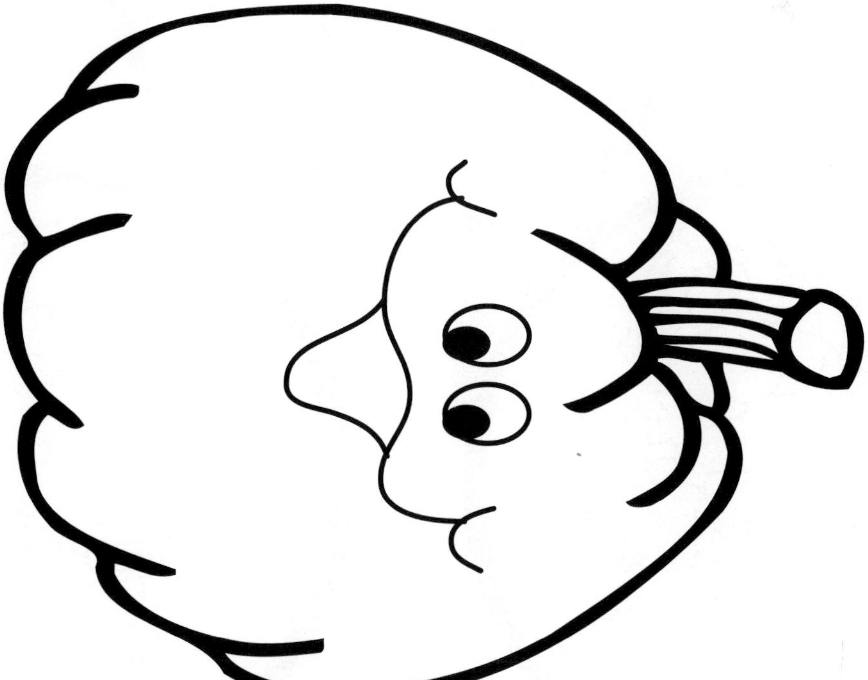

Winter Pictures
Use with "Let It Snow!" on page 279.

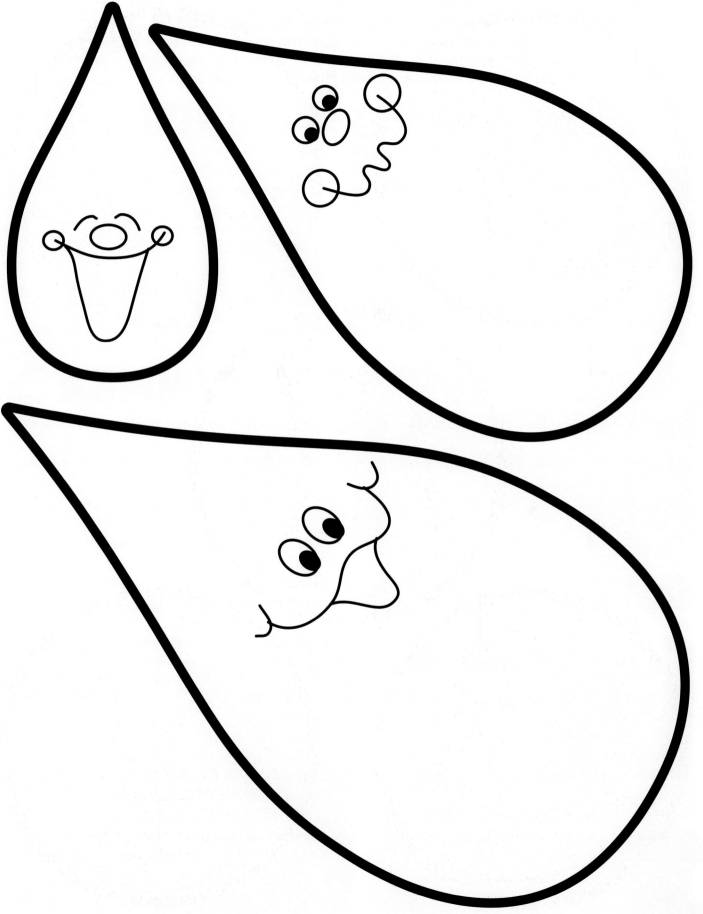

CELEBRATE!

Use the following list of books to celebrate the seasons and holidays. Whether they're used to introduce a unit, to follow up an activity, or simply for storytime enjoyment, these picks just can't be beat!

compiled by Angie Kutzer

FALL

Fall by Ron Hirschi, Cobblehill Books

Fresh Fall Leaves by Betsy Franco, Scholastic Inc.

Marmalade's Yellow Leaf by Cindy Wheeler, Alfred A. Knopf, Inc.

Nuts To You! by Lois Ehlert, Harcourt Brace & Company

Red Leaf, Yellow Leaf by Lois Ehlert, Harcourt Brace & Company

WINTER

Amy Loves The Snow by Julia Hoban, HarperCollins Publishers, Inc.

A Hat For Minerva Louise by Janet Morgan Stoeke, Dutton Children's Books

Here Comes The Snow by Angela Shelf Medearis, Scholastic Inc.

Sledding by Elizabeth Winthrop, HarperCollins Publishers, Inc.

Wake Me In Spring by James Preller, Scholastic Inc.

SPRING

The Garden In Our Yard by Greg Henry Quinn, Scholastic Inc.

My Spring Robin by Anne Rockwell, Macmillan Publishing Company, Inc.

Spring by Chris L. Demarest, Harcourt Brace & Company

The Spring Hat by Madelaine Gill, Simon & Schuster Books For Young Readers

When Spring Comes by Robert Maass, Henry Holt And Company, Inc.

SUMMER

A Beach Day by Douglas Florian, Greenwillow Books

Once Upon A Picnic by John Prater and Vivian French, Candlewick Press

One Hot Summer Day by Nina Crews, Greenwillow Books

Summer by Chris L. Demarest, Harcourt Brace & Company

The Too Hot Day by Beverly Komoda, HarperCollins Publishers, Inc.

HALLOWEEN

Dinosaurs' Halloween by Liza Donnelly, Scholastic Inc.

Halloween Cats by Jean Marzollo, Scholastic Inc.

It's Pumpkin Time! by Zoe Hall, Scholastic Inc.

Popcorn by Frank Asch, Parents' Magazine Press

Scare The Moon by Harriet Ziefert, Candlewick Press

THANKSGIVING

Best Thanksgiving Book by Pat Whitehead, Troll Associates

1, 2, 3 Thanksgiving! by W. Nikola-Lisa, Albert Whitman & Company

Thanksgiving Treat by Catherine Stock, Macmillan Publishing Company, Inc.

Today Is Thanksgiving! by P. K. Hallinan, Ideals Children's Books

A Turkey For Thanksgiving by Eve Bunting, Clarion Books

HANUKKAH

Arielle And The Hanukkah Surprise by Devra Speregen and Shirley Newberger, Scholastic Inc.

The Chanukkah Guest by Eric A. Kimmel, Scholastic Inc.

Grandma's Latkes by Malka Drucker, Harcourt Brace & Company

Light The Lights! A Story About Celebrating Hanukkah And Christmas by Margaret Moorman, Scholastic Inc.

My First Hanukkah Book by Aileen Fisher, Regensteiner Publishing Enterprises, Inc.

CHRISTMAS

Clifford's Christmas by Norman Bridwell, Scholastic Inc.

Jingle Bells illustrated by Normand Chartier, Simon & Schuster Children's

Looking For Santa Claus by Henrik Drescher, Lothrop, Lee & Shepard Books

Merry Christmas Mom And Dad by Mercer Mayer, Western Publishing Company, Inc.

Waiting For Christmas by Monica Greenfield, Scholastic Inc.

KWANZAA

The Gifts Of Kwanzaa by Synthia Saint James, Albert Whitman & Company

Imani's Gift At Kwanzaa by Denise Burden-Patmon, Simon & Schuster Children's

Kwanzaa by A. P. Porter, Carolrhoda Books, Inc.

Kwanzaa by Janet Riehecky, Childrens Press®, Inc.

My First Kwanzaa Book by Deborah M. Newton Chocolate, Scholastic Inc.

VALENTINE'S DAY

Honey, I Love by Eloise Greenfield, HarperCollins Publishers

Little Mouse's Big Valentine by Thacher Hurd, HarperCollins Publishers

Rosie Rabbit's Valentine's Day by Harriet Ziefert, Candlewick Press

Valentine Cats by Jean Marzollo, Scholastic Inc.

A Village Full Of Valentines by James Stevenson, Greenwillow Books

EASTER

Danny And The Easter Egg by Edith Kunhardt, Greenwillow Books

Easter Surprise by Catherine Stock, Bradbury Press

Little Mouse Meets The Easter Bunny by Harriet Ziefert, HarperCollins Publishers

Little Rabbit's Easter Surprise by Kenn and Joanne Compton, Holiday House, Inc.

Spot's First Easter by Eric Hill, G. P. Putnam's Sons

MOTHER'S DAY

Flower Garden by Eve Bunting, Harcourt Brace & Company

I Like It When... by Mary Murphy, Harcourt Brace & Company

I Love You As Much... by Laura Krauss Melmed, Lothrop, Lee & Shepard Books

Just For You by Mercer Mayer, Western Publishing Company, Inc.

Lots Of Moms by Shelley Rotner and Sheila M. Kelly, Penguin Books USA Inc.

FATHER'S DAY

Daddies by Dian Curtis Regan, Scholastic Inc.

Guess How Much I Love You by Sam McBratney, Candlewick Press

I Meant To Tell You by James Stevenson, Greenwillow Books

My Father's Hands by Joanne Ryder, Morrow Junior Books

When Daddy Came To School by Julie Brillhart, Albert Whitman & Company

HOLIDAY MEDLEYS

Here's a list of seasonal musical selections to add to the flavor, fun, and fancy of holidays and special days.

compiled by Mackie Rhodes

SEASONS

"Snowflake"
Rockin' Down The Road (winter)

"The Garden Song"
10 Carrot Diamond (spring)

"Star Sun"
Bahamas Pajamas (summer)

"Hello Winter"
Diamonds & Dragons (all seasons)

HALLOWEEN

Halloween Fun (entire album)

"Halloween Night" *Bahamas Pajamas*

"Halloween On Parade" *Holidays And Special Times*

"Have A Good Time On Halloween Night"
Holiday Songs & Rhythms

"Jack-O-Lantern" *Dinosaur Ride*

"Looking For Dracula" *10 Carrot Diamond*

"Monster" *Can You Sound Just Like Me?*

"Scared As I Can Be"
Mr. Al Sings Friends And Feelings

THANKSGIVING

"Happy Thanksgiving To All"
Holidays And Special Times

"Things I'm Thankful For"
Holiday Songs & Rhythms and
Holiday Magic

WINTER CELEBRATIONS
CHRISTMAS, HANUKKAH, KWANZAA

These recordings include Christmas songs, in addition to the following selections for the special days indicated.

Holiday Magic
"Chanukah, Oh Chanukah"

Holiday Songs & Rhythms
"Hanukkah"

Tis The Season
"Hanukkah Medley: Hanukkah, Oh Hanukkah Hanukkah"

Holiday Times
"Dreidel, Dreidel, Dreidel"

"Harmonica For Hanukkah"

"My Little Blue Dreidel"

"Kwanza Time"

The Christmas Gift
"Little Dreydl Spin"

VALENTINE'S DAY

"If Apples Were Pears" *Imagine That!*

"Love Is…"
Holidays And Special Times

"Valentines Song"
Holiday Songs & Rhythms

EASTER

"Peter Cottontail"
Holidays And Special Times

"Easter Time Is Here Again"
Holiday Songs & Rhythms

MOTHER'S DAY AND FATHER'S DAY

"A Mother Is Forever" and "Hush Little Baby"
Diamonds & Daydreams

"May There Always Be Sunshine" (multilingual) *10 Carrot Diamond*

For more information or to order the listed recordings, contact:

10 Carrot Diamond, Charlotte Diamond,
Hug Bug Records
([604] 931-7375)

Bahamas Pajamas, Joe Scruggs,
Shadow Play Records
(1-800-274-8804)

Can You Sound Just Like Me?,
Red Grammer,
Red Note Records
([315] 676-5516)

Diamonds & Daydreams,
Charlotte Diamond,
Hug Bug Records
([604] 931-7375)

Diamonds & Dragons, Charlotte Diamond,
Hug Bug Records
([604] 931-7375)

Dinosaur Ride, Jim Valley And Friends,
Rainbow Planet Records And Tapes
(1-800-523-2371)

Halloween Fun,
KIMBO® Educational
(1-800-631-2187)

Holiday Magic, Hap Palmer,
Hap-Pal Music Inc.
(1-800-645-3739)

Holiday Songs & Rhythms, Hap Palmer,
Educational Activities, Inc.
(1-800-645-3739)

Holiday Times, Ella Jenkins,
Smithsonian Folkways Recordings
(1-800-410-9815)

Holidays And Special Times, Greg & Steve,
Youngheart Music
(1-800-444-4287)

Imagine That!, Jim Valley And Friends,
Rainbow Planet Records And Tapes
(1-800-523-2371)

Mr. Al Sings Friends And Feelings, Mr. Al,
Melody House
(1-800-234-9228)

Rockin' Down The Road, Greg & Steve,
Youngheart Music
(1-800-444-4287)

The Christmas Gift, Charlotte Diamond,
Hug Bug Records
([604] 931-7375)

Tis The Season, Fred Koch,
Melody House, Inc.
(1-800-234-9228)

YOU'RE A TREAT!

Happy Halloween!

From Your Teacher

©1998 The Education Center, Inc. • TEC458

You add spice to our class.
Happy Thanksgiving!
From Your Teacher

©1998 The Education Center, Inc. • TEC458

Note To The Teacher: Make a construction-paper copy of these cards for each child. Color the cards; then cut them out. If desired, spread glue in the middle of the pie on the Thanksgiving card; then sprinkle on some pumpkin-pie spice, cinnamon, or allspice.

BIRTHDAY WISHES
From Your Teacher
©1998 The Education Center, Inc. • TEC458

Happy Holidays!
From Your Teacher

©1998 The Education Center, Inc. • TEC458

©1998 The Education Center, Inc. • *The Mailbox® Superbook* • *Preschool* • TEC458

Note To The Teacher: Make a construction-paper copy of these cards for each child. Color the cards; then cut them out. If desired, glue wiggle eyes onto the polar bear cub's face and glue candy sprinkles to the cupcake.

U R
SPECIAL
2 ME!

From
Your Teacher

©1998 The Education Center, Inc. • TEC458

HAPPY
ST. PATRICK'S DAY

From
Your
Teacher

©1998 The Education Center, Inc. • TEC458

©1998 The Education Center, Inc. • *The Mailbox® Superbook* • *Preschool* • TEC458

Note To The Teacher: *Make a construction-paper copy of these cards for each child. Color the cards; then cut them out. If desired, attach the valentine to an individual serving-size box of actual conversation hearts. Jazz up the St. Patrick's Day card by gluing green glitter to the shamrock.*

"HOPPY" EASTER

From Your Teacher

©1998 The Education Center, Inc. • TEC458

GOOD LUCK IN "KINDER-GARDEN"!

From Your Teacher

©1998 The Education Center, Inc. • TEC458

Note To The Teacher: Make a construction-paper copy of these cards for each child. Color the cards; then cut them out. If desired, embellish the Easter egg with sequins and glitter.

Programming Suggestions: Use a copy of this page for a newsletter, a parent note, a booklist, or a center game or label.

Programming Suggestions: Use a copy of this page for a newsletter, a parent note, a booklist, or a center game or label.

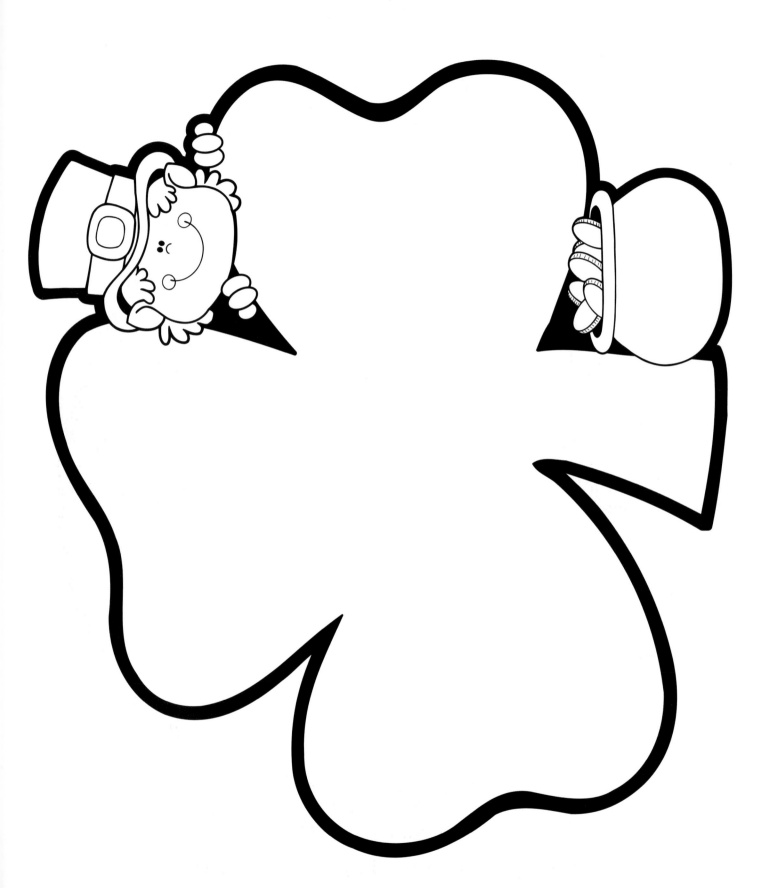

Programming Suggestions: Use a copy of this page for a newsletter, a parent note, a booklist, or a center game or label.

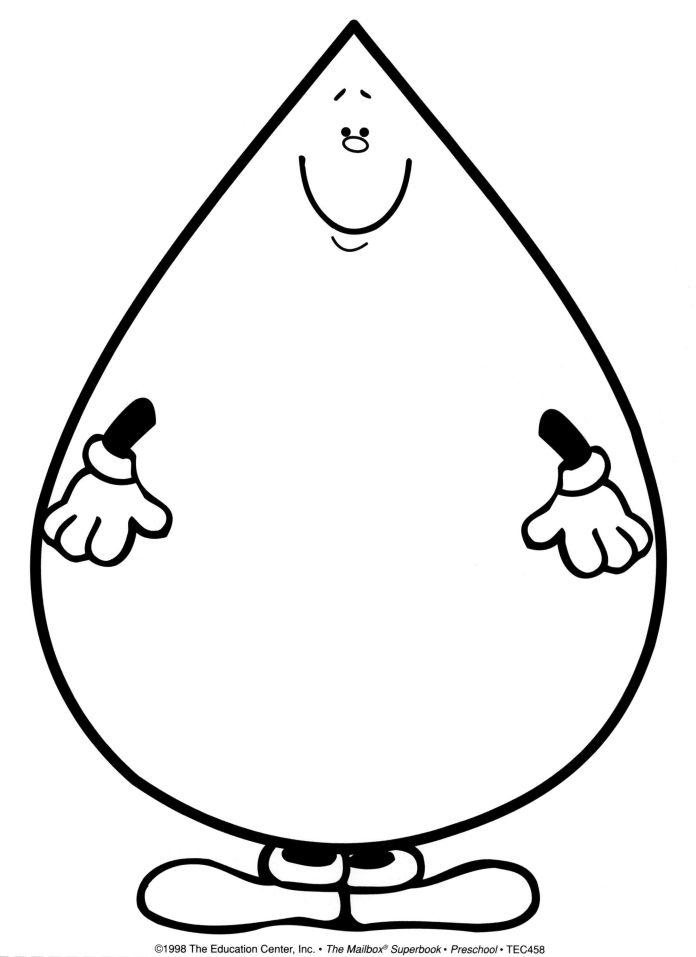

Programming Suggestions: Use a copy of this page for a newsletter, a parent note, a booklist, or a center game or label.

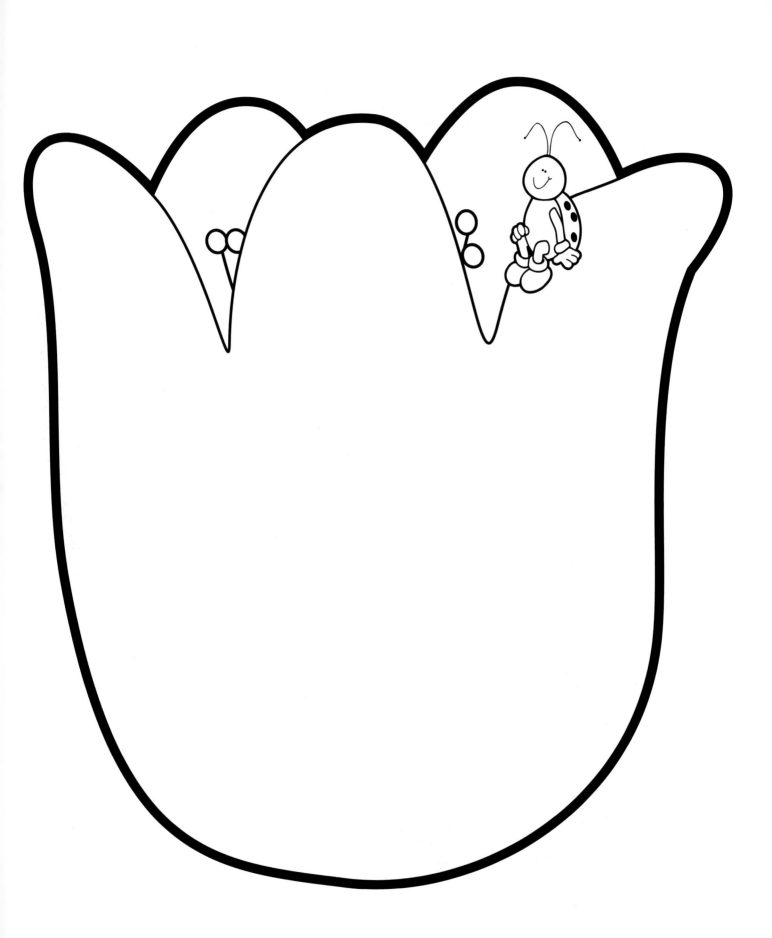

Programming Suggestions: Use a copy of this page for a newsletter, a parent note, a booklist, or a center game or label.

Programming Suggestions: Use a copy of this page for a newsletter, a parent note, a booklist, or a center game or label.

Programming Suggestions: Use a copy of this page for a newsletter, a parent note, a booklist, or a center game or label.

Programming Suggestions: Use a copy of this page for a newsletter, a parent note, a booklist, or a center game or label.

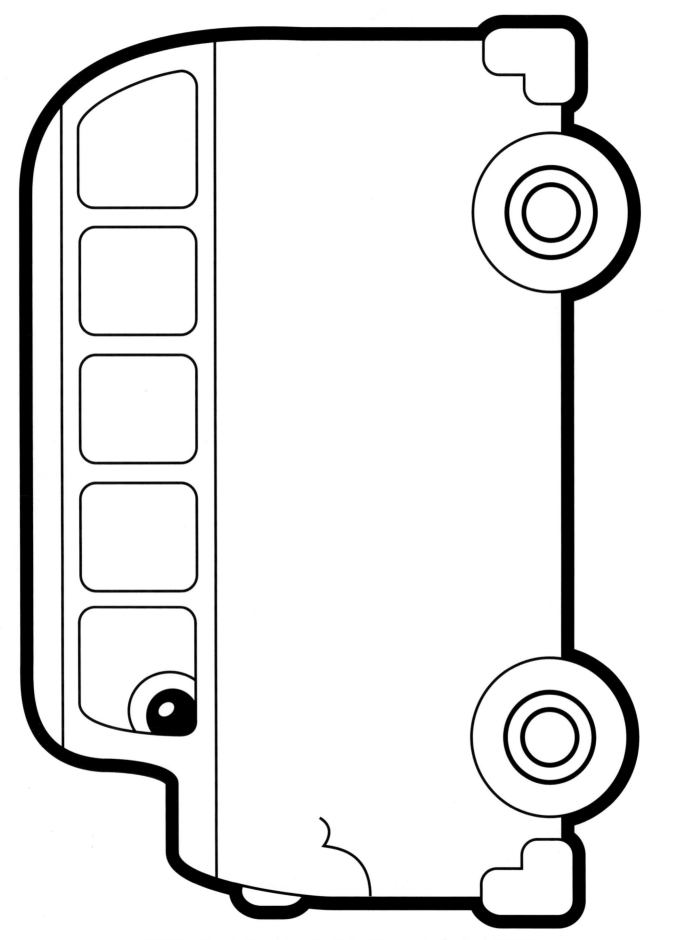

Programming Suggestions: Use a copy of this page for a newsletter, a parent note, a booklist, or a center game or label.

Programming Suggestions: Use a copy of this page for a newsletter, a parent note, a booklist, or a center game or label.

Programming Suggestions: Use a copy of this page for a newsletter, a parent note, a booklist, or a center game or label.

Programming Suggestions: Use a copy of this page for a newsletter, a parent note, a booklist, or a center game or label.

JANUARY

Sunday	Monday	Tuesday	Wednesday	Thursday	Friday	Saturday

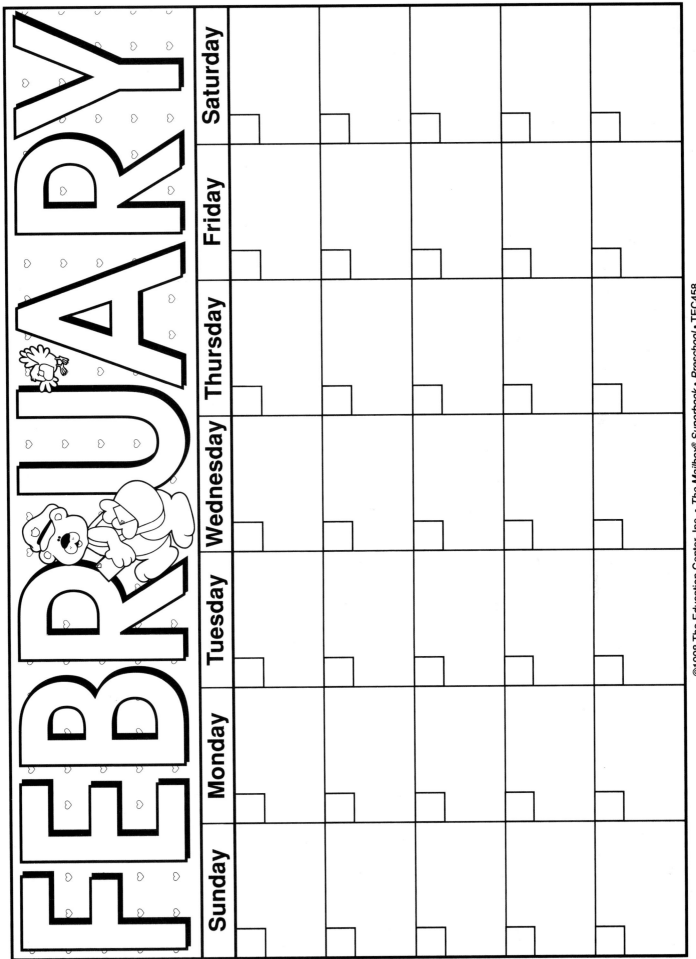

FEBRUARY

Sunday	Monday	Tuesday	Wednesday	Thursday	Friday	Saturday

Sunday	Monday	Tuesday	Wednesday	Thursday	Friday	Saturday

MARCH

Sunday	Monday	Tuesday	Wednesday	Thursday	Friday	Saturday

MAY

Sunday	Monday	Tuesday	Wednesday	Thursday	Friday	Saturday

JUNE

JULY

Sunday	Monday	Tuesday	Wednesday	Thursday	Friday	Saturday

AUGUST

Sunday	Monday	Tuesday	Wednesday	Thursday	Friday	Saturday

SEPTEMBER

Sunday	Monday	Tuesday	Wednesday	Thursday	Friday	Saturday

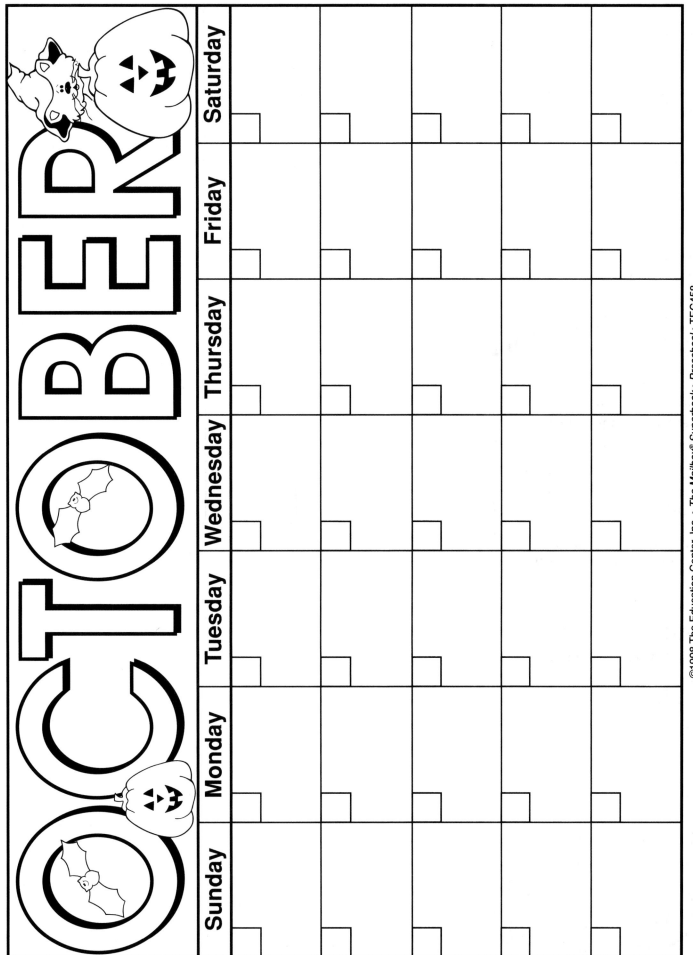

OCTOBER

Sunday	Monday	Tuesday	Wednesday	Thursday	Friday	Saturday

NOVEMBER

Sunday	Monday	Tuesday	Wednesday	Thursday	Friday	Saturday

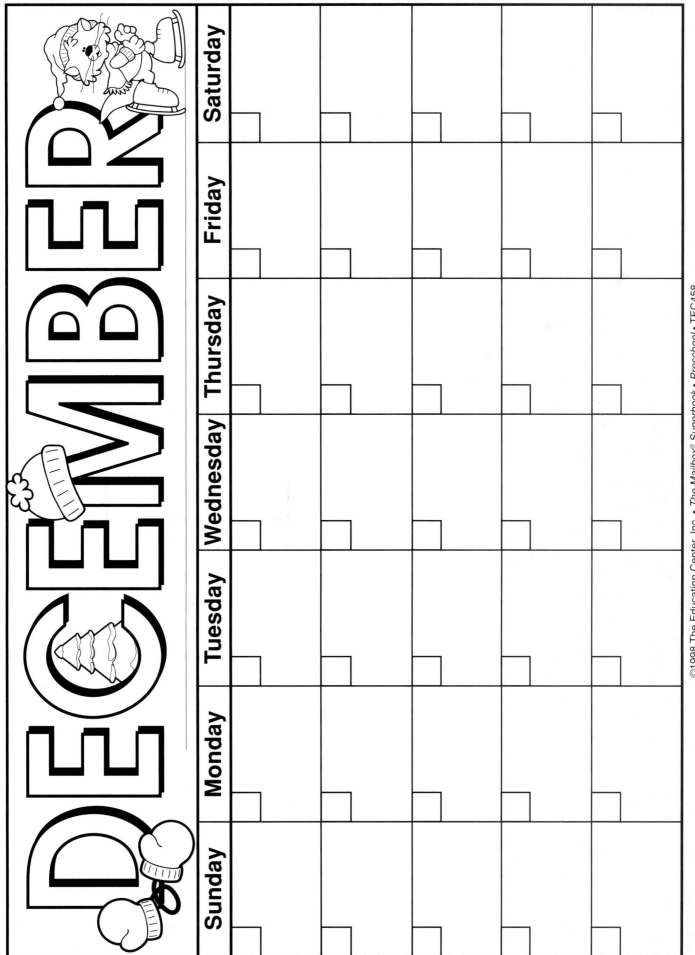

DECEMBER

Sunday	Monday	Tuesday	Wednesday	Thursday	Friday	Saturday